Scholarly Personae in the History of Orientalism, 1870-1930

Scholarly Personae in the History of Orientalism, 1870-1930

Edited by

Christiaan Engberts
Herman Paul

BRILL

LEIDEN | BOSTON

Cover illustration: Christiaan Snouck Hurgronje and the Saudi crown prince Saʿud ibn Abd al-Aziz in Leiden in 1935. Source: Leiden University Library: Or. 8952 L 5:14.

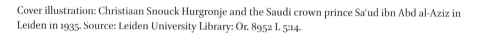

The Library of Congress Cataloging-in-Publication Data is available online at http://catalog.loc.gov

Typeface for the Latin, Greek, and Cyrillic scripts: "Brill". See and download: brill.com/brill-typeface.

ISBN 978-90-04-39523-7 (hardback)
ISBN 978-90-04-40631-5 (e-book)

Copyright 2019 by Koninklijke Brill NV, Leiden, The Netherlands.
Koninklijke Brill NV incorporates the imprints Brill, Brill Hes & De Graaf, Brill Nijhoff, Brill Rodopi, Brill Sense, Hotei Publishing, mentis Verlag, Verlag Ferdinand Schöningh and Wilhelm Fink Verlag.
All rights reserved. No part of this publication may be reproduced, translated, stored in a retrieval system, or transmitted in any form or by any means, electronic, mechanical, photocopying, recording or otherwise, without prior written permission from the publisher.
Authorization to photocopy items for internal or personal use is granted by Koninklijke Brill NV provided that the appropriate fees are paid directly to The Copyright Clearance Center, 222 Rosewood Drive, Suite 910, Danvers, MA 01923, USA. Fees are subject to change.

This book is printed on acid-free paper and produced in a sustainable manner.

Contents

Acknowledgments VII
List of Illustrations VIII
Notes on Contributors IX

Introduction: Scholarly Personae in the History of Orientalism, 1870-1930 1
    Herman Paul

1 The Prussian Professor as a Paradigm
   Trying to "Fit In" as a Semitist between 1870 and 1930 17
      Holger Gzella

2 Multiple Personae
   Friedrich Max Müller and the Persona of the Oriental Scholar 45
      Arie L. Molendijk

3 Epistemic Vice
   Transgression in the Arabian Travels of Julius Euting 64
      Henning Trüper

4 German Indology Challenged
   On the Dialectics of Armchair Philology, Fieldwork, and Indigenous Traditions in the Late Nineteenth Century 99
      Pascale Rabault-Feuerhahn

5 Herbert Giles as Reviewer 118
      T. H. Barrett

6 Orientalism and the Study of Lived Religions
   The Japanese Contribution to European Models of Scholarship on Japan around 1900 143
      Hans Martin Krämer

7 Orientalists at War
   Personae and Partiality at the Outbreak of the First World War 172
      Christiaan Engberts

Index 193

Acknowledgments

The idea for the workshop out of which this volume emerged came from Léon Buskens, at the time director of the Leiden University Center for the Study of Islam and Society (LUCIS). Together with the editors of this volume, both of whom then worked in a research project devoted to scholarly personae, he enthusiastically set out to organize a two-day workshop at Leiden University in January 2016. Although new responsibilities as director of the Netherlands Institute Morocco (NIMAR) in Rabat prevented Professor Buskens from contributing to this edited volume, it is obvious that this publication would not have existed without him. Generous thanks are also due to LUCIS and the Netherlands Organization for Scientific Research (NWO) for providing generous funding and to George MacBeth for his careful copyediting. Finally, the editors owe a special word of thanks to Maurits van den Boogert at Brill – a publishing house to which generations of Orientalists are indebted – for his stimulus, patience, and determination to make this volume happen.

Illustrations

Figures

3.1 Julius Euting, Original Diary, University of Tübingen Library, Md 676-22, 52r, detail   74
3.2 Julius Euting, *Tagbuch*, II, 229, detail: "Making a squeeze of an inscription"   74
3.3 Julius Euting, *Tagbuch*, II, 26, detail: "Drawing by the Prince Mâgid"   75
3.4 Julius Euting, Original Sketchbook 6, University of Tübingen Library, Md 676-32, 30r: "Abdalaziz, Hâjel 29. Nov. 83, since 1897 Emîr of Hâjel"   77
3.5 Julius Euting, Original Sketchbook 7, Md 676-33, 22v-23r, detail: The sandstone formation and proto-Arabic inscription site "Mahagge[h] 11 Feb. 84, from WNW"   80
3.6 Julius Euting, Tagbuch, II, 107, detail: Beginning of Ch. X, "From Hâjel to Teimâ"   81
3.7 Julius Euting, Original Diary, University of Tübingen Library, Md. 676-21, 21r, detail: Caricature of Ḥamûd el-ʿObeid   92

Table

6.1 Main authors of works on Japanese religions in European languages   149

Notes on Contributors

T. H. Barrett
is Professor Emeritus of East Asian History at the School of Oriental and African Studies, London.

Christiaan Engberts
is a lecturer in General History at Leiden University.

Holger Gzella
is Professor of Hebrew and Aramaic at Leiden University.

Hans Martin Krämer
is Professor of Japanese Studies at Heidelberg University.

Arie L. Molendijk
is Professor of the History of Christianity and the Philosophy of Religion at the University of Groningen.

Herman Paul
is Professor of the History of the Humanities at Leiden University.

Pascale Rabault-Feuerhahn
is a researcher at the Centre national de la recherche scientifique, Paris.

Henning Trüper
is a fellow at the Helsinki Collegium for Advanced Studies.

Introduction: Scholarly Personae in the History of Orientalism, 1870-1930

Herman Paul

1 Introduction

In 1884, the Lebanese philologist Ibrāhīm al-Yāziǧī (1847-1906) filed a harsh complaint about Arabic studies in Europe when he reproached the then just-deceased Reinhart Pieter Anne Dozy (1820-1883) for never having visited the Middle East. How could Dozy or any of his colleagues in Europe claim Arabic expertise without ever having heard the language spoken on the street or sought the opportunity to meet and learn from native speakers? Al-Yāziǧī dissociated himself from generations of European Arabists when he concluded:

> In spite of all research proficiency, in spite of the high ambitions, in spite of all patience in observing and writing, the man [Dozy] lacked the best means for understanding the Arabic language, the classical and the modern alike, because, to our knowledge, he has never traveled to one of the Arabic-speaking countries, such as Egypt or Syria, and conversed orally with only few Arabs, but learned the language solely from books, with the help of people among his fellow-countrymen whom are called Orientalists.[1]

By the late nineteenth century, such complaints were voiced not only in the Middle East, but also among younger European Orientalists such as Ignaz Goldziher (1850-1921) and Martin Hartmann (1851-1918).[2] Even at Dozy's *alma mater*, Leiden University, where Michael Jan de Goeje (1836-1909) faithfully built upon Dozy's legacy, disparaging words on Dozy's philological heritage could be heard. Christiaan Snouck Hurgronje (1857-1936) was the most outspoken of these critics. Although his doctoral dissertation on *Het Mekkaansche*

---

[1] Cited after H. L. Fleischer, "Eine Stimme aus dem Morgenlande über Dozy's Supplément aux dictionnaires arabes," in Fleischer, *Kleinere Schriften*, 3 vols. (Leipzig: S. Hirzel, 1885-1888), 3: 615-641, at 619-620 (my translation).

[2] Sabine Mangold, *Eine "weltbürgerliche Wissenschaft": Die deutsche Orientalistik im 19. Jahrhundert* (Stuttgart: Franz Steiner, 2004), 251-256.

feest (1880) still contained a few polite words on his *Doktorgroßvater*, his dissociation from Dozy became apparent when, in 1884, he deemed it necessary to travel to Mecca to do fieldwork in the center of Islam.[3] Such fieldwork required different qualities than manuscript study as practiced by Dozy. It demanded not only active command of, in this case, Arabic, and the ability to gather relevant data, but also, as Snouck's adventures illustrated, social and political skills for acquiring funding, organizing research on foreign territory, and winning support from local communities – not to mention contempt for death in the case of scholars reckless enough to join the Hajj.[4]

Recent scholarship mostly treats this late nineteenth-century dissatisfaction with "armchair philology" as indicative of a paradigm shift that took place in Arabic studies. Suzanne Marchand, for example, distinguishes between the "lonely Orientalists" between 1820 and 1870, who devoted most of their energies to "specialized, historicist study," and a generation of "furious" Orientalists in the decades around 1900, who for various reasons dissociated themselves from a philological heritage and instead attached increasing value to conducting fieldwork, studying contemporary problems, and rendering services to colonial administrations. Consequently, in Marchand's assessment, "going there" became nothing less than a career requirement.[5] Likewise, Sabine Mangold highlights the frustration that German Arabists around 1900 felt about the philological inheritance of especially Heinrich Leberecht Fleischer (1801-1888), the influential Leipzig Orientalist. Drawing on the cases of Carl Heinrich Becker (1876-1933) and Georg Kampffmeyer (1864-1936), among others, Mangold shows how an increasing interest in Arabic *realia* (economics, politics, religion) went hand-in-hand with growing disdain for philological text fetishism.[6]

Obviously, not all fields of Oriental studies underwent the same changes as did Arabic studies around 1900. At the time, Orientalism (*Orientalistik*, *orientalisme*) was the name of a cluster of fields, including but not limited to Islamic, Sanskrit, Indian, Chinese, and Japanese studies.[7] Although these subfields were related, and populated by overlapping groups of scholars, the

---

3 P. S. van Koningsveld, "Snouck Hurgronje zoals hij was: een bijdrage tot de waardering van de Nederlandse oriëntalistiek," *De Gids* 143 (1980), 763-784.
4 For Snouck's adventures abroad, see also Arnoud Vrolijk and Richard van Leeuwen, *Arabic Studies in the Netherlands: A Short History in Portraits, 1580-1950*, trans. Alastair Hamilton (Leiden: Brill, 2014), 117-150.
5 Suzanne L. Marchand, *German Orientalism in the Age of Empire: Religion, Race, and Scholarship* (Cambridge: Cambridge University Press, 2009), 102, 103, 220, 221.
6 Mangold, *Weltbürgerliche Wissenschaft*, 256-266.
7 The title of this volume follows nineteenth-century custom in using "Orientalism" as an umbrella term for the fields covered in the chapters that follow: Arabic, Semitic, Sanskrit, Chinese, and Japanese studies. With his 1978 book *Orientalism*, Edward W. Said would completely

historical trajectories of these emerging disciplines took different forms, depending, among other things, on national contexts, colonial politics, and commercial interests. Chinese studies, for example, underwent a transition almost opposed to that of Arabist studies. Here a philological ethos, defended in terms of *Wissenschaftlichkeit*, only emerged in the early twentieth century, after a period of mostly "practical," linguistically oriented teaching and writing aimed at educating interpreters and civil servants in particular.[8] Field-specific patterns of development and national differences notwithstanding, the Arabist examples mentioned above hint at something important. They suggest that the emergence of new research questions, new methods, or new societal demands could change the very idea and reality of "being an Orientalist." Just as, at Leiden University, Jan Julius Lodewijk Duyvendak (1889-1954) represented a new type of Sinologist, compared to his predecessor Gustaaf Schlegel (1840-1903), so Goldziher, Hartmann, and Snouck represented a generation of Orientalists that conceived of themselves, their academic tasks, and their professional identities in terms that would have been implausible to Fleischer or Dozy.

This raises a question that so far has received only limited attention in the historiography of Orientalism, or in the history of the humanities more broadly: how did scholars experience and define their professional identities?[9] What did it take for them to be a professor, *Privatdozent*, or non-academic researcher in the field of Oriental studies? What talents, virtues, or skills did this require? Also, how were these skills and virtues acquired or molded, especially but not only in educational practices, and what positive or negative models were invoked in contexts of socialization? If the models that Dozy and Fleischer had embodied came to be regarded as old-fashioned, what alternative models did Snouck, Hartmann, and Goldziher put in their place? And how were these different understandings of what it meant to be an Arabist, Egyptologist, or Sinologist related to professional identities in other areas of the *Geisteswissenschaften*, not to mention the emerging social sciences?

Historians of science have developed the concept of "scientific" or "scholarly personae" to capture such different, overlapping, and often conflicting templates of scholarly selfhood that scholars developed, tried to appropriate, and sought to instill in their students. In what follows, I will (1) briefly introduce

---

change the meaning of the term – but that chapter in the history of Orientalism falls outside the scope of this volume.

8 Barend ter Haar, "Between the Dutch East Indies and Philology (1919-1974)," in *Chinese Studies in the Netherlands: Past, Present and Future*, ed. Wilt L. Idema (Leiden: Brill, 2014), 69-103.

9 See, however, Henning Trüper, "Dispersed Personae: Subject-Matters of Scholarly Biography in Nineteenth-Century Oriental Philology," *Asiatische Studien* 67 (2013), 1325-1360.

this concept in its three main variants, (2) explain why scholarly personae need to be studied empirically, in different fields of study, (3) make a case for Orientalism as a suitable case study for trying out this concept, and (4) briefly summarize how the chapters brought together in this volume contribute to this project.

2   Scholarly Personae

The newly founded journal *Persona Studies* represents a first approach to our subject: an approach that is largely rooted in cultural studies but appeals to scholars throughout the humanities. Central to this approach is the assumption that social life requires people to present themselves in ways that are recognizable to others as well as effective in granting people "identities" that help them navigate the demands of social life. Drawing on the old Latin *persona*, which among other things could refer to a mask worn by theater actors, advocates of this first approach conceive of *personae* as shorthand for identities that people articulate or "perform" in contextually sensitive ways. Although adherents of this first approach acknowledge that identities are not created *ex nihilo*, but are indebted to social traditions that make certain public identities appear as more plausible than others, the founding editors of *Persona Studies*, P. David Marshall and Kim Barbour, highlight the agency of individuals to shape their own *personae*. For Marshall and Barbour, then, *personae* are performances of identity, acts of self-fashioning, or tools for public "impression management" (to borrow a term from Erving Goffman).[10] Accordingly, their analysis of the use and function of *personae* focuses near-exclusively on how individuals "produce," "perform," "enact," "inhabit," "negotiate," and "manage" their identities – in personalizing their game avatars or through playful mixture of professional role identities in work environments.[11]

Applied to the history of scholarship (or the history of science, as long as this is understood to cover the social sciences and humanities, too), this first approach encourages research on what Richard Karwan calls "scholarly self-fashioning."[12] A noteworthy contribution to this research agenda comes from Mineke Bosch, who highlights the importance of scholarly self-fashioning in

---

10   Erving Goffman, *The Presentation of Self in Everyday Life* (Garden City, NY: Doubleday, 1959).
11   P. David Marshall and Kim Barbour, "Making Intellectual Room for Persona Studies: A New Consciousness and a Shifted Perspective," *Persona Studies* 1 (2015), 1-12.
12   *Scholarly Self-Fashioning and Community in the Early Modern University*, ed. Richard Karwan (Farnham: Ashgate, 2013).

the claiming of academic authority. To be accepted as a trustworthy member of a scientific community, scholars not only need to engage in serious research, but also have to follow social conventions extending well beyond the realm of ideas. In Bosch's own words,

> The scholarly identity makes use of specific bodily practices such as dietetics and routines of physical conduct (sexuality and sports for instance), but also of dress and other tools to keep up the appearance of a "truth-speaker" – beards and moustaches, or for women "ascetic dress" or "comfortable footwear" instead of high heels.[13]

Bosch thus uses the persona concept to draw attention to how scholars present themselves to each other, not only verbally, but also with their bodies and through their "emotion management." Like Marshall and Barbour, Bosch acknowledges the importance of culturally shared repertoires, but highlights the unique touches that individuals add in adapting such models to their own purposes. Consequently, she can attribute *personae* to individuals, speaking for instance about "[Robert] Fruin's scholarly persona" and "[Pieter] van Winter's scholarly persona."[14]

This would be inconceivable within the second approach that must be mentioned here – an approach inspired by the anthropology of Marcel Mauss, but articulated most forcefully by Lorraine Daston and H. Otto Sibum in a seminal 2003 theme issue of *Science in Context*. For Daston and Sibum, scientific *personae* are cultural templates for the social role of a *Gelehrter*, *savant*, man of learning, or scientist. Although these templates can be adapted to new circumstances or even disappear in favor of others, as happened to the *Naturforscher* and the *femme savant*, they usually change at a slow or even very slow pace. As time-, place-, and discipline-transcending models of how to be a scientist, *personae* belong to what historians of science, with a nod to Fernand Braudel, call a *histoire de longue durée*.[15] Consequently, *personae* are best regarded as

---

13   Mineke Bosch, "Scholarly Personae and Twentieth-Century Historians: Explorations of a Concept," *Low Countries Historical Review* 131, no. 4 (2016), 33-54, at 43.

14   Ibid., 45, 48. See also Mineke Bosch, "Persona and the Performance of Identity: Parallel Developments in the Biographical Historiography of Science and Gender, and the Related Uses of Self Narratives," *L'Homme* 24, no. 2 (2013), 11-22.

15   Frederick L. Holmes, "The Longue Durée in the History of Science," *History and Philosophy of the Life Sciences* 25 (2003), 463-470; Heiko Stoff, "Der aktuelle Gebrauch der 'longue durée' in der Wissenschaftsgeschichte," *Berichte zur Wissenschaftsgeschichte* 32 (2009), 144-158; Mathias Grote, *What Could the "longue durée" Mean for the History of Modern Science?* (Paris: Fondation Maison des sciences de l'homme, 2015).

collective entities, of which Daston and Sibum claim that they ontologically precede individual social existence:

> To understand personae in this sense is to reject a social ontology that treats only flesh-and-blood individuals as real, and dismisses all collective entities as mere aggregates, parasitic upon individuals. Personae are as real or more real than biological individuals, in that they create the possibilities of being in the human world, schooling the mind, body, and soul in distinctive and indelible ways.[16]

Applying Daston's and Sibum's definition of scientific *personae* to the world of early modern learning, Gadi Algazi likewise treats *personae* as "materials that persons are made of." As his discussion of Johannes Kepler suggests, men of learning in early modern Europe could navigate between several *personae*. But as Kepler found out, they could not easily transform them: the power of these cultural institutions was too large for individuals to challenge. As collective representations, *personae* could not be changed "by force of personal decision."[17]

This implies that real differences exist between the first and second approaches to the concept of scholarly *personae*. While the first one revolves around self-fashioning and self-presentation, the second one focuses on broadly shared images of what it takes to be a scientist or man of learning. While the former zooms in on individuals in specific cultural settings, the latter engages in macro-level analysis, tracing scholarly *personae* across centuries. And if Daston and Sibum are right about the social ontologies underlying these persona concepts, these are more than differences in emphasis. Insofar as the two approaches are rooted in different anthropological assumptions, or different metaphysical views of human agency, they are irreconcilable.

Yet as Algazi rightly notes, we are not left with these alternatives.[18] There is a third approach – a conception of scholarly *personae* of which Algazi is not entirely uncritical, but one that has the advantage of occupying a middle-range position between the biographical and the social, or between individuals engaged in "impression management," on the one hand, and powerful cultural institutions, on the other. This third approach, to which most chapters in this volume relate, is specifically tailored to situations of disagreement or uncertainty about the marks of a good scholar. Treating scholarly personae as

---

16 Lorraine Daston and H. Otto Sibum, "Introduction: Scientific Personae and Their Histories," *Science in Context* 16 (2003), 1-8, at 3-4.
17 Gadi Algazi, "*Exemplum* and *Wundertier*: Three Concepts of the Scholarly Persona," *Low Countries Historical Review* 131, no. 4 (2016), 8-32, at 17, 23.
18 Ibid., 10-11.

INTRODUCTION 7

"models" of what a scholar is, characterized by distinct combinations of talents, virtues, and/or skills, this third approach is premised on the assumption that personae never come in the singular. The persona that Dozy embodied became visible only when it was contrasted with others – when al-Yāziǧī and others began to criticize it, when Snouck began to adopt a different model of "how to be a scholar," or, much earlier, when Dozy and his colleagues advocated philological criticism as a mark of *Wissenschaftlichkeit* over against older, theologically-inspired modes of Arabic scholarship.[19]

Personae, in this third definition, are models, past or present, inherited or invented, of what it takes to be a scholar. Usually, they are attributed to influential individuals, who thereby come to serve as their embodiments, positively or negatively. Thus, for Carl Heinrich Becker, "Fleischer's era" referred to a time in the history of Orientalism when philological criticism such as practiced by Fleischer was regarded as the defining mark of an Orientalist scholar.[20] This is not to say that Fleischer created his own persona, as the first approach would say, but rather that, for various reasons, the name Fleischer came to serve as shorthand for a persona that assigned great significance to source critical attitudes. The proper name was thus turned into a generic one, sometimes (not necessarily in Fleischer's case) even to the point of becoming a stereotype that no longer maintained a clear relation to its name-giver.[21]

The third approach encourages research on how personae served as models for imitation, emulation, and dissociation alike. It draws attention to how virtues, vices, skills, and talents were associated with specific individuals – the name of Heinrich Ewald (1803-1875) being widely perceived as synonymous to dogmatism and arrogance, for instance[22] – and how such embodied personae were remembered, positively or negatively, for the sake of advocating (or criticizing) certain constellations of virtues and skills. Also, it examines why scholarly personae were often defined in contrastive terms, as means for remedying the perceived shortcomings of other personae. Scholarly personae are thus a conceptual tool for distinguishing between competing models of how to be a scholar, as defined by historical agents or as distinguished in hindsight by historians of science. This implies that the third approach is particularly suited to examining clashes or tensions between generations, schools, traditions, or

---

19   On which see Mangold, *Weltbürgerliche Wissenschaft*, 29-77.
20   Carl Heinrich Becker, *Vom Werden und Wesen der islamischen Welt: Islamstudien*, 2 vols. (Leipzig: Quelle & Meyer, 1924-1932), 2: 484.
21   Herman Paul, "The Virtues of a Good Historian in Early Imperial Germany: Georg Waitz's Contested Example," *Modern Intellectual History* 15 (2018), 681-709.
22   Christiaan Engberts, "Gossiping about the Buddha of Göttingen: Heinrich Ewald as an Unscholarly Persona," *History of Humanities* 1 (2016), 371-385.

cultures, each with their own expectations regarding the virtues or skills characteristic of a scholar.[23]

3 Case Studies

To what extent, then, did al-Yāziǧī's criticism of Dozy, with which I started, reflect a clash between different, perhaps even incompatible personae? Admittedly, the persona cultivated by al-Yāziǧī and his Arabic nationalist compatriots in the Syrian Scientific Society, among other associations, cannot be neatly classified as a *scholarly* persona (one that only professional scholars could appropriate). This, however, was the whole point of al-Yāziǧī's criticism: the philologist, poet, and journalist that was al-Yāziǧī had little patience for "bookish" scholars such as Dozy. His ideal of philological scholarship in the service of Arabic nationalism made him rebel against what he perceived as a much too narrow persona.[24]

At the same time, academic Orientalists defended "narrow" professional identities by dissociating themselves from "accidental Orientalists," or from non-academic authors writing about their experiences in the Near or Far East.[25] Clearly, such criticism served purposes of academic boundary work.[26] However, as Max Müller (1823-1900) experienced, such demarcation strategies could also be employed within the academic world, even against famous Orientalists. When Müller, a prolific author of popular books on Hinduism and Sanskrit literature, was criticized for "cater[ing] to the public so long that scholarly work had become of only secondary consequence,"[27] this showed that at least part of his work was seen as not befitting an Oxford professor. In Arie L. Molendijk's analysis, Müller's problem was that he tried to combine a scholarly persona with the persona of a sage in a time and place where this was deemed inappropriate.[28] Likewise, Dozy's controversial study of the Israelites in Mecca,

---

23 Herman Paul, "The Virtues and Vices of Albert Naudé: Toward a History of Scholarly Personae," *History of Humanities* 1 (2016), 327-338.
24 Bassam Tibi, *Arab Nationalism: Between Islam and the Nation-State*, 3rd ed. (Basingstoke: Macmillan, 1997), 103-104.
25 Barbara Spackman, *Accidental Orientalists: Modern Italian Travelers in Ottoman Lands* (Liverpool: Liverpool University Press, 2017).
26 On which see T. F. Gieryn, "Boundary-Work and the Demarcation of Science from Non-Science: Strains and Interests in Professional Ideologies of Scientists," *American Sociological Review* 48 (1983), 781-795.
27 "Max Müller," *The Nation* 71 (1900), 343-344, at 343.
28 Arie L. Molendijk, *Friedrich Max Müller and the Sacred Books of the East* (Oxford: Oxford University Press, 2016).

published in 1864, elicited critical feedback from colleagues who believed that speculation did not befit a serious student of Arabic – one that Dozy had been, judging by his *Recherches sur l'histoire politique et littéraire de l'Espagne pendant le moyen âge* (1848). The persona at stake in this controversy, then, was one that Dozy himself was perceived as having embodied in an earlier phase of his life.[29]

What these examples show is that scholarly personae can be located, or indeed were located, at different levels: within fields of research, in and outside of academic scholarship, as well as geographically, between Europe and the Arab world. If scholarly personae are often defined in contrastive terms, this implies that the contrasts can be drawn at different levels of generalization. This, in turn, suggests that a concept like scholarly personae is better not defined in the abstract. Empirical historical research is needed for adding muscle and flesh to the bones of the concept, that is, for showing when, how, and why historical agents felt a need to distinguish between different models of being a scholar.

4   Orientalism

Orientalism is obviously not the only field of study in which the scholarly persona concept (in the third variant) can be tested. In the past few years, attempts have been made to apply and refine the concept in fields as diverse as nineteenth-century history[30] and twentieth-century statistics.[31] In the meantime, stimulating work has been done on how funding agencies in the early twentieth century helped shape scholarly personae.[32] Still, the work has only just begun: comparisons with other disciplines, in and outside of the *Geisteswis-*

---

29   Herman Paul, "Virtue Language in Nineteenth-Century Orientalism: A Case Study in Historical Epistemology," *Modern Intellectual History* 14 (2017), 689-715.

30   Herman Paul, "The Heroic Study of Records: The Contested Persona of the Archival Historian," *History of the Human Sciences*, 26, no. 4 (2013), 67-83; Daniela Saxer, *Die Schärfung des Quellenblicks: Forschungspraktiken in der Geschichtswissenschaft 1840-1914* (Munich: De Gruyter Oldenbourg, 2014), esp. 140-141, 172. See also *How to Be a Historian: Scholarly Personae in Historical Studies, 1800-2000*, ed. Herman Paul (Manchester: Manchester University Press, 2019).

31   In September 2018, the British Society for the History of Science hosted a session at its annual conference on "Scientific Personae and the (Dis-)Unity of Modern Statistics in Comparative Perspective, c. 1860-1960."

32   Pieter Huistra and Kaat Wils, "Fit to Travel: The Exchange Programme of the Belgian American Educational Foundation: An Institutional Perspective on Scientific Persona Formation (1920-1940)," *Low Countries Historical Review*, 131, no. 4 (2016), 112-134.

senschaften, are as of yet hardly possible. There are three reasons, then, why Orientalism in its late nineteenth and early twentieth-century European incarnations seems an interesting case for further exploring and testing the persona concept.

First, just like other emerging humanities disciplines at the time, late nineteenth-century Orientalism went through processes often referred to as "professionalization." Concretely, this meant that a field in which academic scholars had always found themselves accompanied by "a broad range of explorers, adventurers, and travelers: missionaries, theologians, and preachers; eccentrics, frauds, and crackpots; social reformers, political advocates, soldiers, spies, and diplomatic representatives of various European regimes"[33] tried to define itself in more academic terms. As Suzanne Marchand puts it: "Part of this effort was focused on pushing out, or at least getting around, the aristocrats, missionaries, and diplomats who still contributed much to Oriental studies": they were perceived as embodying different personae than those befitting a serious Orientalist.[34]

Secondly, Orientalism was a field fraught with religious, political, and ideological struggles, with perennial disagreement not only over the boundaries, but also over the very essence of what constituted Oriental studies. The degree of divergence was even such that, in Robert Irwin's assessment, "there was hardly an Orientalist type or a common Orientalist discourse" in Europe.[35] Regardless of whether this is true or not, correspondences in which Oriental scholars continuously evaluated each other's scholarly conduct – not only their academic output, but also their teaching and their political engagement – suggest that issues of scholarly selfhood ranked high on the agenda, perhaps precisely because agreement was hard to reach. Time and again, Orientalists quarreled over the relation between academic reputation and popularizing work, the desirability of studying living languages, or the pros and cons of doing advisory work for colonial administrations.[36]

A third and final reason as to why Oriental studies in the decades around 1900 is an interesting case study for testing the concept of scholarly personae is that intercultural exchanges such as al-Yāziǧī's criticism of Dozy were more

---

33 Lawrence I. Conrad, "The Dervish's Disciple: On the Personality and Intellectual Milieu of the Young Ignaz Goldziher," *Journal of the Royal Asiatic Society of Great Britain and Ireland* 2 (1990), 225-266, at 265.
34 Marchand, *German Orientalism*, 161.
35 Robert Irwin, *For Lust of Knowing: The Orientalists and Their Enemies* (London: Penguin, 2007), 197.
36 See, e.g., Martin Kramer, "Arabistik and Arabism: The Passions of Martin Hartmann," *Middle Eastern Studies* 25 (1989), 283-300.

likely to occur there than in history or statistics. In comparison to other humanities disciplines in Europe, Oriental studies was a field that found itself more frequently subjected to critical evaluation from outside of Europe.[37] Did al-Yāziǧī's criticism of Dozy and his colleagues "whom are called Orientalists" have any impact on what it meant to be an Orientalist? How was the Orientalist persona affected by fieldwork in countries far away from European libraries and universities?

5 This Volume

This volume thus approaches the world of Oriental studies between, roughly, 1870 and 1930 through the prism of scholarly persona. Its key question is a heuristic one: to what extent does the persona concept (in the third variant) contribute to a better understanding of unity and disunity among European Orientalists around 1900? In pursuing this question, the chapters that follow touch upon a range of sub-questions. What were the crucial factors that made some scholarly personae more successful, or at least more visible, than others? How did scholarly personae relate to non-scholarly ones, or to hybrid role identities like the "missionary–scholar," the "political professor," and the "public intellectual"? How did such personae affect day-to-day practices, such as the writing of book reviews – a genre in which evaluative standards often became quite explicit? And how different or similar were the subfields of Arabic, Semitic, Sanskrit, Chinese, and Japanese studies in these respects? Although this volume cannot possibly pretend to address these questions in satisfactory depth, it tries to put them on the agenda, so to speak, by showing in some detail what kind of historical analysis can be done through the prism of scholarly personae.

In his opening chapter, Holger Gzella shows how late nineteenth- and early twentieth-century German Semitists (Hebraists and Aramaicists) struggled with the emerging persona of a "secular" university professor. Although this persona with its corresponding intellectual virtues was recognized as a new professional ideal across the discipline, it posed difficult dilemmas for scholars whose confessional loyalties made them prefer different configurations of the "sacred" and the "secular." Drawing on the cases of Gustav Bickell (1838-1906), Jacob Barth (1851-1914), Mark Lidzbarski (1868-1928), and Hans Bauer

---

[37] As documented in a fascinating recent collection of essays: *The Muslim Reception of European Orientalism: Reversing the Gaze*, ed. Susannah Heschel and Umar Ryad (London: Routledge, 2019).

(1878-1937), Gzella shows how different German Semitists responded differently to these tensions, thereby suggesting that, for them, scholarly personae served as points of orientation more than as models for imitation.

As Arie L. Molendijk shows in his chapter on Max Müller, transgressing standards of conduct embodied by scholarly personae was not without consequences. Although Müller in many respects personified the philological virtues that late nineteenth-century students of Sanskrit perceived as marks of scholarly virtuosity, his popular lectures and publications targeted at "young ladies and easy-going people" (as one critic phrased it) were not seen as befitting a real academic. Likewise, the entrepreneurial qualities that Müller needed for successfully carrying out his *Sacred Books of the East* project (50 vols., 1879-1910) did not fit a philological persona. Like other nineteenth-century pioneers in "big humanities" projects, then, Müller had to navigate between multiple personae, thereby invariably invoking criticism from colleagues committed to distinguishing sharply between "scholarly" and "non-scholarly" personae.

Henning Trüper explores the moral dilemmas in which Orientalists could get entangled by presenting themselves and their colleagues as virtuous scholars, even in cases where this was less than obvious. When the Strasbourg Semitist Enno Littmann (1875-1958) edited the travel diary of the German Orientalist Julius Euting (1839-1913) from his journey to "Inner Arabia" in 1883-1884, Littmann tried to present Euting as an epitome of scholarly virtue, even if this required editing or reworking problematic passages in Euting's manuscript. Ironically, then, Littmann's defense of scholarly virtue required committing a philological vice – an observation that clearly challenges rigid distinctions between scholarly virtues and vices.

If Littmann was an arduous scholarly traveler – in the early 1900s, he conducted fieldwork in Eritrea and Ethiopia – so was the German-born Iranologist and Indologist Martin Haug (1827-1876). As Pascale Rabault-Feuerhahn shows in her chapter on Haug, German Indology underwent a transition similar to Arabic studies in that "armchair philology" was increasingly perceived as an old-fashioned mode of Orientalist scholarship. Yet, as illustrated by the opposition that Haug met with among his German colleagues after his Indian travels, this development was neither linear nor uncontested. The emergence of new scholarly personae might be better understood in terms of accumulation than in terms of succession.[38]

Timothy Barrett's chapter on Herbert Giles (1845-1935), the second Professor of Chinese at Cambridge University, nonetheless shows that certain scholarly

---

[38] As suggested by Lorraine Daston and Peter Galison, *Objectivity* (New York, NY: Zone Books, 2007), 423 n. 18.

practices, such as hostile book reviews in *ad hominem* language, became increasingly rare, and therefore more spectacular when they still made it into print. During Giles's lifetime, the lonely Sinologist, working in splendid isolation from others, was gradually replaced by a new persona: a university professor with colleagues and students, working in professional environments where "old-fashioned warriors" like Giles himself were no longer given much space. What this example shows, among other things, is that scholarly personae have to be understood against their social backgrounds. A discipline with journals and conferences requires more collegiality, and therefore different standards of public evaluation, than the non-institutionalized field that was Sinology in Giles's young years.

Just like Chinese studies, Japanese studies was a field to which Christian missionaries actively contributed. Also, in the closing decades of the nineteenth century, Buddhist priests from Japan played a major part in furthering the study of Japanese religion. This leads Hans Martin Krämer to wonder to what extent the category of *scholarly* personae can be applied to the founding fathers of Japanese studies. Isn't the adjective too restrictive, especially if "scholarly" is treated as synonymous with "academic"? A persona perspective nonetheless enables Krämer to distinguish between three groups of actors in early Japanese studies: European philologists like August Pfizmaier (1808-1887) and Léon de Rosny (1837-1914), Japanese scholars and practitioners of Buddhism such as Akamatsu Renjō (1841-1919), Nanjō Bun'yū (1849-1927), and Kasawara Kenju (1852-1883), and, finally, European missionaries *cum* fieldworkers like Robbins Brown (1810-1880), James C. Hepburn (1815-1911), and Hans Haas (1868-1934).

Christiaan Engberts, finally, examines how classic tensions between nationalism and internationalism, such as experienced most dramatically in times of war, affected the scholarly persona as defined by Dutch and German Semitists in the 1910s. During World War I, Carl Heinrich Becker and Christiaan Snouck Hurgronje came to disagree sharply, not only on Germany's colonial politics, but also, more importantly, on the relation between scholarly work and nationalist commitments. Was Snouck's scholarship still respectable when the Leiden Orientalist, much to Becker's annoyance, failed to acknowledge Germany's world historical role? Was international cooperation, for instance in the *Encyclopaedia of Islam* (1913-1938), still possible when its contributors found themselves taking different political stances?

Scholarly personae, then, were invoked at different occasions and contrasted in different ways. As shown by the chapters in this volume, personae were not etched in stone: they took shape in response to circumstances that varied across time and place. Often, they were articulated in response to perceived threats, or held up as alternatives to "others" in time (old-fashioned armchair philology), place (non-European learning), or social position (amateurism). This is hardly surprising: only when a mode of being a scholar was perceived as being under threat, or as new and not yet sufficiently accepted, did its defining features have to be articulated and defended. Interestingly, this not only explains why scholarly personae were debated most explicitly in contexts of controversy, but also why relative outsiders such as Ibrāhīm al-Yāziǧī often had a sharp eye for them.

This, finally, reveals one of the most important historiographical differences that looking at scholarship through the prism of scholarly personae can make. While existing literature on the history of Orientalism and the history of the humanities more broadly often focuses on *diachronic development*, especially in employing teleological categories like "professionalization" and "specialization," the prism of scholarly personae encourages historians to acknowledge *synchronic variety*, especially insofar as scholarly identities are concerned. Consequently, it is much better equipped to deal with non-European scholars like al-Yāziǧī, or with Buddhist students of Japanese religion as discussed in Krämer's chapter, than are histories that focus on the "development" of Western scholarship. Even if only applied to European case studies, the prism of scholarly personae naturally draws attention to "internal subaltern" groups, such as the Jewish and Catholic scholars examined by Gzella. If only for this reason, the promise of the perspective adopted in this volume reaches well beyond the field of Oriental studies.[39]

Bibliography

Algazi, Gadi. "*Exemplum* and *Wundertier*: Three Concepts of the Scholarly Persona." *Low Countries Historical Review* 131, no. 4 (2016): 8-32.

Becker, Carl Heinrich. *Vom Werden und Wesen der islamischen Welt: Islamstudien*. 2 vols. Leipzig: Quelle & Meyer, 1924-1932.

Bosch, Mineke. "Persona and the Performance of Identity: Parallel Developments in the Biographical Historiography of Science and Gender, and the Related Uses of Self Narratives." *L'Homme* 24, no. 2 (2013): 11-22.

---

[39] A version of this introduction was presented at the École normale supérieure in Paris on 15 December 2017. Thanks to Pascale Rabault-Feuerhahn for hosting this event (together with Michel Espagne), to the participants for helpful feedback, and to the Netherlands Organization for Scientific Research (NWO) for generous funding.

Bosch, Mineke. "Scholarly Personae and Twentieth-Century Historians: Explorations of a Concept." *Low Countries Historical Review* 131, no. 4 (2016): 33-54.

Conrad, Lawrence I. "The Dervish's Disciple: On the Personality and Intellectual Milieu of the Young Ignaz Goldziher." *Journal of the Royal Asiatic Society of Great Britain and Ireland* 2 (1990): 225-266.

Daston, Lorraine and H. Otto Sibum. "Introduction: Scientific Personae and Their Histories." *Science in Context* 16 (2003): 1-8.

Daston, Lorraine and Peter Galison. *Objectivity.* New York, NY: Zone Books, 2007.

Engberts, Christiaan. "Gossiping about the Buddha of Göttingen: Heinrich Ewald as an Unscholarly Persona." *History of Humanities* 1 (2016): 371-385.

Fleischer, H. L. "Eine Stimme aus dem Morgenlande über Dozy's Supplément aux dictionnaires arabes." In Fleischer, *Kleinere Schriften*, 3 vols. Leipzig: S. Hirzel, 1885-1888, 3: 615-641.

Gieryn, T. F. "Boundary-Work and the Demarcation of Science from Non-Science: Strains and Interests in Professional Ideologies of Scientists." *American Sociological Review* 48 (1983): 781-795.

Goffman, Erving. *The Presentation of Self in Everyday Life.* Garden City, NY: Doubleday, 1959.

Grote, Mathias. *What Could the "longue durée" Mean for the History of Modern Science?* Paris: Fondation Maison des sciences de l'homme, 2015.

Heschel, Susannah and Umar Ryad, eds. *The Muslim Reception of European Orientalism: Reversing the Gaze.* London: Routledge, 2019.

Holmes, Frederick L. "The Longue Durée in the History of Science." *History and Philosophy of the Life Sciences* 25 (2003): 463-470.

Huistra, Pieter and Kaat Wils. "Fit to Travel: The Exchange Programme of the Belgian American Educational Foundation: An Institutional Perspective on Scientific Persona Formation (1920-1940)." *Low Countries Historical Review* 131, no. 4 (2016): 112-134.

Irwin, Robert. *For Lust of Knowing: The Orientalists and Their Enemies.* London: Penguin, 2007.

Karwan, Richard, ed. *Scholarly Self-Fashioning and Community in the Early Modern University.* Farnham: Ashgate, 2013.

Kramer, Martin. "Arabistik and Arabism: The Passions of Martin Hartmann." *Middle Eastern Studies* 25 (1989): 283-300.

Mangold, Sabine. *Eine "weltbürgerliche Wissenschaft": Die deutsche Orientalistik im 19. Jahrhundert.* Stuttgart: Franz Steiner, 2004.

Marchand, Suzanne L. *German Orientalism in the Age of Empire: Religion, Race, and Scholarship.* Cambridge: Cambridge University Press, 2009.

Marshall, P. David and Kim Barbour. "Making Intellectual Room for Persona Studies: A New Consciousness and a Shifted Perspective." *Persona Studies* 1 (2015): 1-12.

Molendijk, Arie L., *Friedrich Max Müller and the Sacred Books of the East* (Oxford: Oxford University Press, 2016).

N. N., "Max Müller," *The Nation* 71 (1900), 343-344.

Paul, Herman. "The Heroic Study of Records: The Contested Persona of the Archival Historian." *History of the Human Sciences* 26, no. 4 (2013): 67-83.

Paul, Herman. "The Virtues and Vices of Albert Naudé: Toward a History of Scholarly Personae." *History of Humanities* 1 (2016): 327-338.

Paul, Herman. "Virtue Language in Nineteenth-Century Orientalism: A Case Study in Historical Epistemology." *Modern Intellectual History* 14 (2017): 689-715.

Paul, Herman. "The Virtues of a Good Historian in Early Imperial Germany: Georg Waitz's Contested Example." *Modern Intellectual History* 15 (2018): 681-709.

Paul, Herman, ed. *How to Be a Historian: Scholarly Personae in Historical Studies, 1800-2000*. Manchester: Manchester University Press, 2019.

Saxer, Daniela. *Die Schärfung des Quellenblicks: Forschungspraktiken in der Geschichtswissenschaft 1840-1914*. Munich: De Gruyter Oldenbourg, 2014.

Spackman, Barbara. *Accidental Orientalists: Modern Italian Travelers in Ottoman Lands*. Liverpool: Liverpool University Press, 2017.

Stoff, Heiko. "Der aktuelle Gebrauch der 'longue durée' in der Wissenschaftsgeschichte." *Berichte zur Wissenschaftsgeschichte* 32 (2009): 144-158.

ter Haar, Barend. "Between the Dutch East Indies and Philology (1919-1974)." In *Chinese Studies in the Netherlands: Past, Present and Future*, edited by Wilt L. Idema. Leiden: Brill, 2014: 69-103.

Tibi, Bassam. *Arab Nationalism: Between Islam and the Nation-State*. 3rd ed. Basingstoke: Macmillan, 1997.

Trüper, Henning. "Dispersed Personae: Subject-Matters of Scholarly Biography in Nineteenth-Century Oriental Philology." *Asiatische Studien* 67 (2013): 1325-1360.

van Koningsveld, P. S. "Snouck Hurgronje zoals hij was: een bijdrage tot de waardering van de Nederlandse oriëntalistiek." *De Gids* 143 (1980): 763-784.

Vrolijk, Arnoud and Richard van Leeuwen. *Arabic Studies in the Netherlands: A Short History in Portraits, 1580-1950*. Translated by Alastair Hamilton. Leiden: Brill, 2014.

CHAPTER 1

The Prussian Professor as a Paradigm

Trying to "Fit In" as a Semitist between 1870 and 1930

Holger Gzella

Semitics, the most conservative subfield of what used to be called Oriental studies and direct heir of Christian Hebraism during the Reformation era, took on its present shape during the nineteenth century.[1] Being traditionally governed by comparative philology as the dominant method and Protestant academic culture as its natural habitat, it flourished above all in Lutheran Germany and has maintained a somewhat uneasy but unbroken relationship with theology ever since, especially with Biblical exegesis and church history. Hence it is only natural that an affinity with, or escape from, religious convictions based on the Bible had, and to some extent still has, an impact on people's choice to devote their lives to the study of the Semitic languages.

The present paper explores how the underlying professional ideal affected the biographies of some leading Hebraists and Aramaicists during the late nineteenth and early twentieth centuries. Semitics absorbed such different figures as the sensitive student of Syriac literature Gustav Bickell (1838-1906), whose appreciation of the continuity of Christian thought estranged him from the high castle of Protestant orthodoxy in which he grew up;[2] the hard-working epigraphist and connoisseur of Mandaean religion Mark Lidzbarski (1868-1928), descendant of a Chassidic family in Poland, who, with great perseverance, made his way into Prussian academe;[3] and the historical-comparative gram-

---

1 Since the now outdated notion "Oriental studies," as opposed to "Semitics" (or "Semitic philology"), has no unified method or topic, this term will be avoided here, even though it continued to play a role as a structuring concept in university teaching well into the twentieth century.
2 Ernst Ludwig Dietrich, "Gustav Wilhelm Hugo Bickell," in *Lebensbilder aus Kurhessen und Waldeck*, vol. 4, ed. Ingeborg Schnack (Marburg: Elwert, 1950), 25-39, to be supplemented by the scholar's autobiographical account "Gustav Bickell," in *Convertitenbilder aus dem neunzehnten Jahrhundert*, vol. 3/2, ed. David August Rosenthal (Schaffhausen: Hurter, 1870), 415-464. For his works and further biographical notes, see Johannes Laichner, "Gustav Wilhelm Hugo Bickell," in *Personenlexikon zur Christlichen Archäologie. Forscher und Persönlichkeiten vom 16. bis zum 21. Jahrhundert*, ed. Stefan Heid and Martin Dennert (Regensburg: Schnell und Steiner, 2012), 186.
3 Enno Littmann, "Mark Lidzbarski (1868-1928)," in *Ein Jahrhundert Orientalistik: Lebensbilder aus der Feder von Enno Littmann und Verzeichnis seiner Schriften*, ed. Rudi Paret and Anton

marian Hans Bauer (1878-1937), a former Catholic priest of humble Bavarian descent who refused to bring the intellectual sacrifice of renouncing modernism, rather involuntarily drifted away into open waters, and became one of the pioneers of a new period in Semitic linguistics.[4]

These three scholars distinguished themselves in the most important areas of specialisation within Semitics during an age of increasing professionalism, that is, the study of Syriac and Arabic manuscripts, West Semitic inscriptions, and grammatical analysis. They dealt with basically the same language subgroups, received a largely identical academic training, thought about similar problems using common epistemic skills, and participated in shared scholarly networks, spending their days reading widely, trying to make accurate observations, and contributing new matter.[5] Their individual lives and works, however, all illustrate the tension between confessional loyalties and an increasingly secular environment. While Lidzbarski and Bauer converted to Protestantism during their studies in Berlin, Bickell took the opposite direction and joined the service of the Roman Church after graduation in Marburg. A striking example of acculturation, by contrast, is Jacob Barth (1851-1914), a student of Fleischer's and later teacher of Carl Heinrich Becker. Barth operated successfully within the same paradigm as his contemporaries and yet taught at the Berlin Orthodox Jewish Seminary. He was part of an environment otherwise largely cocooned from the historical-positivist approach then current at state universities and thereby bridged the gap between the secular, the scholarly, and the observant religious milieus.[6]

Schall (Wiesbaden: Harrassowitz, 1955), 46-51; Walter Bauer, "Mark Lidzbarksi zum Gedächtnis," *Nachrichten von der Gesellschaft der Wissenschaften zu Göttingen: Geschäftliche Mitteilungen* (1928/29), 71-77; see also *Auf rauhem Wege: Jugenderinnerungen eines deutschen Professors* (Giessen: Töpelmann, 1927), published anonymously, and Ludmila Hanisch, *Aufzeichnungen von Mark Lidzbarski (1868-1928): Aus den Nachlässen der Deutschen Morgenländischen Gesellschaft* (Halle: Universitäts- und Landesbibliothek Sachsen-Anhalt, 2015).

4 Holger Gzella, "Hans Bauer und die historisch-vergleichende Semitistik," in *Studien zur Semitistik und Arabistik: Festschrift für Hartmut Bobzin zum 60. Geburtstag*, ed. Otto Jastrow, Shabo Talay, and Herta Hafenrichter (Wiesbaden: Harrassowitz, 2008), 141-182.

5 Reviews, obituaries, references for *Habilitation* and appointment procedures, and personal letters attest to a fairly consistent set of academic virtues in Semitics and the hierarchical relations between them for this period: excellent knowledge of languages and texts was central, acumen and originality generally outranked mere learning and industry, at least if compatible with judgment and common sense, but oversophistication, pretension, and mere eclecticism were frowned upon.

6 There are only very few and brief biographical sketches of Barth; particularly useful and based on personal knowledge is Carl Heinrich Becker, "Jacob Barth," *Der Islam* 6 (1915), 200-202.

The four different cases addressed here thus exemplify the complex interaction of Near Eastern studies with distinct denominational identities during a formative period. They show how personalities from various backgrounds gravitated towards the ideal of a professional scholar with its particular intellectual virtues, and how they responded to the resulting dilemmas. Documents such as private letters (obviously the main form of long-distance communication then), personal reminiscences (especially in the often-extensive obituaries in periodicals or the transactions of learned societies), or even autobiographical reflections (as in the case of Bickell and Lidzbarski) furnish immediate insights into their lives and concerns. The topics they chose to discuss, or to avoid, offer further, albeit indirect, clues as to their self-understanding and can at times be supplemented by iconographic information:[7] for instance, photographs of Barth, Lidzbarski, and Bauer, despite their very different biographies, show that they dressed in a similar fashion, just like most other German nineteenth-century professors, and the beard styles of Barth and Bauer also resemble each other, as do the glasses of Bauer and Lidzbarski.[8] Yet Barth's kippah explicitly marks him as an Orthodox Jew, whereas Bickell conformed to the conventions of the Roman Catholic diocesan clergy of his time by being clean-shaven and wearing a priestly robe, whilst at the same time sporting his Austrian Order of Merit.[9] Even their attributes, then, suggest that the dilemmas they all experienced have common roots in the shift from "sacred" to "secular" philology in nineteenth-century Semitics. In order to understand the distinct personal reactions prompted by the professionalization of the field, it is essential to briefly sketch the changes in subject matter, approach, and infrastructural underpinnings that it underwent during this period.[10]

---

[7] An in-depth study of the often highly-stylized pictorial representations of scholars in the nineteenth and early twentieth centuries, their dress code, haircut, attributes, and pose, would no doubt lead to interesting results. Much suitable comparative material is readily available in, e.g., Wilhelm Rau, *Bilder 135 deutscher Indologen*, 2nd ed. (Wiesbaden: Steiner, 1982).

[8] Already A. E. Housman, "The Application of Thought to Textual Criticism," *Proceedings of the Classical Association* 18 (1922), 67-84, addressed the proverbial cliché of "Teutonic professors" with their "goggle eyes behind large spectacles, and ragged moustaches saturated in lager beer" (71).

[9] Dietrich, "Bickell," plate before page 25; <https://de.wikipedia.org/wiki/Mark_Lidzbarski#/media/File:Lidzbarski_Mark.jpg> (last accessed 28 January 2019); Hans Wehr, "Nachruf auf Hans Bauer," *Zeitschrift der Deutschen Morgenländischen Gesellschaft* 91 (1937), 175-184, plate before page 177; and Gzella, "Bauer," 182 (drawing) <https://upload.wikimedia.org/wikipedia/commons/7/78/YaakovBarthPhoto.jpg> (last accessed 28 January 2019).

[10] For a recent survey with further bibliography, see Holger Gzella, "Expansion of the Linguistic Context of the Hebrew Bible / Old Testament: Hebrew Among the Languages of

The academic investigation of Semitic idioms arose in Early Modern Europe chiefly as a means to gain a deeper understanding of the original Hebrew and Aramaic text of the Old Testament. Cognate "classical" languages such as Syriac, Arabic, and Ethiopic that produced long-standing literary traditions were studied for determining the precise meaning of particular lexemes in the Biblical corpus (the exact nuance is still debated for those many cases where a word occurs but rarely or in ambiguous contexts) and for making the ancient Bible translations accessible as a source of information for textual criticism (because they may preserve indirect reflexes of the correct reading or interpretation of a certain passage that was subsequently obscured in the transmission of the original). Linguistic analysis was focused on grammar and lexicon and had a strongly functional character. The most popular formats of scholarly production in this area were thus teaching grammars with practical chrestomathies, dictionaries of single languages, and comparative lists of parallel features or words; they paved the way for the great Polyglot Bibles as the towering achievements of Semitic learning in the seventeenth century.[11]

Under the influence of Enlightenment thought, however, Hebrew was dethroned first by a "secular" study of Arabic, as embodied in the works of Johann Jacob Reiske (1716-1774),[12] and then by the many new findings of the nineteenth century: manuscripts were acquired, archaeological sites and inscriptions uncovered, scripts and languages deciphered. These discoveries offered, for the first time, a source-based access to the grand pristine civilizations of the Near East. The combined heritage of Enlightenment and Romanticism also produced a novel understanding of the Biblical text as a human and historical artefact that was shaped by continuous editing. Progress in comparative linguistics eventually provided a rational historical framework for the classification and mutual relations of the individual Semitic languages, thereby singling them out as a coherent object of study from other "Oriental" idioms like

---

the Ancient Near East," in *Hebrew Bible / Old Testament: The History of its Interpretation, Vol. III: From Modernism to Post-Modernism: The Nineteenth and Twentieth Centuries, Part 1: The Nineteenth Century – a Century of Modernism and Historicism*, ed. Magne Sæbø (Göttingen: Vandenhoeck & Ruprecht, 2012), 134-167.

11 See also Holger Gzella, "Wilhelm Gesenius als Semitist: Das 'Lehrgebäude' in seinem wissenschaftsgeschichtlichen Kontext," in *Biblische Exegese und hebräische Lexikographie: Das "Hebräisch-deutsche Handwörterbuch" von Wilhelm Gesenius als Spiegel und Quelle alttestamentlicher und hebräischer Forschung, 200 Jahre nach seiner ersten Auflage*, ed. Stefan Schorch and Ernst-Joachim Waschke (Berlin: De Gruyter, 2013), 184-208, esp. 185-189.

12 Aptly summarized by Johann Fück, *Die arabischen Studien in Europa bis in den Anfang des 20. Jahrhunderts* (Leipzig: Harrassowitz, 1955), 108-124; note Reiske's self-confessed indifference to the *philologia sacra* (reference on p. 111). A full biography of this intriguing man remains to be written.

Persian and Turkish.[13] The late nineteenth and early twentieth centuries then saw a cleavage between a traditional, strictly empirical, style of Semitic philology, championed by Theodor Nöldeke (1836-1930) and his many students, and the more modern, evolutionary, approach of Carl Brockelmann (1868-1956).[14] While established nomenclature and inherited encyclopaedic interests faded but gradually (even today, departments and degree programs all over the world quite regularly contain the term "Oriental," and Brockelmann, like several of his contemporaries, was also a highly competent classical Turkologist), these new methodological underpinnings mark an important break in terms of the self-conceptualisation of the discipline, in relation to the older *studia orientalia*.

Such developments had a lasting impact on the infrastructural embedding of the field. The investigation of Hebrew and other Semitic idioms was no longer confined to, but still entrenched in, theological curricula that remained faithful to the Reformers' emphasis on the study of Scripture in the original version. Numerous decentralized Protestant faculties supported competition and diversity, especially in northern Germany, fuelled by the attractive career perspectives of vicars. Simultaneously, Semitics was firmly anchored in academe by means of its own professorships, journals, and learned societies. It cemented its reputation as an elite discipline that demanded mastery of several difficult languages, with their diverging scripts, and wide learning as well as precision and judgment. Old Testament exegesis, by contrast, especially in the form of historical, or "higher," criticism in Germany, emerged only then as a proper and respected academic subject governed by wide-ranging historical imagination rather than grammatical exactness.[15] Nonetheless, the boundaries were fuzzy: various scholars still operated successfully in both fields, such as August Dillmann (1823-1894), at the same time the leading expert on Classical Ethiopic and an authority in Pentateuchal criticism. Indeed, many theologians learned at least some Syriac and Arabic besides Biblical Hebrew in the course of their studies, because their fathers, teachers, or other role models had once done so as well.

---

13   Gzella, "Expansion," 135-140.
14   Ibid., 156-167.
15   Ibid., 140-145. On the rise of source criticism, see Thomas Römer, "'Higher Criticism': The Historical and Literary-critical Approach – with Special Reference to the Pentateuch," in *Hebrew Bible / Old Testament: The History of its Interpretation, Vol. III: From Modernism to Post-Modernism: The Nineteenth and Twentieth Centuries, Part 1: The Nineteenth Century – a Century of Modernism and Historicism*, ed. Magne Sæbø (Göttingen: Vandenhoeck & Ruprecht, 2012), 393-423, and Rudolf Smend, "The Work of Abraham Kuenen and Julius Wellhausen," ibid., 424-453.

In addition, at least some Biblical Hebrew was offered at many *Gymnasia* as the third classical language besides Latin and Greek, in particular in Germany and in the Netherlands, and was taught with a similarly strong emphasis on grammar.[16] The standardized school curriculum thereby provided early experience with the Near East as the original context of the Bible and Christianity to the sons of teachers, doctors, civil servants, vicars, merchants, and professionals in commerce and industry who chiefly populated the *Gymnasia* of those days. It offered a suitable challenge even for bright pupils who did not have a religiously-motivated interest in Scripture – like Theodor Nöldeke or Justus Olshausen (1800-1882) – but wanted something more "exotic," perhaps more difficult, but still familiar, than the rather mainstream study of Ancient Greece and Rome.[17] Prestige, visibility, and scope thus buttressed the standing of Semitics in the late-nineteenth-century academic landscape dominated by a Protestant middle class that defined itself by shared intellectual and cultural values.

As the chief goal of traditional philology in the strict sense is "to get it right" – be it the original reading of a text transmitted in manuscripts, a bewildering grammatical detail, or the etymology and meaning of a specific word – the study of Semitic languages is ideologically neutral and could play different roles in the struggle between scientific method and confessional identity.[18] Either, it could be instrumental in rigorously placing Sacred Scripture into its historical context by unlocking comparative sources or individuating different layers in a composite text on grounds of linguistic variation. When applied to this end, it would undermine a flat reading of the Doctrine of Inspiration and

---

16   It was not grouped together with the ancient languages but with religious education, however, cf. *Centralblatt für die gesamte Unterrichtsverwaltung in Preußen* 1867: 13-14; 1898: 688-689. I am not aware of any comprehensive study of the teaching of Biblical Hebrew in secondary schools since the Reformation period, but it is a topic that would certainly merit a monograph.

17   On the social background, education, and daily lives of Protestant vicars in particular, who constituted an important part of the German middle class in the nineteenth century (and amounted to ca. 25 percent of all academics in Germany around 1850), see, e.g., Oliver Janz, *Bürger besonderer Art: Evangelische Pfarrer in Preußen 1850-1914* (Berlin: De Gruyter, 1994), with copious bibliographical references. Jürgen Kocka, "Bildungsbürgertum – Gesellschaftliche Formation oder Historikerkonstrukt?," in *Bildungsbürgertum im 19. Jahrhundert, Teil IV: Politischer Einfluß und gesellschaftliche Formation*, ed. Jürgen Kocka (Stuttgart: Klett-Cotta, 1989), 9-20, at 15. For the role of the classical grammar school in providing access to the typically German *Bildungsbürgertum* and its increasing permeability towards the end of the nineteenth century, see ibid., 19.

18   For an outline focused on Anglophone scholarship, see James Turner, *Philology: The Forgotten Origins of the Modern Humanities* (Princeton, NJ: Princeton University Press, 2014), 210-229; 357-368; 375-378.

its fundamental role in Jewish, Catholic, and indeed conservative Protestant orthodoxy.[19] That was the path chosen by, above all, the renegade Hebrew Bible scholar and historian Julius Wellhausen (1844-1918), who, despite his linguistic prowess and purposeful move from a Chair in Old Testament to a Professorship in Semitic languages, never became a grammarian of the technical sort.[20] Or, it could provide a safe haven for those who, like Bickell and later Barth, did not wish to deviate from their respective religious orthodoxy by reducing Scripture to a purely historical document and thus confined their interest in language to textual, grammatical, and lexical analysis at the word-level. Finally, it could offer a lasting application of the scholarly virtues of the exegete, such as close and sensitive reading, an empirical mindset, and intellectual honesty, to a related subject-matter and thus enable those who strayed from Jewish or Christian orthodoxy, like Lidzbarski or Bauer, to continue to make good use of their familiarity with Biblical languages and texts, even if they could no longer subscribe to the premises of a certain confessional framework but avoided to critically engage with it. Philology is where all these paths met.

How exactly, then, did Bickell, Lidzbarski, Bauer, and Barth as Semitic Philologists relate to the persona of the nineteenth-century "Prussian" professor, i.e., to the higher civil servant publicly entrusted with research on and teaching of a certain subject who was part of an academic community united by an often similar family background, culture as well as lifestyle (cemented by close-knit social networks and shared interests in "canonical" literature, music, and the visual arts), and adherence, with varying degrees, to the basic tenets that values and meaning are embodied in pure learning, that reality is always historically conditioned, and that truth can be pursued by transcending subjective judgments in which the objective spirit subsists?[21] And how did their

---

19 Cf. Gerald P. Fogarty, "The Catholic Church and Historical Criticism of the Old Testament," in *Hebrew Bible / Old Testament: The History of its Interpretation, Vol. III: From Modernism to Post-Modernism: The Nineteenth and Twentieth Centuries, Part 1: The Nineteenth Century – a Century of Modernism and Historicism*, ed. Magne Sæbø (Göttingen: Vandenhoeck & Ruprecht, 2012), 244-261; Edward Breuer and Chanan Gafni, "Jewish Biblical Scholarship between Tradition and Innovation," ibid., 262-303.

20 Wellhausen's own account of his alienation from theology surfaces in several of his letters, especially in his request for Justus Olshausen's advice about a future career path in 1880. See Rudolf Smend, ed., *Julius Wellhausen: Briefe* (Tübingen: Mohr Siebeck, 2013), n. 65. The various passages illustrating Wellhausen's stance on Semitics vis-à-vis theology have been assembled and analyzed in Holger Gzella, "Review of Smend (ed.), *Briefe*," *Bibliotheca Orientalis* 73 (2016), 482-491.

21 For a dense description of the attitudes of German professors and their social background during the period in question as self-conscious bearers of culture that ennobled the state

respective choices of topics interact with their biographical decisions? One should stress that this ideal was not a permanent achievement; rather, it had to be constantly renewed in everybody by means of tireless work, regular contact with high culture, and what was agreed to be proper conduct.

Bickell's main dilemma was, as he so eloquently writes in his "confessions" from 1870, the clash between his fascination with philology in general and Protestant theology with its traditional focus on source languages and history as the natural intellectual habitat in which he grew up on the one hand, and a growing contempt of the Lutheran doctrine of grace and redemption, which he had considered a break with pristine Christian thought since he was seventeen, on the other. By contrast, he was attracted by the logical coherence of Catholic teaching, its appeal to common sense, and its historical pedigree in ecclesiastical tradition. At the same time, he could not accommodate his firm belief in the divine inspiration of Scripture and his dislike of subjective exegesis with the view, then increasingly accepted in liberal academic circles in Germany, that the Biblical text in its transmitted form has been compiled from many different sources in the course of several centuries and bears the mark of distinct, even contradictory, theological agendas.[22]

Both convictions had a major impact on his personal and professional life and alienated him from the milieu in which he no doubt could have made a splendid career. Even if his personal account is to some extent colored by the apologetic discourse of the day and its clichés, there is little reason to doubt its overall sincerity. These intense ponderings accompanied what otherwise looks like a fairly standard academic record. Gustav Bickell was born in Kassel in 1838 as the son of the conservative professor of church law and later minister of justice Johann Wilhelm Bickell (1799-1848). He studied theology and Semitic as well as Indo-European languages in Marburg and Halle, taught the latter two subjects as a *Privatdozent* since his *Habilitation* in 1862 in Marburg and the following year also in Giessen.

When editing a manuscript containing Ephrem's Syriac *Carmina Nisibena* in London, however, his historical sense was immediately captured by the antiquity of the belief in the Immaculate Conception that he inferred from those

---

and justified its existence, see Fritz K. Ringer, *The Decline of the German Mandarins: The German Academic Community, 1890-1933* (Cambridge, MA: Harvard University Press, 1969), esp. 14-127.

22 *Convertitenbilder*, 418-436 (on his reservations against the Lutheran *sola fide* doctrine); 436-445 (on his sense of historical continuity in the Christian tradition); 451-455 and 457-459 (on his preference for an objective and authoritative interpretation of the divinely-revealed Scriptures grounded in apostolic succession).

beautiful poems.[23] As a consequence, he converted to Catholicism in 1865 after a long struggle with his denominational identity – the final step was delayed by exposure to anti-Catholic bias in his social environment – and entered the diocesan seminary in Fulda, being ordained to the priesthood already in 1867. Converts with a full university training in Protestant theology were apparently so warmly appreciated that diocesan bishops did not necessarily require them to undergo the full Catholic curriculum (let alone internships) and gave them much liberty in following their academic interests. Bickell subsequently continued his scholarly vocation as extraordinary professor of Oriental languages in Münster from 1871, as professor of Christian archaeology and Semitic languages at the Theological Faculty in Innsbruck (then firmly in the hands of the Society of Jesus) from 1874, and, finally, as professor of Semitics at the Philosophical Faculty of the University of Vienna from 1891 until his death in 1906.

Bickell's choice of academic subjects reflects his personal decisions. His fine *Grundriß der hebräischen Grammatik* (Leipzig: Brockhaus, 1869/1870; later also translated into English and French) with its clear historical approach along the lines of Olshausen's earlier work may still bear witness to his original training, since Hebrew grammar and historical-comparative philology were by no means subjects in which Catholics excelled.[24] Yet, like Barth several decades later, he purposefully avoided questions of higher criticism, excepting his *Der Prediger über den Wert des Daseins* (Innsbruck: Wagner, 1884), an eccentric contribution on the original composition of the Book of Qohelet, whose position in the Biblical canon is far from central anyway. Instead, he rigorously subordinated the human element in Scripture to ecclesiastical authority and focused, as far as the Biblical writings are concerned, on textual detail and on putting Biblical poetry into the straightjacket of regular verse patterns. "Lower criticism," after all, was not to the same extent affected by the historical turn that characterized the more ambitious approaches in Protestant exegesis, especially the growing consensus that large parts of the Pentateuch had to be assigned to the post-exilic period and hence could not be of Mosaic authorship, and therefore did not undermine the role of Scripture as the foundation of dogmatic and moral tenets sanctioned by divine authority.[25]

While these works of his are now long forgotten, Bickell achieved lasting fame as a student of Syriac literature. (One may speculate that Syriac, with its

---

23   Ibid., 454.
24   See Gzella, "Expansion," 161, for a brief characterization of this useful little work.
25   Suspicion about historical criticism in official Catholic teaching lasted far into the twentieth century; see Fogarty, "Catholic Church," 246-257.

fixed metres, also influenced his views on Hebrew verse.) His editions of Ephrem's *Carmina Nisibena* (Leipzig: Brockhaus, 1866),[26] the collected works of Isaac of Antioch, *Opera omnia* (Giessen: Ricker, 1873-1877), and the extremely corrupted manuscript of *Kalilag und Damnag* (Leipzig: Brockhaus, 1876), for which he collaborated with the renowned Göttingen Sanskritist Theodor Benfey (1809-1881), are still important, and without his *Conspectus rei Syrorum litterariæ* (Münster: Theißing, 1871), Anton Baumstark's *Geschichte der syrischen Literatur* (Bonn: Marcus and Weber, 1922), the fullest handbook even today, could not have been written.[27]

Editing Syriac and Arabic texts was a highly respected occupation in the late nineteenth and early twentieth centuries, because doing it well required excellent knowledge of languages and contents, patience, meticulousness, and judgment, that is, it displayed all the uncontested philological virtues.[28] Moreover, written sources served as the basis of all further historical examination, hence competent editions, like dictionaries and grammars, occupied a prominent place in the hierarchy of scholarly genres and enjoyed a much greater prestige than specialized topical studies. (The latter would, once one had obtained a doctorate and a *Habilitation*, normally appear in the form of journal articles, then considered less weighty than books – which were also considerably more arduous to write before the advent of electronic word processing.) Bickell's contributions are particularly remarkable for their accuracy, their elegant translations, and, in the case of the *Carmina Nisibena*, the thorough introduction that places Ephrem's poems in their historical and dogmatic context. The author clearly carved out the niche he had selected for himself to very good results.

The study of the Syriac tradition also more generally bespeaks his own interest in Christian antiquities, which he depicts so vividly in his autobiographical sketch – and which sets him apart from leading Syriacists with little appreciation of Syriac literature itself, such as Nöldeke, who only got into that field because the university library at Kiel had acquired a suitable amount of relevant books.[29] However, it was also a Catholic enterprise in a similar way to how

---

26 The comment on p. 1 on Ephrem's excellence among the Syriac writers thanks to his "venerable antiquity, elegant diction, and weighty reasoning" (*cum veneranda antiquitate, sermonis elegantia, argumenti gravitate*) seems to bear witness to Bickell's "Damascus road experience" in London.

27 Unsurprisingly, Baumstark (1872-1948), one of the founding fathers of the comparative study of liturgical traditions, was a Catholic, too, though the son of a convert from Protestantism.

28 Cf. Housman's praise of the textual critic in "Application of Thought."

29 Nöldeke's letters brim with remarks that show his disdain for the contents of Syriac (and Arabic) writings, see, e.g., his comparison of reading Ephrem's poems with the strains of

source criticism of the Bible was a Protestant one.[30] With its basically identical doctrine of the Sacraments, its participation in the apostolic succession, its similar moral guidelines, its solemn liturgy, and its esteem for the saints, above all the Virgin Mary, Syriac Christianity feels very close to Roman Catholicism, yet without much of the historically- and politically-conditioned polemics that had put a long-standing strain on relations with the Greek and Russian Orthodox churches. No wonder, then, that the investigation of Eastern Christianity and the historical-comparative study of its traditions as well as liturgical practices chiefly evolved in Catholic scholarship during the late nineteenth and early twentieth centuries. As an area of specialization, it was dogmatically as unproblematic as language teaching and the study of the ancient translations of the Bible, and it served ecclesiastical politics.[31] The same interests as in Bickell's research – Hebrew grammar and textual criticism, Syriac, and other Aramaic languages – also feature prominently in his university classes.[32]

And yet, despite the proof of personal convictions that must have seemed shockingly unenlightened in a field predominantly steeped in secularized Protestant academic culture such as Semitics, especially during the *Kulturkampf* of the last decades of the nineteenth century, and his engagement in confessional polemics, such as the publication of his ardent defence of Papal Infallibility (*Gründe für die Unfehlbarkeit des Kirchenoberhauptes nebst Widerlegung der Einwürfe* [Münster: Russel, 1870]), Bickell was by no means a loner among his peers. His centrifugal position to liberal Protestantism did not tarnish his reputation as a scholar of Syriac who attained the highest standards of craftsmanship.[33] The rationalist Nöldeke, who made no secret of his admira-

---

moving his household in a letter to Lidzbarski from 1914, reproduced in Hanisch, *Aufzeichnungen*, 29-34. Similarly the communications in Bernhard Maier, *Gründerzeit der Orientalistik: Theodor Nöldekes Leben und Werk im Spiegel seiner Briefe* (Würzburg: Ergon-Verlag, 2013), unfortunately often abbreviated, e.g., 298 (to Hoffmann, 1903) and 390 (to Snouck Hurgronje, 1921): reading Syriac is a penalty for sins committed in a former life, and Ephrem only has an important place in the history of human folly!

30 Gzella, "Expansion," 141-142.
31 Ancient Near Eastern languages and archaeology were thus pillars of research and teaching when, in 1909, the Pontifical Biblical Institute was founded in order to keep pace with progress in Protestant exegesis, see Holger Gzella, "Il rapporto tra l'esegesi biblica e gli studi orientali alla soglia di un nuovo millennio," *Acta Pontificii Instituti Biblici* 11/2009-10 (2010), 731-747, esp 731-734, and Maurice Gilbert, *The Pontifical Biblical Institute. A Century of History (1909-2009)*, trans. Leo Arnold (Rome: Biblical Institute Press, 2009), 11-30.
32 Wolfdieter Bihl, *Orientalistik an der Universität Wien. Forschungen zwischen Maghreb und Ost- und Südasien: Die Professoren und Dozenten* (Vienna: Böhlau, 2009), 60.
33 His edition of *Kalilag und Dimnag*, for instance, earned high praise from colleagues, including the notoriously critical Theodor Nöldeke, see, e.g., the latter's review in *Zeitschrift der Deutschen Morgenländischen Gesellschaft* 30 (1876), 752-772.

tion for Darwin, excluded him from the "sane Orientalists" ("zurechnungsfähigen Orientalisten"), to be sure, but at the same time called him "outstanding" ("vortrefflich").[34] The likewise anti-ecclesiastical and anti-theological Wellhausen, in many ways Bickell's polar opposite, highly respected him as a "learned, hard-working, and perceptive man" ("gelehrter, fleißiger und scharfsinniger Mann") and even nominated him, successfully, for a membership of the Göttingen Academy in 1901.[35] Such a gesture first and foremost confirms Wellhausen's unbiased eye for scholarly quality, but it is also indicative of the considerable common ground in an elite discipline with rather few serious practitioners in an age when everybody read everything relevant. Despite the stereotype of bourgeois narrow-mindedness, nineteenth-century academic culture breathes an egalitarian spirit, insofar as a proven ability according to uncontroversial benchmarks could compensate for personal views and a lifestyle that may have seemed eccentric to the majority: whoever knew his languages and primary sources counted as "one of us."

By focussing on Syriac religious literature, Bickell thus successfully combined the scholarly virtues of learning, precision, and unlocking new knowledge with aesthetic appreciation, a romantic sense of the past, and an unbroken fidelity to the pristine Christian tradition. His position as a Catholic priest teaching Semitic languages mostly at Austrian universities was marginal in both German-speaking Semitic scholarship (where Catholic practitioners were rare throughout the nineteenth and early twentieth centuries)[36] and Catholic Theology (where Semitics was much less prominent than in Protestant circles, because the authoritative Biblical text was the Latin Vulgate). However, in competently editing and translating Syriac manuscripts, he applied one of the most widely accepted genres of scholarly production in the field and, owing to the importance of the authors and texts of his preference, participated in an academic discourse that extended beyond confessional

---

34   Maier, *Gründerzeit*, 171 (296 on Nöldeke's esteem for Darwin and 320, 322, and 377 on his self-professed rationalism).

35   See Smend (ed.), *Briefe*, nos. 119 and 595. It is not quite clear what Wellhausen meant when he said, in his letter of nomination, that Bickell had been "bitterly disappointed" by the Catholic Church in his old age (letter no. 595: "Ich gönne dem alten Mann sehr ein Zeichen der Sympathie; er ist ihrer werth und bedarf ihrer. Er hat sich in seiner Jugend dem Katholicismus zugewandt, ist aber jämmerlich enttäuscht worden und sitzt nun zwischen zwei Stühlen"), or whether he simply wanted to make the nominee more palatable to a learned society that would generally have had little sympathy for passionate ultramontanism.

36   One of the few exceptions was Hubert Grimme (1864-1942) of Münster; see Franz Taeschner, "Hubert Grimme," *Zeitschrift der Deutschen Morgenländischen Gesellschaft* 96 (1942), 381-392.

boundaries. He is thus an example of how personal religious beliefs can determine the specific choice of an academic subject and yet lead to results that are perfectly acceptable even outside that particular denominational framework. His biographical decisions were nonetheless incompatible with the type of the "Prussian professor" and secular Protestantism as the governing intellectual *Leitkultur*; they made him "bail out" rather than "fit it."

Not so Lidzbarski, Bickell's junior by thirty years. He sacrificed his entire youth to attain the life of a "Prussian professor" that would have been at Bickell's fingertips and put all of his seemingly boundless energy into consolidating the fields of Semitic epigraphy and Mandaic literature. Born as Mordechai Lidzbarski to Chassidic parents in 1868 in Płock, then part of Poland under Russian sway, he underwent a strict Talmudic education from early childhood. His interest in language, as documented in his autobiography, and the keen desire to learn "something modern," however, made him exchange, at the age of fourteen, his home for the Protestant grammar school in Posen, a bulwark of German culture, and a supplementary education in Berlin for coming to grips with Latin and Greek as well as guided self-study in several Semitic languages. That was quite an achievement, since *Gymnasium* pupils would normally enrol at the age of nine or ten, and the rigid classical curriculum made it difficult to transfer from other school types. Eventually, he severed his family ties, immersed himself in German language and life and converted to Protestantism as a student. Determined to become a professor, he read Semitics in Berlin in penurious conditions. After his doctorate in Berlin under Sachau and Schrader in 1893, his *Habilitation* in Kiel in 1896, both on Arabic subjects, and years of uninterrupted hard work, he obtained professorships in Greifswald (1907), and, finally, in Göttingen (1917), where he died in 1928.

In concentrating on the flourishing area of West Semitic epigraphy during the first part of his professional career, Lidzbarski practiced Semitics in a very modern form: only in the closing decades of the nineteenth century did the discovery of Hebrew, Phoenician, Aramaic, and other inscriptions provide a rigorously historical framework for Biblical Hebrew and the classical varieties of Aramaic, all of which have only been transmitted in much later manuscript traditions, and made it possible to study peoples mentioned in the Bible on the basis of primary sources.[37] His main contributions to this area chime with such recent developments in bearing a decisively empirical mark: the two-volume *Handbuch der nordsemitischen Epigraphik nebst ausgewählten Inschriften* (Weimar: Felber, 1898) with its comprehensive survey of the history of research,

---

37 Gzella, "Expansion," 135-137; Holger Gzella, *A Cultural History of Aramaic: From the Beginnings to the Advent of Islam* (Leiden: Brill, 2015), 6-9.

a bibliography of no less than 1163 titles between 1616 and 1896, editions of the most important texts with analyses of their script, language, and contents as well as their material underpinnings, and the three-volume *Ephemeris für semitische Epigraphik* (Giessen: Töpelmann, 1900-1915), which extensively documents all new discoveries and the discussion about readings and interpretations. Lidzbarski's epigraphic work was largely devoted to assembling secondary literature, sifting through countless proposals, and separating the wheat from the chaff. Hard palaeographic, grammatical, and archaeological evidence was more to his taste than Biblical source criticism or rabbinic exegesis, which he consistently avoided, as he did with Biblical philology.[38] It is revealing how he contrasts Nöldeke's grammatical excellence and Julius Euting's (1839-1913) keen eye for palaeography with the many "insignificant articles by amateurish vicars" ("unbedeutende Aufsätze dilettantischer Reverends").[39]

As in the case of Bickell, however, Lidzbarski did not blot out his intellectual heritage, he transformed it. While even his contributions to epigraphy may ultimately owe something to Talmudic reasoning (ambiguous readings would have to be sorted out, the meanings of unknown words and expressions established, missing parts reconstructed, and plausible historical contexts proposed), it is the main focus of his last years, Mandaic language and literature, that profited most immediately from his Jewish Orthodox education. For Mandaic, the Aramaic variety in which the writings of the religious group of the Mandaeans are composed, is, due to a common origin in Southern Mesopotamia and despite the different script, linguistically very close to Jewish Babylonian Aramaic, that is, the idiom of the Aramaic parts of the Babylonian Talmud.[40] It has previously been overlooked that it must have been chiefly due to his familiarity with Jewish Babylonian Aramaic language and texts that Lidzbarski was able to so accurately edit and translate such an impressive amount of Mandaic writings, often only preserved in faulty manuscripts that require regular emendation. As a result, he was the first to make accessible this erstwhile marginal subject (the only reliable tool was then Nöldeke's magisterial *Mandäische Grammatik* [Halle: Verlag der Buchhandlung des Waisenhauses, 1875], based on but a small corpus) to students of Gnostic religion and historians of Early Christianity and thus to create a firm footing for a more

---

38   His contributions to Gotthelf Bergsträsser's *Hebräische Grammatik* (Leipzig: Hinrichs, 1918-1929) merely concern the passages on script and epigraphy (see the preface to vol. 2, 1 n. 2).
39   Lidzbarski, *Handbuch*, vol. 1, 109.
40   Gzella, *Cultural History*, 330-366, esp. 348-366. Note also Wellhausen's perceptive remark in a letter to Nöldeke: "so ein großer Rabbiner und Mandäer Lidzbarski auch ist" (Smend, ed., *Briefe*, no. 1063, 22 February 1916).

historical evaluation of Mandaism:[41] *Das Johannesbuch der Mandäer* (Giessen: Töpelmann, 1905-1915); *Mandäische Liturgien* (Berlin: Weidmann, 1920); and *Ginza: Der Schatz oder das große Buch der Mandäer* (Göttingen: Vandenhoeck & Ruprecht and Leipzig: Hinrichs, 1925). His editions enjoy a lasting value, and his index-cards with Mandaic vocabulary have been incorporated into the only real lexicon of the language currently available.[42]

Lidzbarski's ability to rely on an intimate knowledge of Jewish Babylonian Aramaic for making sense of Mandaic was a rare skill among academics in those days. After all, Jewish varieties of Aramaic other than Biblical and Targumic Aramaic were not normally taught in Protestant or secular curricula, hence even professional Aramaicists like Nöldeke had to consult informants, often students of theirs, with a traditional Jewish upbringing in order to integrate Talmudic and other Rabbinic evidence into their comparative perspective.[43] Hence Lidzbarski's work at the cutting-edge of Semitic scholarship of his time was to some extent ultimately indebted to his Chassidic education in Płock. Of course, the little-known Mandaic script and its idiosyncratic spelling did not pose any problems to such an expert epigrapher.

At the height of his career, Lidzbarski had become the doyen of Semitic epigraphy and of Mandaic studies and contributed like no other individual to their coming-of-age as independent sub-disciplines. Prestigious formal distinctions such as his membership of the Göttingen Academy in 1912 (first as a corresponding, since 1918 as an ordinary member), the warm words of authorities like Wellhausen,[44] and exchanges of letters with, among others, Nöldeke and his fellow-epigrapher Euting[45] attest to his sterling reputation. Still, the strictly matter-of-fact tone of his epistolary correspondence, which avoids all personal remarks to an extent quite untypical even for an early twentieth-century scholar,[46] and the single-handed way in which he ran the *Ephemeris*, the

---

41   For a brief outline of the history of Mandaic studies, see Charles G. Häberl, *The Neo-Mandaic Dialect of Khorramshahr* (Wiesbaden: Harrassowitz, 2009), 13-29.
42   Ethel S. Drower and Rudolf Macuch, *A Mandaic Dictionary* (Oxford: Oxford University Press, 1963), v.
43   See Gzella, "Expansion," 142-143.
44   See Smend, ed., *Briefe*, nos. 931, 974, and 975.
45   Both collections are still unpublished, but his correspondence with Nöldeke is preserved in the archive of the Deutsche Morgenländische Gesellschaft in Halle, and the one with Euting in the University Library at Strasbourg, see Hanisch, *Aufzeichnungen*, 6-7. Nöldeke's appreciation of Lidzbarski also emerges from a letter to Snouck Hurgronje from 1920, see Maier, *Gründerzeit*, 377 (in the same letter, Nöldeke stresses his own total lack of interest in Mandaean religion).
46   Note also Hanisch, *Aufzeichnungen*, 20: "Die Schreiben dokumentieren die gegenseitige Anerkennung der Kompetenz und zeigen zugleich, dass sich Lidzbarski in Briefen auf

most important periodical on Semitic inscriptions, breathe a markedly lonely air; there is also something tense in his critique of others.[47]

Such a reserved attitude may be the permanent scar of a conversion that was not restricted to changing one's religious convictions but also encompassed one's entire social environment and even academic interests. Lidzbarski, for one, appears to have purposefully abandoned any interest in rabbinic literature after he had re-invented himself,[48] but never seems to have been completely integrated into academic or other social life following the decades after his conversion.[49] As a result, one gets the impression of a very private man who adopted the persona of the "Prussian professor" with such zeal that he was completely absorbed by his solitary work at the forefront of a prestigious discipline that, like no other arts subject, embodied the main virtues of empirical philological scholarship, technical mastery, and scientific objectivity. He seems to have derived much of his energy from the desire to always prove himself. Similar to the amiable Bickell, but with greater determination, he selected the topics he pursued in a way that corresponded to his biographical choices. It is from the vantage point of his life's goal, leading the existence of a German professor as the culmination of upward social mobility, that he looked back on his youth when he published, a year before his death, his autobiography and recapitulated where he came from and how far he made it.[50] Even the title, *Auf rauhem Wege*, might echo the final stanza of the much-loved seventeenth-century Protestant hymn *Was Gott tut, das ist wohlgetan*: "Es mag mich auf die rauhe Bahn Not, Tod und Elend treiben, so wird Gott mich ganz väterlich in seinen Armen halten. Drum laß' ich ihn nur walten" ("On the rough road I may be driven by need, death, and misery, yet God will hold me in his arms like a father. Therefore I yield him all power").

Sachfragen konzentrierte und persönliche Mitteilungen vermied." Other Semitists, by contrast, regularly mention, e.g., health problems, family matters, travel impressions, and their own views on politics.

47 Littmann, "Lidzbarski," 49, even detects, quite appropriately, the attitude of an "Alleinherrscher."
48 The only Semitist at Berlin whose classes he never attended was, tellingly, the Orthodox Jew Barth, see Bauer, "Lidzbarski," 71; cf. also Hanisch, *Aufzeichnungen*, 24.
49 See Littmann, "Lidzbarski," 50: "Er fühlte sich heimatlos und einsam." Similarly, Bauer, "Lidzbarski," 76-77, on his lack of a social life and very rare attendance of the Göttingen Academy meetings. Both Littmann and Walter Bauer could rely on personal knowledge of Lidzbarski. However, this is not the place to speculate about reasons why he remained a life-long bachelor.
50 Omitting his name from such a personal document might simply result from his reserved character, but apparently, he still considered it an important enough testimony of his achievements to publish.

While an element of determination appears central to both Bickell's and Lidzbarski's ways into the field and their respective styles of practicing it, the third convert portrayed here, Johann Baptist (later Hans) Bauer, is a different case.[51] His modest origins as the early-orphaned son of a lower-class peasant from a village near Bamberg in rural Bavaria, where he was born in 1878, partly align him with the young Lidzbarski. However, Bauer could profit from the career opportunities offered by the Catholic Church to young men without sufficient means but with the interest in and aptitude for an academic study. The *Aufseesianum*, a Catholic boarding school in Bamberg, provided him with a sound secondary education. Upon graduation, his excellent record paved the way to his training for the priesthood at the German-Hungarian College and the Pontifical Gregorian University in Rome, then the best instruction available to those diocesan seminarians of whom bishops had particularly high hopes. The seven-year philosophical and theological curriculum was governed by the Neo-Scholastic tradition with its terminological sophistication as well as abstract thinking and accompanied by an almost military discipline in daily life.[52]

After his return as a priest to his home diocese of Bamberg in 1904, Bauer served as curate for two years and was subsequently given permission to study Near Eastern languages at Berlin and Leipzig, the latter in particular being a mecca of Arabic philology ever since Reiske. He used this opportunity to the full, immersed himself in his studies (which covered many different humanities subjects), and obtained a doctorate in 1910 with a revolutionary thesis on the Semitic verb as well as a *Habilitation* in 1912 on the teachings of the Arabic philosopher al-Ghazali, parts of whose work he later translated. In between these two formal qualifications, he spent some time in Beirut and Jerusalem and thereby also gained acquaintance with the modern Near East. There is evidence that he was groomed to take a professorship in Old Testament exegesis at the Catholic Theological Faculty in Bamberg in due course.

However, his life in a predominantly secular environment and his exposure to academic topics that must have been unsettling to an intellectually curious clergyman whose prior education had largely isolated him from the challenges of the modern world, triggered or at least reinforced a painful process of alienation from the Catholic Church and its teaching. Berlin of all places was at that time not only a vibrant capital but, under the Assyriologist Friedrich Delitzsch

---

[51] Gzella, "Hans Bauer," offers a recent and reasonably extensive biography also based on archival documents and a full study of Bauer's works; hence it is not necessary to repeat all the details here.

[52] Ibid., 142-145.

(1850-1922), also the center of "Panbabylonism," that is, the now obsolete idea that all concepts and institutions of Ancient Israelite religion were patterned after Mesopotamian models; Heinrich Zimmern (1862-1931) at Leipzig held similar views. This approach, radical though it was, bespoke the strictly philological and historical training that Bauer received in other branches of Semitics and eventually questioned his belief in the divine inspiration of Scripture. Stranded in a worldly society, with no spiritual environment to provide a counter-balance to his doubts, his identity as a priest was no longer a given. Other Catholic religious students in Berlin faced similar experiences, too.[53]

When finally required to take the oath against "modernism" in 1911, an obligatory measure to safeguard the intellectual and moral loyalty of Catholic clergy members in responsible positions, such as a soon-to-become professor, Bauer followed his conscience and refused. The reasons are reported in a letter sent in 1937 by prelate Theodor Geiger of Bamberg to the then rector of the German College, Fr. Karl Klein SJ, who solicited information about Bauer and the way things worked out for him a short while after his death. Geiger's reply cites from Bauer's original request, submitted in 1911, to step down from his priestly duties; it constitutes the only relevant personal testimony of Bauer's inner motives currently known.[54] In his study of Old Testament exegesis, he had, as he candidly admits, "seen too many things that he could not accommodate with the holiness and truthfulness of God" and, consequently, "had reservations about the Doctrine of Inspiration" and "could no longer perform a priestly function."[55]

In the following two years, Bauer was on sick leave for depression but continued his academic work, became a freemason in 1913, and, when confronted with this clear transgression of canon law in 1916, replied that he "could no longer accept all the articles of faith of the Catholic Church." So, while he "previously had no reason to seek a formal breach with the Church," he requested "not to consider him any longer a member of the diocesan clergy and the Catholic Church," and confirmed that he acted as he felt he should before God and

---

53   On Thaddäus Hyazinth Engert (1875-1945) and his fate, see Otto Weiß, *Der Modernismus in Deutschland: Ein Beitrag zur Theologiegeschichte* (Regensburg: Pustet, 1995), 292-314.

54   In the archive of the German College at Rome, "Briefsammlung 20. Jahrhundert," 10 April 1937.

55   In the original wording: "daß er die Ableg[un]g des Antimodernisten-Eides nicht mit seiner Überzeug[un]g vereinbaren könne. Somit könne er auch in Zukunft kein geistliches Amt mehr annehmen [und] sei genötigt, eine andere Stelle zu suchen. Seine Hauptschwierigkeiten lägen auf dem Gebiete der Exegese, besonders des Alten Testamentes. Bei seiner Beschäftig[un]g mit demselben habe er zu viel gesehen, was er mit der Heiligkeit [und] der Wahrhaftigkeit Gottes nicht in Einklang zu bringen wisse. So stellten sich naturgemäß Bedenken gegen die Inspirationslehre ein."

his conscience.[56] In the end, he was excardinated and formally converted to Protestantism in July 1916, married in 1920 – his wife Eugenie (née Kerschbaumer) came from a Catholic family nonetheless – and served as professor of Semitic language at Halle from 1922 until his death in 1937.

Contrary to Bickell, who passionately embraced the life that Bauer abandoned, the latter did not select and pursue his academic targets strictly in accordance with a prior religious conviction. Rather, he gradually, and apparently not always consciously, drifted away from an established career path under the influence of his studies, especially the radically secular approaches to Scripture that were on the upswing in his student days. And contrary to Lidzbarski, who had identified a German professorship as his life's goal and worked toward the same objective with utter resolution, ending up in that kind of position was apparently something that simply overcame Bauer.[57] Prelate Geiger had no doubt a point when he blamed Bauer's former superiors for allowing him to study, without any clear target, at universities with a Protestant signature, because faith is usually consolidated by regular contact with other believers, and it easily fades away in a non-religious environment without proper cultivation.

Even though Bauer's growing scepticism about Catholic doctrine was thus nourished by his immersion in the study of the Bible and Ancient Israel in a secular historical framework (no doubt in addition to his exposure to anti-Catholic bias in Prussia), he did not further pursue that line. Instead of becoming a source critic or historian of Near Eastern religion like Wellhausen, he mainly concentrated on historical-comparative philology and decided to stay away from Biblical exegesis altogether. The groundwork for all his later contributions was laid in lectures, seminars, and independent reading at Berlin and Leipzig, since his former training in Catholic theology would be of little direct help. Only in his publications on Arabic philosophy and its intellectual system could he make use of his acquaintance with Neo-Scholastic thought, which enabled him to handle definitions and abstract concepts with considerable ease.[58]

---

56 The gist of this letter, too, is preserved in Geiger's reply from 1937: "Darauf schrieb er, April 1916, d[a]ß es ihm nicht mehr möglich sei, alle Glaubenssätze der kath. Kirche anzuerkennen. Einen förmlichen Bruch mit der Kirche zu suchen habe er aber bis jetzt keine Veranlassung gehabt. Auf die an ihn nunmehr gestellten Fragen hin sehe er sich aber veranlaßt, an das Generalvikariat die Bitte zu richten, ihn nicht mehr als Mitglied der kath. Kirche [und] des Klerus der Diözese zu betrachten. Er tue genau das, was er vor Gott und seinem Gewissen tun zu müssen glaube, sodaß er damit seinen früheren guten Vorsätzen keineswegs untreu werde. – Daraufhin wurde er am 1. Mai 1916 suspendiert [und] exkardiniert...."
57 Gzella, "Hans Bauer," 142-145.
58 Ibid., 178-180.

In contradistinction to Lidzbarski, Bauer did not confine himself to the sober empiricism of the epigraphist, although his achievements in the latter domain are remarkable, and his participation, in 1930, in the decipherment of Ugaritic, the newly-discovered local language of a Syrian city state in the Late Bronze Age transmitted in a formerly unknown writing system, even bears the mark of genius.[59] His principal contribution to the field, however, are the two major reference grammars of Biblical Hebrew and Biblical Aramaic which he co-authored with Pontus Leander, the *Historische Grammatik der hebräischen Sprache des Alten Testamentes* (Halle: Niemeyer, 1922) and the *Grammatik des Biblisch-Aramäischen* (Halle: Niemeyer, 1927). Building upon several specialized studies that appeared throughout the preceding years, they were the first to analyze these two languages within a rigorously historical framework based on a systematic association of the attested grammatical forms with their reconstructed ancestors by way of phonetic laws.[60] He thereby departed from the older descriptive grammatical empiricism in the spirit of Nöldeke and employed a paradigm introduced from Indo-European into Semitics by his predecessor in Halle, Brockelmann.[61] After a period of growth of the material basis thanks to the publication of many new inscriptions and manuscripts as well as ongoing infrastructural consolidation during the late nineteenth century, Bauer inaugurated a new phase of historical-comparative Semitic linguistics. He even ventured into the emerging discipline of phonology and corresponded with its founder Nikolai Trubetzkoy (1890-1938) in the thirties, thus being one of the first Semitists to apply the concept of the phoneme.[62]

Being an outsider apparently enabled him to think independently and disregard the traditional boundaries of Semitics more easily. Despite his struggles with the Doctrine of Inspiration, however, none of his published works seems to be at variance with Catholic doctrine in the end. Bauer's ten-year journey from a Bavarian priest to a Prussian Protestant professor, during which he became a *Privatdozent* teaching a secular subject, a freemason, a convert, and a married man and father of two, can be best interpreted as a gradual and partly uncontrolled process of alienation from one lifestyle and gravitation toward another. It is not the execution of a biographical and scholarly program as it was the case with Bickell, Lidzbarski, or indeed Wellhausen (though with very

---

59   Ibid., 156; 175-178.
60   Ibid., 153-175.
61   Gzella, "Expansion," 166-167; for the most rigorous application of the "Neogrammarian" method to Hebrew currently available, see Benjamin D. Suchard, "The Development of the Biblical Hebrew Vowels" (PhD thesis, Leiden University, 2016).
62   Klaas-Hinrich Ehlers, *Strukturalismus in der deutschen Sprachwissenschaft: Die Rezeption der Prager Schule zwischen 1926 und 1945* (Berlin: De Gruyter, 2005), 175.

different outcomes in each of these cases). Bauer's study is situated at the front-line of his field, but the man henceforth circumvented the very topics that once caused the gap between him and the Church.

Whereas the biographies of Bickell, Lidzbarski, and Bauer all involve religious conversion, Jacob Barth, like them, practiced historical-comparative philology as part of an academic discourse that transcended confessional borders, and yet he remained a firmly Orthodox Jew. A native of Flehingen (1851) in Baden-Württemberg with its old Jewish community and a graduate of the *Gymnasium* in Karlsruhe, he received a philological training that was as solid as it could be: he studied Semitic languages in Berlin and under Fleischer in Leipzig, where he also obtained his doctorate in 1873, and worked for some time with Nöldeke in Strasbourg.[63] Subsequently, he served as a lecturer in Biblical exegesis and Jewish philosophy at the Orthodox Rabbinical Seminary in Berlin since 1874, since 1876, following his *Habilitation*, also at the state university, where he became an extraordinary professor in 1880 (Jews were still excluded from full professorships there), and led a productive scholarly life until his death in 1914. His environment was congenial to bridging the gap between orthodox faith and historical-comparative grammar. The Orthodox Seminary was established, like the Pontifical Biblical Institute in Rome for the Catholic clergy several decades later, for preparing rabbis with a traditional orientation to face the challenges of the modern world.[64] Marrying Rosa Hildesheimer, the daughter of the Seminary's founder, further cemented his affiliation with this institution and its objective.

Barth engaged actively and successfully with the secular, historical-comparative style of Semitic scholarship of his time by strictly focusing on grammar as an end in itself.[65] Especially his standard works on the nominal and pronominal systems of the Semitic languages, *Die Nominalbildung in den semitischen Sprachen* (Leipzig: Hinrichs, 1894) and *Die Pronominalbildung in den semitischen Sprachen* (Leipzig: Hinrichs, 1913), won him high acclaim. In addition,

---

63 Leipzig and Strasbourg were suitable places for someone with Barth's background and tenets, since Fleischer and Nöldeke each had many Jewish students. See Holger Preißler, "Heinrich Leberecht Fleischer: Ein Leipziger Orientalist, seine jüdischen Studenten, Promovenden und Kollegen," *Bausteine einer jüdischen Geschichte der Universität Leipzig*, ed. Stephan Wendehorst (Leipzig: Leiziger Universitätsverlag, 2006) 245-268.
64 Cf. Mordechai Breuer, *Jüdische Orthodoxie im Deutschen Reich 1871-1918* (Frankfurt: Jüdischer Verlag bei Athenäum, 1986), 120-133.
65 Becker, "Barth," emphatically portrays his teacher as a grammarian *pur sang* and thereby stresses the underlying conviction that, for Barth, philological competence was the basis of everything else.

he competently edited several Arabic texts[66] and authored numerous articles on the origin of individual grammatical morphemes as well as on the etymology of certain words in the light of comparative evidence. Even though they are not always convincing in their general conclusions, they brim with valuable and not otherwise easily accessible material gleaned during a lifetime of attentive reading. Representative examples appeared together as *Etymologische Studien zum semitischen insbesondere zum hebräischen Lexicon* (Leipzig: Hinrichs, 1893), *Wurzeluntersuchungen zum hebräischen und aramäischen Lexicon* (Leipzig: Hinrichs, 1902), and *Sprachwissenschaftliche Untersuchungen zum Semitischen* (Leipzig: Hinrichs, 1907-1911). He was also the first to formulate a principle later known as "Barth's Law," a rational account of the systematic variation between *a* and *i* in the vowel in the "imperfect" preformative of several Semitic languages, that is, the difference between, e.g., Classical Arabic *yaktubu* and Hebrew *yiḵtoḇ*, "he writes."[67]

This last success notwithstanding (in Semitics, only very few phonetic laws are named after an individual and thereby immortalize their discoverer), Barth approached the development of grammatical forms in the way that he learned as a student, i.e., by means of *ad hoc* analogies, spontaneous phonetic changes, and logical deduction, not in the modern fashion against the background of invariable phonetic regularities as championed by Brockelmann and then Bauer.[68] His epistolary correspondence with the leading secular, albeit generally conservative, Semitists and Arabists of his time – besides Nöldeke (to whom he remained particularly attached),[69] Zimmern, Snouck Hurgronje, and de Goeje – about grammatical and etymological problems as well as readings and translations of difficult passages shows that he was well-integrated into

---

66 Wellhausen's verdict that Barth was "kein Held im Arabischen" (Smend, ed., *Briefe*, n. 70) therefore seems unfair, but it was not necessarily colored by any overt anti-Semitic prejudice. On this latter, difficult, point, see Gzella, Review of Smend (ed.), *Briefe*, 485.
67 Jacob Barth, "Zur vergleichenden semitischen Grammatik," *Zeitschrift der Deutschen Morgenländischen Gesellschaft* 48 (1894), 1-21, esp. 4-6. Cf. Suchard, "Development," 207-208.
68 In several letters to Nöldeke, especially the one dated to 2 March 1913 (now part of the "Briefnachlass Theodor Nöldeke" in the University Library at Tübingen, no. Md 782-A12), Barth explicitly critiques Brockelmann's *Grundriß der vergleichenden Grammatik der semitischen Sprachen* (Berlin: Reuther & Reichard, 1908-1913): "Polemiken habe ich, wie Sie ja sehen, tunlichst unterlassen. Bei Brockelmann machte ich darum öfter e/e Ausnahme (ich hätte es viel häufiger tun können), weil sein Buch wegen seines Umfangs Vielen fälschlich als Autorität gilt, und weil er solche Aufstellungen, die von einer ihm nicht angenehmen Seite kommen, mit dem Ellbogen bei Seite zu schieben sucht" (last page). These words express antipathy rather than mere disagreement over the facts.
69 Documented, e.g., by his charming note in a letter dated to 28 April 1913 (now in the Tübingen collection, last page) that he celebrated the fortieth anniversary of their meeting with a "Mai-Bowle."

the more traditional echelons of the field. By contrast, he remained loyal to his orthodox conviction in refusing to engage with source criticism in his lectures on the Bible (excepting the different authorship of Deutero-Isaiah, which he thought had a Talmudic pedigree)[70] and in confining his publications to comparative grammar and Arabic textual criticism. Neither did the West Semitic inscriptions or Assyriology, which document the historical context of the Old Testament, occupy any prominent place in his work, and he also avoided textual criticism of the Bible. He thereby combined his religious and his scholarly identity the same way Bickell did by putting the focus on Syriac and Hebrew metre, that is, by practising a base-level style of old-fashioned philology that could more easily be squared with the concept of a divinely-inspired text.[71] An empirical attitude also underlies his popularizing critique of Panbabylonism in *Babel und israelitisches Religionswesen: Vortrag* (Berlin: Mayer and Müller, 1902). There he argued rationally, not apologetically, for the non-derivative character of Israelite religion and its institutions by disproving many of the Panbabylonist challenges and communicated his orthodox viewpoint in a suitable academic format. In the absence of further insights into his personal ideas, this lecture may serve as an illustration of the way he dealt with the aggressively secular approaches to Scripture in his day.

A comparative look at the personal and professional biographies of these four leading Hebraists and Aramaicists of the period between 1870 and 1930 thus confirms the initial hypothesis that they represent four different reactions to the persona of the "Prussian professor," more specifically the "secular Semitist," as it emerged under the influence of nineteenth-century historicism and increasing specialization. Bickell renounced it, despite what may almost seem a birthright bestowed on him thanks to his family background and education, and instead chose to follow his religious impulse. Lidzbarski fully embraced it, even though he was a foreigner from a minority group, and, like many a *homo novus*, paid the price of loneliness and an often but lukewarm social acceptance in return. Bauer slowly drifted toward it, such a persona being the most readily available form of leading an intellectual existence after he could no longer accept the tenets of his prior life as a Catholic priest. And Barth partly

---

70 Breuer, *Orthodoxie*, 172-173. A student described his piety as "von einer, ich möchte sagen, bäuerlichen Naivität getragen, die es ihm erlaubte, ohne Problemen nachzujagen oder vor Problemen zu flüchten, sich mit allem, auch den modernsten Anschauungen und Dingen zu befassen" (ibid., 173).

71 Due to the authority of the transmission, even textual criticism was only hesitatingly adopted by nineteenth-century Jewish scholars, cf. Breuer and Gafni, "Jewish Biblical Scholarship," 266-277.

adopted it, like a dress, but ultimately remained a resident alien in Prussian academe whose true spiritual home was Jewish Orthodoxy.

To all of them, philology provided a common set of intellectual virtues, linguistic skills, and objects of study, yet they employed it to ends that were each more or less influenced by distinct biographical choices. Bickell excelled in a comprehensive investigation and aesthetic appreciation of fresh Syriac Christian sources that were so close to his personal Catholic faith. Lidzbarski focused on the hard base-level data of inscriptions and manuscripts instead of complex theological systems, but he could nonetheless employ his knowledge of Jewish Babylonian Aramaic and Talmudic literature in order to gain access to Mandaean religious lore. Bauer came to terms with the challenges of historicism by delving deep into the objective facts of the historical phonology and morphology of Hebrew and Aramaic from the highly modern vantage point of an evolving linguistic organism. And Barth, unwavering in his loyalty to Orthodox Jewish practice, edited Arabic manuscripts and compared grammatical and etymological details in a traditional style in which acute observations were more important than rigorous method. None of them, however, engaged in any way with the predominant current in liberal academic Protestantism, that is, a markedly historical – and at times even iconoclastic – approach to Scripture that attempted to portray the Biblical texts as a merely human artefact and explain their genesis in a fashion quite different from age-old convictions shared by Jewish and Christian orthodoxy. Biblical source criticism remained a blind spot for all four of them, including the converts to Protestantism Bauer and Lidzbarski; they deliberately avoided the debate about a central discourse of avant-garde scholarly exegesis of the day.[72]

Such are the powers of philology, then: that it can integrate seamlessly into these diverse denominational outlooks, academic interests, and human personalities and make possible a rational discussion between them, as is still the case when exploring the meaning of Biblical texts in an interreligious setting. The modern heirs of the nineteenth-century Orientalists often pretend, for better or for worse, to be historians instead of philologists. History, however,

---

[72] Hence it does not come as a surprise that the most extreme form of a secular approach to Scripture, Panbabylonism, was considered a "genuinely Protestant" topic in confessional polemics. One may especially note the passionate tirade with which the Jesuit priest Anton Deimel, one of the founding fathers of Sumerology, attacked Jensen, Zimmern, and others, even though he did acknowledge their merits as philologists: *Pantheon babylonicum* (Rome: Biblical Institute Press, 1914), viii (*in impetum desinit caeco odio ac genuine furore protestantico conceptum adversus Christi divinitatem eiusque dignitatem in terris vicarii ... quamdiu nimirum philologos agunt, magna praestant; cum primum philosophari coeperunt, lumen iis mentis exstinguitur*).

needs to be founded on serious textual study, just as philological detail requires the resounding space of historical context.[73] This is the timeless core of the scholarly persona independent of conditioning social and cultural factors. Even today, obtaining a mastery of languages and sources and pursuing, with utmost determination, one's innermost impulse in the choice of one's topics produces the most sustainable results in the humanities.

Bibliography

Barth, Jacob. "Zur vergleichenden semitischen Grammatik." *Zeitschrift der Deutschen Morgenländischen Gesellschaft* 48 (1894): 1-21.

Bauer, Walter. "Mark Lidzbarksi zum Gedächtnis." *Nachrichten von der Gesellschaft der Wissenschaften zu Göttingen: Geschäftliche Mitteilungen* (1928/29): 71-77.

Becker, Carl Heinrich. "Jacob Barth." *Der Islam* 6 (1915), 200-202.

Bergsträsser, Gotthelf. *Hebräische Grammatik*. Leipzig: Hinrichs, 1918-1929.

Bickell, Gustav. "Gustav Bickell." In *Convertitenbilder aus dem neunzehnten Jahrhundert*, vol. 3/2, edited by David August Rosenthal, 415-464. Schaffhausen: Hurter, 1870.

Bihl, Wolfdieter. *Orientalistik an der Universität Wien: Forschungen zwischen Maghreb und Ost- und Südasien: Die Professoren und Dozenten*. Vienna: Böhlau, 2009.

Breuer, Edward and Chanan Gafni. "Jewish Biblical Scholarship between Tradition and Innovation." In *Hebrew Bible / Old Testament: The History of its Interpretation, Vol. III: From Modernism to Post-Modernism: The Nineteenth and Twentieth Centuries, Part 1: The Nineteenth Century – a Century of Modernism and Historicism*, edited by Magne Sæbø, 262-303. Göttingen: Vandenhoeck & Ruprecht, 2012.

Breuer, Mordechai. *Jüdische Orthodoxie im Deutschen Reich 1871-1918*. Frankfurt: Jüdischer Verlag bei Athenäum, 1986.

Deimel, Anton. *Pantheon babylonicum*. Rome: Biblical Institute Press, 1914.

Dietrich, Ernst Ludwig. "Gustav Wilhelm Hugo Bickell." In *Lebensbilder aus Kurhessen und Waldeck*, vol. 4, edited by Ingeborg Schnack, 25-39. Marburg: Elwert, 1950.

Drower, Ethel S. and Rudolf Macuch. *A Mandaic Dictionary*. Oxford: Oxford University Press, 1963.

Ehlers, Klaas-Hinrich. *Strukturalismus in der deutschen Sprachwissenschaft: Die Rezeption der Prager Schule zwischen 1926 und 1945*. Berlin: De Gruyter, 2005.

---

73 The present writer can only agree emphatically with Josef van Ess's perceptive conclusion in his "From Wellhausen to Becker: The Emergence of *Kulturgeschichte* in Islamic Studies," in *Islamic Studies: A Tradition and Its Problems*, ed. Malcolm H. Kerr (Malibu: Undena Publications, 1980), 27-51, esp. 51.

Fogarty, Gerald P. "The Catholic Church and Historical Criticism of the Old Testament." In *Hebrew Bible / Old Testament: The History of its Interpretation, Vol. III: From Modernism to Post-Modernism: The Nineteenth and Twentieth Centuries, Part 1: The Nineteenth Century – a Century of Modernism and Historicism*, edited by Magne Sæbø, 244-261. Göttingen: Vandenhoeck & Ruprecht, 2012.

Fück, Johann. *Die arabischen Studien in Europa bis in den Anfang des 20. Jahrhunderts.* Leipzig: Harrassowitz, 1955.

Gilbert, Maurice. *The Pontifical Biblical Institute: A Century of History 1909-2009.* Translated by Leo Arnold. Rome: Biblical Institute Press, 2009.

Gzella, Holger. "Hans Bauer und die historisch-vergleichende Semitistik." In *Studien zur Semitistik und Arabistik: Festschrift für Hartmut Bobzin zum 60. Geburtstag*, edited by Otto Jastrow, Shabo Talay, and Herta Hafenrichter, 141-182. Wiesbaden: Harrassowitz, 2008.

Gzella, Holger. "Il rapporto tra l'esegesi biblica e gli studi orientali alla soglia di un nuovo millennio." *Acta Pontificii Instituti Biblici* 11/2009-10 (2010): 731-747.

Gzella, Holger. "Expansion of the Linguistic Context of the Hebrew Bible / Old Testament: Hebrew Among the Languages of the Ancient Near East." In *Hebrew Bible / Old Testament: The History of its Interpretation, Vol. III: From Modernism to Post-Modernism: The Nineteenth and Twentieth Centuries, Part 1: The Nineteenth Century – a Century of Modernism and Historicism*, edited by Magne Sæbø, 134-167. Göttingen: Vandenhoeck & Ruprecht, 2012.

Gzella, Holger. "Wilhelm Gesenius als Semitist: Das 'Lehrgebäude' in seinem wissenschaftsgeschichtlichen Kontext." In *Biblische Exegese und hebräische Lexikographie: Das "Hebräisch-deutsche Handwörterbuch" von Wilhelm Gesenius als Spiegel und Quelle alttestamentlicher und hebräischer Forschung, 200 Jahre nach seiner ersten Auflage*, edited by Stefan Schorch and Ernst-Joachim Waschke, 184-208. Berlin: De Gruyter, 2013.

Gzella, Holger. *A Cultural History of Aramaic: From the Beginnings to the Advent of Islam.* Leiden: Brill, 2015.

Gzella, Holger. "Review of Smend (ed.), *Briefe.*" *Bibliotheca Orientalis* 73 (2016): 482-491.

Häberl, Charles G. *The Neo-Mandaic Dialect of Khorramshahr.* Wiesbaden: Harrassowitz, 2009.

Hanisch, Ludmila. *Aufzeichnungen von Mark Lidzbarski (1868-1928): Aus den Nachlässen der Deutschen Morgenländischen Gesellschaft.* Halle: Universitäts- und Landesbibliothek Sachsen-Anhalt, 2015.

Housman, A. E. "The Application of Thought to Textual Criticism." *Proceedings of the Classical Association* 18 (1922): 67-84.

Janz, Oliver. *Bürger besonderer Art: Evangelische Pfarrer in Preußen 1850-1914.* Berlin: De Gruyter, 1994.

Kocka, Jürgen. "Bildungsbürgertum – Gesellschaftliche Formation oder Historikerkonstrukt?" In *Bildungsbürgertum im 19. Jahrhundert, Teil IV: Politischer Einfluß und gesellschaftliche Formation*, edited by Jürgen Kocka, 9-20. Stuttgart: Klett-Cotta, 1989.

Laichner, Johannes. "Gustav Wilhelm Hugo Bickell." In *Personenlexikon zur Christlichen Archäologie: Forscher und Persönlichkeiten vom 16. bis zum 21. Jahrhundert*, edited by Stefan Heid and Martin Dennert. Regensburg: Schnell und Steiner, 2012.

Littmann, Enno. "Mark Lidzbarski (1868-1928)." In *Ein Jahrhundert Orientalistik: Lebensbilder aus der Feder von Enno Littmann und Verzeichnis seiner Schriften*, edited by Rudi Paret and Anton Schall, 46-51. Wiesbaden: Harrassowitz, 1955.

[Lidzbarski, Mark]. *Auf rauhem Wege: Jugenderinnerungen eines deutschen Professors*. Giessen: Töpelmann, 1927.

Maier, Bernhard. *Gründerzeit der Orientalistik: Theodor Nöldekes Leben und Werk im Spiegel seiner Briefe*. Würzburg: Ergon-Verlag, 2013.

Nöldeke, Theodor. "Review of Gustav Bickell, Kalilag und Damnag." *Zeitschrift der Deutschen Morgenländischen Gesellschaft* 30 (1876): 752-772.

Preißler, Holger. "Heinrich Leberecht Fleischer: Ein Leipziger Orientalist, seine jüdischen Studenten, Promovenden und Kollegen." In *Bausteine einer jüdischen Geschichte der Universität Leipzig*, edited by Stephan Wendehorst, 245-268. Leipzig: Leiziger Universitätsverlag, 2006.

Rau, Wilhelm. *Bilder 135 deutscher Indologen*, 2nd ed. Wiesbaden: Steiner, 1982.

Ringer, Fritz K. *The Decline of the German Mandarins: The German Academic Community, 1890-1933*. Cambridge, MA: Harvard University Press, 1969.

Römer, Thomas. "'Higher Criticism': The Historical and Literary-Critical Approach – with Special Reference to the Pentateuch." In *Hebrew Bible / Old Testament: The History of its Interpretation, Vol. III: From Modernism to Post-Modernism: The Nineteenth and Twentieth Centuries, Part 1: The Nineteenth Century – a Century of Modernism and Historicism*, edited by Magne Sæbø, 393-423. Göttingen: Vandenhoeck & Ruprecht, 2012.

Smend, Rudolf. "The Work of Abraham Kuenen and Julius Wellhausen." In *Hebrew Bible / Old Testament: The History of its Interpretation, Vol. III: From Modernism to Post-Modernism: The Nineteenth and Twentieth Centuries, Part 1: The Nineteenth Century – a Century of Modernism and Historicism*, edited by Magne Sæbø, 424-453. Göttingen: Vandenhoeck & Ruprecht, 2012.

Smend, Rudolf, ed. *Julius Wellhausen: Briefe*. Tübingen: Mohr Siebeck, 2013.

Suchard, Benjamin D. "The Development of the Biblical Hebrew Vowels." PhD thesis, Leiden University, 2016.

Taeschner, Franz. "Hubert Grimme." *Zeitschrift der Deutschen Morgenländischen Gesellschaft* 96 (1942): 381-392.

Turner, James. *Philology: The Forgotten Origins of the Modern Humanities*. Princeton, NJ: Princeton University Press, 2014.

van Ess, Josef. "From Wellhausen to Becker: The Emergence of *Kulturgeschichte* in Islamic Studies." In *Islamic Studies: A Tradition and Its Problems*, edited by Malcolm H. Kerr, 27-51. Malibu: Undena Publications, 1980.

Wehr, Hans. "Nachruf auf Hans Bauer." *Zeitschrift der Deutschen Morgenländischen Gesellschaft* 91 (1937): 175-184.

Weiß, Otto. *Der Modernismus in Deutschland: Ein Beitrag zur Theologiegeschichte*. Regensburg: Pustet, 1995.

CHAPTER 2

Multiple Personae

Friedrich Max Müller and the Persona of the Oriental Scholar

Arie L. Molendijk

1   Introduction

The concept of the "scientific persona" or "scholarly persona" has been introduced to open a new field of research in the study of the history of the sciences and humanities.[1] The persona is located between the individual biography and the social institution. In a pioneering volume, Lorraine Daston and H. Otto Sibum defined it as "a cultural entity that simultaneously shapes the individual in body and mind and creates a collective with a shared and recognizable physiognomy."[2] Daston and Sibum mentioned various "bases" for the persona: a social role (e.g., the mother), a profession (the physician), an anti-profession (the flâneur), a calling (the priest). Personae are to be viewed as historically conditioned: they emerge and disappear within specific contexts. Daston and Sibum focused on the emergence of distinct types of scholars: "A nascent [scientific] persona indicates the creation of a new kind of individual, whose distinctive traits mark a recognized social species."[3] Daston and Sibum also pointed in this respect to the role that a coming-of-age ritual may play, such as the induction into certain religious orders or – an example they don't give – the defence of a PhD thesis and the acceptance of the concomitant rights and obligations of the new doctor, who recently also has to take an oath in the Netherlands.

To be seen as a scholar, one has to meet certain requirements, perform according to a template. Scientific statements must be verifiable and backed-up by experiments and statistical evidence. Historical treatises must provide precise information about which archives and other sources were consulted, whereas cultural anthropologists define themselves by their fieldwork and notebooks, in which they keep track of their conversations and observations.

---

1   This paper draws on Arie L. Molendijk, *Friedrich Max Müller and the Sacred Books of the East* (Oxford: Oxford University Press, 2016). Quoted with permission of Oxford University Press.
2   Lorraine Daston and H. Otto Sibum, "Introduction: Scientific Personae and Their Histories," *Science in Context* 16 (2003), 1-8, at 2.
3   Ibid., 3.

The criteria that define scholarship may be disputed, especially in times of transition. On the level of theory and paradigms this point is nicely illustrated by the insight of the German physicist Max Planck, who famously said: "A new scientific truth does not triumph by convincing its opponents and making them see the light, but rather because its opponents eventually die, and a new generation grows up that is familiar with it."[4] Young scholars are socialized into the new approach and techniques.

Much research, therefore, focuses on the history of influential scientists and scholars, on new approaches, techniques and instruments, and also on the new discoveries, innovative theories and paradigm shifts. Historians of the history of scholarship also have a predilection for the study of institutions such as the Royal Society and "grand projects" such as the *Monumenta Germaniae Historica*. The scholarly persona, however, has only recently been "discovered" and put on the research agenda. And, of course, it makes good sense to study models of scholarship and the ethos of this once rare, but nowadays widespread species. It is evident that there may be competing types of scholarly personae, for instance the allegedly "detached" philologist versus the Orientalist who travels and studies contemporary issues. A new generation denounces the previous generation as "arm-chair" scholars. Notwithstanding its creative potential it is not always easy to apply the concept of a persona in historical research. At which level of abstraction can it be meaningfully used? The "scientist" is a useful concept, whereas the "cook" or the "biological chemist" are not according to Daston and Sibum. Is the "Oriental scholar" really a distinct type? Another tricky aspect of the notion of the persona is that it tends to focus on ideals and to overlook the work on the ground where practical circumstances, such as a shortage of time combined with the imperative to come quickly to results, may be as influential as the norms and values of the profession.

In this chapter I will follow the angle suggested by Herman Paul. He has defined scholarly personae as "models, either past or present, inherited or invented, of what it takes to be a scholar."[5] Which are the pursued goods, which are the guiding values and skills, what are the rewards? Also helpful is Paul's suggestion that the individual scholars find themselves confronted with a variety of models, which they accept, reject, revise, and merge to fit their own situation.[6] Of course, it is wise to say that personae have to be seen as ideal-types

---

4 Max Planck, *Scientific Autobiography and Other Papers* (1948), trans. F. Gaynor (New York, NY: Philosophical Library, 1950), 33.
5 Herman Paul, "What Is a Scholarly Persona? Ten Theses on Virtues, Skills, and Desires," *History and Theory* 53 (2014), 348-371.
6 Herman Paul, "The Virtues and Vices of Albert Naudé: Toward a History of Scholarly Personae," *History of Humanities* 1 (2016), 327-338.

that don't exist in pure forms in reality. On the other hand, Paul's inclination to give ample space for "individualizing"[7] comparisons between scholarly personae may lead to problems of demarcation, if every single scholar in the end moulds his or her own way of being a scholar. In that case it will also be difficult to detect major historical transitions in the ways the scholarly persona has been perceived and constructed. I will take the case of Max Müller (1823-1900) to see how far the new tool brings us.

2 Max Müller as an Oriental Scholar

Friedrich Max Müller's long career spanned various branches of learning. First, he gained fame as a Sanskritist, who edited and translated the *Rig-Veda*. At Oxford he was appointed Taylorian Professor of Modern European Languages and Literature and became interested in comparative philology, which laid the ground for his famous and controversial studies in the "Science of Language." His 1861 lectures on language at the Royal Institution made him a star in England. The ensuing book went through fourteen editions during his lifetime and was translated into French, German, Italian, Russian, Swedish, and Dutch. He gave the Hibbert and Gifford Lectures and he is still seen as the founder of the comparative study of religion. His main biographer divides Müller's scholarly work into the areas of language and thought, comparative mythology, the "science of religion," missions, and philosophy of religion.[8]

Although Max Müller was at the cross-roads of several (emerging) disciplines, it also makes sense to see him as an Oriental scholar. Looking back at his arrival in Oxford in the 1840s, he casually ranked himself as a "young Oriental scholar."[9] The edition of the *Rig-Veda* in six volumes, and, especially, the series of the translations of the *Sacred Books of the East* (50 vols, 1879-1910) at the Clarendon Press added much to his prestige in this respect. "Famous Orientalist Passes Away at Oxford" was the subtitle of the obituary in the *New York Times*.[10] Müller spoke at Oriental Congresses and chaired sessions, and he was no doubt a respected and at the same time controversial authority in this field.

---

7   Paul, "What Is a Scholarly Persona?" 365.
8   Lourens P. van den Bosch, *Friedrich Max Müller: A Life Devoted to the Humanities* (Leiden: Brill, 2002).
9   F. Max Müller, *My Autobiography: A Fragment* (London: Longmans, Green, and Co, 1901), 279.
10 N. N., "Prof. Max Mueller Dead," *New York Times* (29 October 1900). One day before the *New York Times* had announced that Professor Max Müller "[was] sinking fast."

2.1 Assessments

Many assessments of Müller's work, however, are not very specific and address his importance in very general terms. In a memorial meeting at the University of Columbia right after he had died, Müller was called the greatest scholar of his generation, whereas his biggest American opponent, the Sanskritist and linguist William Dwight Whitney, thought him "one of the great humbugs of the century."[11] Müller's friend Moncure Conway disputed the impression given in a New York paper that Müller was "somewhat vainglorious." Conway admitted that Müller's appearance ("his erect mien, his handsome, courtly look") could perhaps lead to such an impression but argued that he actually was a very hospitable man with many friends from all over the world. Although much praise was lavished upon "one of the giants of learning," remarkably critical pieces appeared in the *New York Times* just after Müller's death. An unsigned column spoke of lack of sound judgment on the part of the deceased scholar.[12] Another piece in the same issue of the *New York Times* was similarly critical and spoke of the "triviality of many of his writings."[13]

This sort of critique is echoed in later appreciations. Typical is probably Ferdinand de Saussure's remark in his posthumously edited *Course in General Linguistics*: "Max Müller popularised the subject in a series of brilliant if somewhat superficial lectures (*Lectures on the Science of Language*, 1861), but it is not by too much conscience that he sinned."[14] Only in India Müller seems to be still held in high esteem. In his biography of Müller, the famous Bengali writer Nirad C. Chaudhuri tells his readers how as a child he came to know about him. He had learned from his father who "was not a highly educated man in the formal sense" how Müller had established "that our languages and the European languages belonged to the same family…; and that we Hindus and the

---

[11] Moncure D. Conway, *Autobiography: Memories and Experiences of Moncure Daniel Conway*, 2 vols. (London: Cassell, 1904), 2: 280; Stephen G. Alter, *William Dwight Whitney and the Science of Language* (Baltimore, MD: Johns Hopkins University Press, 2005), 201. The controversy between Max Müller and his American opponent Whitney may explain some of the harsh comments about Müller in the New York Times. The *New York Times* of 1 November 1900 announced the memorial meeting at 7 November, 4.30 p.m., in the Schermerhorn Hall: <http://query.nytimes.com/mem/archive-free/pdf?res=F50F12F93E5B11738DDDA80894D9415B808CF1D3> (last accessed 29 January 2019).

[12] N. N., "Max Mueller," *New York Times* (3 November 1900).

[13] Montgomery Schuyler, Jr., "Max Muller's Service to Science," *New York Times* (3 November 1900).

[14] Ferdinand de Saussure, *Cours de linguistique générale* (Paris: Payot, [1916] 1980), 16; English version: *Course in General Linguistics*, trans. Roy Harris (London: Duckworth, 1983), 3. The second half of the sentence is missing in the translation; cf. Ferdinand de Saussure, *Writings in General Linguistics*, trans. Simon Bouquet et al. (Oxford: Oxford University Press, 2006), 186.

Europeans were both peoples descended from the same original stock."[15] This "discovery" – as well as his edition of the *Rig-Veda* – gave a boost to Indian self-understanding, Hindus now seeing their country as the cradle of higher civilization *tout court*. Another example of Müller's fame here is the fact that during her state visit to the German Democratic Republic in 1976 the Indian prime minister Indira Gandhi proposed a toast to Max Müller (who was born in Dessau in Eastern Germany), which caused some embarrassment among her hosts, who were not aware of their famous, or infamous, compatriot.

Although it was Max Müller's ambition to put an end to all amateurism, many of his colleagues were rather critical of him. Various things played a role here, but it stands out that his many popular expositions did his scholarly reputation no good. In 1872 the secretary of the London Philological Society wrote to Whitney:

> As to M. M. [Max Müller], at our Society he is not set very high ... But M. has a nice style, and writes books that young ladies and easy-going people read with pleasure, fancying themselves thereby enlightened, and so they are, which results in M. M. being greatly glorified in society. But behind the scenes he's not much thought of.[16]

Already in 1867, Müller's friend Matthew Arnold had reported from Berlin to the British government department of education that Müller "was losing all scientific importance" in the German capital because of his focus on "secondary and popular aims."[17] It is hard to say how popular Müller exactly was, but probably he was one of the most publicly visible intellectuals of his day. In this last respect he may even be compared to Richard Dawkins, who since the publication of the *Selfish Gene* in 1976 has moved away from his specialist scientific work. Max Müller, however, would have denied that his later work concerning mythology, religious studies, and philosophy was merely popular and not "scientific."

---

15   Nirad C. Chaudhuri, *Scholar Extraordinary: The Life of Professor the Rt. Hon. Friedrich Max Müller P. C.* (Delhi: Oxford University Press, 1974), 5. Actually this discovery had been made earlier by William Jones (1746-1794), but is attributed here to Müller, which testifies again to Müller's prestige in India.

16   Frederick J. Furnivall to Whitney, 27 December 1872, quoted in Alter, *Whitney*, 177, 303, note 13.

17   Matthew Arnold, *The Letters of Matthew Arnold*, 6 vols., ed. Cecil Y. Lang (Charlottesville, VA: University Press of Virginia, 1996-2001), 3: 125 (19 March 1867 to Henry John Roby).

What further harmed his reputation were his "often wild and fantastic"[18] theories about the origins of myth and language. Müller famously located the origin of languages in a limited number of roots, technically "phonetic types." These are "simply ultimate facts," compared by Müller with the Platonic ideas. If he had left it at this, he would not have been ridiculed as much as has been the case. However, he engaged in speculations about how these roots had come into existence. He explained this by the analogy that each metal – if struck – has a particular sound. In a similar way primitive man must have responded to impressions from the outside by forming "vocal expressions."[19] Müller spoke of "the creative faculty," which gave to each general concept, "as it thrilled for the first time through the brain, a phonetic expression."[20] This idea was mockingly called the "Ding Dong Theory."

With the exception of his edition of the *Rig-Veda*, the history of Sanskrit Literature and some more technical studies, Max Müller's work was overall deemed popular and, thus, unscientific by many of his Oriental colleagues around 1900. "He had catered to the public so long that scholarly work had become of only secondary importance."[21] Many reviewers thought his theories absurd. He "pushed out frail structures of theory far beyond the safe realm of facts."[22] The criticism was that he did not respect the facts and lacked self-criticism. Put in a slightly ironical fashion: "[h]e always aided his chosen science by his poetic insight and suggestiveness."[23] The verdict was that Müller's imagination took over and was insufficiently checked by reason and facts.[24] In this way Oriental scholars and comparative linguists framed Müller's deficiencies. His Germanic upbringing in circles of Romanticists may have contributed to this "perception," especially among Anglo-Saxon colleagues. One obituary attributed this flaw in Müller to "defects of mental constitution."[25] Some opponents – impressed by the bitter battle between Müller and Whitney – described Müller's character in defiant, dishonest, and even "insultingly unfair" terms.[26]

---

18 Schuyler, Jr., "Max Muller's Service to Science."
19 F. Max Müller, *Lectures on the Science of Language*, 2 vols., 7th ed. (London: Longmans, Green & Co, 1873), 440, note 57.
20 Ibid., 441.
21 E. W. Hopkins, "Max Müller," *The Nation* 71 (1900), 343-344, reprinted in *Portraits of Linguists: A Biographical Source Book for the History of Western Linguistics, 1746-1963*, ed. Thomas A. Sebeok, 2 vols. (Westport, CT: Greenwood Press, [1966] 1976), 1: 395-399, at 397; Schuyler, "Max Muller's Service."
22 N. N., "Max Mueller."
23 Hopkins, "Max Müller," 396.
24 N. N., "Max Mueller."
25 Ibid.
26 Schuyler, "Max Muller's Service," and Hopkins, "Max Müller," 397.

The quotations above no doubt give a one-sided impression (many contemporaries saw Müller as a high-ranking scholar), but they clearly show a trait of the "scholarly persona" as favoured by his Orientalists and linguists at the time. Müller's prestige as a serious and outstanding scholar was damaged by his speculative and popular work. He may have attracted broad audiences of uninformed "young ladies," but this was a sign that he did not any longer belong predominantly to the scholarly guild, who define themselves by serious work that sticks to the facts. His publications and lectures for broad audiences, especially, as well as his popularity in general, harmed Müller's scholarly prestige. His reputation as a "scientist" – here used in the most general sense – was at stake.

2.2   *How Did Max Müller Define His Scholarly Work?*

The *first* thing to be noted here is that Friedrich Max Müller spent most of his working life reading, editing, translating and interpreting ancient texts. It was his strong conviction that without such texts, we cannot understand ancient civilizations and religions. In a similar way as fieldwork nowadays defines the modern cultural anthropologist, the study and mastery of languages defined in the nineteenth century textual scholars such as Müller. *Secondly*, although the edition of ancient texts was important in itself, for Müller it finally served a higher goal: the understanding of ancient (religious) history. The discovery of old manuscripts in the recent past and their critical edition provided the basis for the scholarly study of history, especially of religious history, as these texts primarily concerned religious practices and ideas.[27] One could even claim that these very texts made the new "science of religion," as Müller termed the comparative study of religions, possible. Müller described the new task of the scholarly study of religions in an almost reverential way:

> It [is] the duty of those who have devoted their life to the study of the principal religions of the world in their original documents, and who value religion and reverence it in whatever form it may present itself, to take possession of this new territory in the name of true science, and thus to protect its sacred precincts from the inroads of those who think that they have a right to speak on the ancient religions of mankind, whether those of the Brahmans, the Zoroastrians, or Buddhists, or those of the

---

[27]   F. Max Müller, "Buddhism" (1862) in F. Max Müller, *Chips from a German Workshop*, vol. 1 (London: Longmans, Green & Co, 1867), 182-231, at 186-187 about the necessity to study religions on the basis of their "original documents" and the fact that these texts were only recently discovered.

Jews and Christians, without ever having taken the trouble of learning the languages in which their sacred books are written.[28]

Amateurs without proper linguistic skills are to be kept away from the new "territory," as Müller preferred to call it, which was laid bare by the "discovery" of these ancient texts. True scholars who have to be respectful of their subject of study must claim this field and protect it from intruders who are not entitled to go there, because they don't know the original languages of the documents.

Thirdly, Müller saw this type of scholarship as a "science," which was basically defined by the use of the comparative method. Famously, he said that "all higher knowledge is acquired by comparison, and rests on comparison."[29] Comparison as such has an older history, but here it is more than just comparing similar things. It is defined as a strict method of comparing, as it stands for an evidence-based way of investigation *tout court*. The comparative approach "really means that our researches are based on the widest evidence that can be obtained, on the broadest inductions that can be grasped by the human mind."[30] The introduction of the comparative approach was seen in the 1850s and 1860s as a break-through in the study of man.[31] Finally disciplines such as linguistics, history, law, political economy, ethnology and the study of religions – sometimes referred to simply by the term "comparative religion" – got a firm "scientific" basis. In the study of language, the comparative approach put an end, according to Müller, to the "philological somnambulism" of previous times.[32] He himself polemicized against theory and abstract reasoning.[33] This self-understanding and self-modelling as a fact-based scholar explains at least to some extent why Müller had great difficulties understanding his opponent's criticism of his own allegedly overly fantastic theories.

---

28 F. Max Müller, *Introduction to the Science of Religion* (London: Longmans, Green & Co, 1873), 35.

29 F. Max Müller, *op cit.*, 12. Max Müller was a serious and important scholar and is treated as such in major histories of linguistics and the study of religion. The term 'science' is put between quotation marks, because it refers to Müller's own understanding of his work, which was in his view similar to the 'natural sciences' (for instance, formulating laws of development).

30 Ibid.

31 Stefan Collini, Donald Winch, and John Burrow, *That Noble Science of Politics: A Study in Nineteenth-Century Intellectual History* (Cambridge: Cambridge University Press, 1983), 209.

32 Müller, *Introduction to the Science of Religion,* 12.

33 F. Max Müller, *Natural Religion,* Gifford Lectures Glasgow 1888 (London: Longmans, Green, and Co, 1889), 196.

2.3 Mixed Categories?

A major challenge in analysing the work of Max Müller as an Oriental scholar is the fact that he clearly transgressed the domain of scholarship or science properly spoken. On the one hand, he posed as a detached scholar, mastering Oriental languages, and critically editing texts, but he wanted more than "just" scholarly recognition. His work had to make a practical impact as well. One way to achieve this aim was to frame Müller in his capacity of editor of the *Rig-Veda* as a scholarly sage. In the biography of her deceased husband, Georgina wrote that at the end of the 1850s "the natives of India" began to speak of Max Müller as "Moksha Mûlara," "which was thus explained by one of their Pundits: 'He who by publishing the *Veda* for the first time in a printed form gave (*ra*) the root, (*mûla*) the foundation, the knowledge of final beatitude (*moksha*), he is called Moksha Mûlara.'"[34] His biographer Nirad Chaudhuri, however, tells another story. He recalled the fact that Müller was often named this way in Bengali magazines and books and assumed that this had been done in India by Indians, until he learned that in the first volume of the edition of the *Rig-Veda* Müller himself had Sanskritized his name as "Moksha Mûlara."[35] Müller prided himself in his role of providing the East with – purified – editions of their own religious traditions, which may even define a nation or civilization.[36]

Müller was consulted by Indians about religious matters that were subject to controversy. It would be inaccurate to say that they asked Müller for advice solely in his capacity as an Oriental scholar and expert in Sanskrit, although his expertise in these fields was deemed important. In my view it points to another important role that Müller fulfilled – his role as a what I would call a sage. One could speak here about a mixed *persona* of scholar and sage (or authoritative religious expert). Although the precise term was not used, it makes sense to argue that Müller was explicitly staged as a sage. In the *Thoughts on Life and Religion* published a few years after Müller's death, for instance, his wife Georgina collected sayings from his published work and private letters and diaries that could console readers.[37] She clearly wanted to provide consolation and wisdom.

---

34 F. Max Müller, *The Life and Letters of the Right Honourable Max Müller*, 2 vols., ed. [Georgina Müller] (London: Longmans, Green, and Co, 1902), 1: 225. Cf. ibid., 2: 87, Müller to Emerson, 19 April 1880: "The translator of the *Upanishads*, Moksha Mulara, sends greetings and best wishes to his American Guru, Amarasunu, on his seventy-seventh birthday."

35 Chaudhuri, *Scholar Extraordinary*, 140. The interpretation by the pundits is according to Chaudhuri "an etymological flight."

36 Peter van der Veer, *Imperial Encounters: Religion and Modernity in India and Britain* (Princeton, NJ: Princeton University Press, 2001), 119 and passim.

37 F. Max Müller, *Thoughts on Life and Religion*, ed. [Georgina Müller] (London: Archibald Constable and Company, 1906), vi: "My earnest desire is that this little book may prove a

This genre is later termed "sage writing," a concept forged by John Holloway to re-evaluate the work of Victorian writers such as Thomas Carlyle, Matthew Arnold, and John Ruskin.[38] The work of contemporary American writers such as Henry David Thoreau and Ralph Waldo Emerson is also captured under this heading. Müller was familiar with the work of these writers and entertained many of them at his house, as they visited Oxford. Other "sages" from India (*yogins, samnyasins,* as Müller referred to them) frequently visited his house. In the second series of *Auld Lang Syne* he recollected memories of his many Indian friends,[39] and shortly before his death he edited a small volume with sayings of the "Indian Saint," the mystic Ramakrishna (1836-1886), which had to show the high level of Indian spirituality and philosophy.[40]

The concept of the Victorian sage is used by John Holloway to point to the value of their "moralizing" and "prophetic" discourse and to overcome a blatantly negative appreciation of their work, as had been given by the Modernists. Many of the Victorian sages drew on the Old Testament prophets, whereas Müller tried to warm his readers to Indian traditions as well. The persona of the sage is defined by his orientation towards wisdom and his wish to share ancient sayings and proverbs with his readers and even followers. Müller is not the prototypical Victorian "sage," as most of his work was "scientific." He did much more to cultivate his scholarly persona, by stressing the importance of methodologically sound research and reasoning. Scholarly and edifying work were not as sharply separated in the Victorian age as they are supposed to be nowadays. At the Chicago Parliament of World Religions in 1893 the two roles were not yet clearly differentiated.[41] Still Müller was aware of the difference between his scholarly persona and his persona as a sage, teacher or religious

---

help and comfort to many exposed to like trials, and strengthen those whose path now stretches before them as a sunny avenue, to meet the sorrows that almost surely await them as life advances."

38   John Holloway, *The Victorian Sage: Studies in Argument* (London: MacMillan, 1953).
39   F. Max Müller, *Auld Lang Syne*, 2 vols. (London: Longmans & Green, 1898-1899).
40   F. Max Müller, *Ramakrishna: His Life and Sayings* (London: Longmans, Green, and Co, 1898), v. See also Vivekananda's discussion of this booklet in "Ramakrishna: His Life and Sayings," in *The Complete Works of Swami Vivekananda*, 8 vols. (Calcutta: Advaita Ashrama, 1973-1979), 4: 409-421. Cf. Thomas J. Green, *Religion for a Secular Age. Max Müller, Swami Vivekananda and Vedānta* (Farnham: Ashgate, 2016).
41   Arie L. Molendijk, "The First Conferences on the History of Religions: Religious Dialogue versus Scholarly Study," *NTT: Journal for Theology and the Study of Religion* 72 (2018), 211-224. In this article I discuss the differentiation between scholars of religion and those interested in religious understanding and dialogue by analyzing the divergence of their respective milieu – i.e. conferences. Cf. Arie L. Molendijk, "'To Unite Religion against all Irreligion': The 1893 World Parliament of Religions," *Journal for the History of Modern Theology* 18 (2011), 228-50.

expert, but they could also be closely related, as his success as a speaker, for instance, depended on a mingling of the two. His lectures provided not only knowledge, but wisdom.

The tension here can be explained by the fact that Müller was deeply convinced that scientific work would and should have practical consequences. This is most evident in the "science" (the word is used to stress how rigid and trustworthy the new endeavour is) of religion. The most well-known quotation here is probably the following one: "The Science of Religion may be the last of the sciences which man is destined to elaborate; but when it is elaborated, it will change the aspect of the world, and give a new life to Christianity itself."[42] Müller saw the tracing of the origins of religious thought as one of the most fascinating endeavours of science. "Science" is defined here predominantly by the comparative or historical method – terms that are used interchangeably by Müller.[43] It is stressed that real research is by no means a theoretical endeavour and has nothing to do with Hegelian laws of thought or Comtian epochs.[44] This type of investigation has to be done in "in a bold, but scholar like, careful, and reverent spirit."[45] These formulations stem from 1873 and show Müller's undiminished excitement about what was to be achieved. It also betrays the tension between bold and careful, scholarly and reverent. Hypotheses about historical developments have to be kept in check by textual evidence and scholars should treat these ancient texts respectfully. In these and similar formulations Müller went beyond the ideals of many of his Oriental colleagues who focused on texts and did not aim at presenting a more wide-ranging history of religions – let alone a normative ideal of what religion really is about. Certainly they did not publish extensive volumes on these topics.

The preliminary conclusion must be that Müller not only represented various personae, which is to be expected (he was also a father), but – more specifically – various professional personae. These are not neatly separated from each other but are related to one another. Sometimes, but not always, they clearly interfere with each other. In the *Thoughts on Life and Religion* it is clearly the sage who is speaking, whereas in other publications the voice of the scholar is dominant. Of course, it is possible to clearly distinguish between ideal types of personae, as I have tried to do above, but still this is not sufficient to analyse the way the persona of the "scholar" for instance is qualified by that of the "sage." Most of the times they don't have the same weight. One could

---

42 Müller, *Chips*, vol. 1, xix-xx.
43 Molendijk, *Friedrich Max Müller*, ch. 4.
44 Müller, *Chips*, vol. 1, ix.
45 Müller, *Introduction to the Science of Religion*, ix.

even argue against my tentative analysis above that the scholar who also presents a worldview is a special type of the scholarly persona. Do we really need the model of the "sage," which has at least anachronistic aspects? In my own perception Müller's performance has so many aspects of the "sage," that it makes sense to introduce it here. Looking at Müller's magnificent career, spanning such a long time and so many fields of research and interests, we could evoke other models and personae as well.

No doubt related here is the persona of the "public intellectual" – a term that became commonly used with the Dreyfus affair in the late nineteenth century[46] – who offers orientation for a broader public. As far as his presence in the media is concerned, Max Müller was doubtless one of the great Victorian intellectuals of his time. His articles could be found in journals all over Europe and the United States, and he spoke to audiences on a large range of topics, not only in the fields he was most well-known for, but also on themes such as "how to work?" and "why I am not an agnostic." He was a regular contributor to the London *Times*, his trips and lecture tours were covered by the international media, and he also presented his views on educational, social, and political issues. His public correspondence with the famous German historian and Nobel Prize winner Theodor Mommsen on the Boer War stirred a lot of attention.[47]

Whereas the persona of the sage is related to wisdom and individual morality, the persona of the public intellectual suggests a more future-oriented, rational and critical analysis of issues of public concern. Is the "intellectual" the "secularized" counterpart of the "sage"? The sage having access to ancient, especially religious, traditions; the intellectual using his knowledge and cognitive powers to come to grips with political and societal issues? These deliberations show how various intellectual personae are part of a larger semantic field, which calls for reflection beyond the scholarly persona. The first lesson is that the scholarly persona has to be understood in a field of related concepts, models and personae. The second – related – lesson is that that conceptual histories of isolated personae (the sage, the intellectual) are insufficient, as categories may overlap and become confused and blurred – in the sense that they are not used ideal typically, but interchangeably in some contexts by some participants and observers.

---

46 *Historisches Wörterbuch der Philosophie*, ed. J. Ritter, vol. 4 (Basel: Schwabe, 1976), 454-458.
47 *The Question of Right between England and the Transvaal: Letters by the Right Hon. F. Max Müller with Rejoinders by Professor Theodor Mommsen* (Westminster: Imperial South African Association, 1900). Cf. Van den Bosch, *Müller,* 170-171 and Johannes H. Voigt, "Die Auseinandersetzung zwischen Theodor Mommsen und Max Müller über den Burenkrieg [The Discussion between Mommsen and Max Müller about the Boer War]," *Geschichte in Wissenschaft und Unterricht* 17 (1966), 65-77.

3 The Rise of "Big Science" and the Persona of the Entrepreneur

Grand editorial projects such as the *Oxford English Dictionary*, the Migne edition of the church fathers, the *Monumenta Germaniae Historica*, and the ninth edition of the *Encyclopaedia Britannica* (under the supervision of the famous Old Testament scholar William Robertson Smith), are important objects of study. They signalled the emergence of large-scale scholarship in the humanities as well as the importance of entrepreneurship and stamina of individual leaders, who initiated and conducted these cooperative ventures with great personal effort and dedication. Not all editors had the commercial genius of the abbé Jacques Paul Migne, who published according to his biographer a book every ten days for thirty years,[48] but a solid financial basis was crucial for success. Just like big industry, big science (*Großwissenschaft*) needs working capital.[49]

With some caution, Müller's editions of the *Rig-Veda* and the *Sacred Books of the East* can be studied in the context of the rise of "big science."[50] The edition of the *Sacred Books of the East* was funded by both the private money of Oxford University Press and the India Office of the British Empire. The – often distinguished – scholars were paid a small amount per page, which bore no relation to their time-consuming work. Only Müller as editor-in-chief received a substantial emolument from the Press. Scholars from different nations were recruited by Müller, and in this respect the series was a token of the ongoing internationalization of – Oriental – scholarship. Internationalization is in my view an important, but not in itself distinguishing, element of the emergence of big science. The contributors all worked in their own studies or libraries and did not cooperate closely. Of course, there were all kinds of relationships – they met at conferences, and corresponded with each other, and, of course, even more frequently with the editor-in-chief –, but they did it all on an individual basis and did not meet as a team. There was no local concentration of work, nor staff members who managed the edition. Yet the series remained a collective effort by an international group of scholars, funded by extra financial means, and involving a steady flow of publications. In these respects, the

---

48 R. Howard Bloch, *God's Plagiarist: Being an Account of the Fabulous Industry and Irregular Commerce of the Abbé Migne* (Chicago, IL: University of Chicago Press, 1994), 1.
49 Adolf von Harnack, "Antrittsrede in der Preußischen Akademie der Wissenschaften [Inaugural Address in the Prussian Academy of Sciences]," in *Adolf von Harnack als Zeitgenosse*, ed. Kurt Nowak, 2 vols. (Berlin: Walter de Gruyter, 1996), 1: 976-982, at 982.
50 The classical book on this subject, Derek J. de Solla Price, *Little Science, Big Science … and Beyond* (New York, NY: Columbia Press, [1963] 1986), does not take any notice of the humanities, and overlooks the importance of the huge editions of classical scholarship.

series is an important step in the establishment of big science, which emerged in full shape around 1900.

These grand projects required new skills of the editors involved, such as fundraising and organizing ("people management") and convincing colleagues to invest their time in translating texts. Max Müller, of course, was aware of the fact that these editions required extra money and manpower. In his autobiography, prefaces, and dedications he honoured the influential men who provided the funds. He was also very much aware of the need to cooperate. In his address to the Second Congress of Orientalists, held at the Royal Institution in London in 1874, Müller had pointed to the necessity "to carry out great works" by joint effort (*viribus unitis*).[51] His organizational skills were acknowledged by his contemporaries, but not without criticism. Müller was said to be "pushful"[52] and one colleague even spoke of Müller's "inability for real attachment." "We all knew that he only valued us so far as we could be of use to him."[53] All the credit went to Müller, whereas – according to some of his critics – he did only a small part of the actual work.[54] Another appraisal, however, stated that "every page [passed] through his hands for revision before final publication."[55]

Here it is not my goal to assess these – often contrary – judgments, but to see according to which standards and ideals Müller's editorial work has been evaluated. His "faculty of making others work with him"[56] implies a tight-rope walk. Pushing for results and correcting their work – including the English of the non-native speakers – was "often taken in bad part by the translator."[57] Müller has been accused of more or less exploiting young scholars, in particular his "assistants," and claiming the credit of their editorial work for himself.[58]

---

[51] F. Max Müller, "Address [to the Aryan Section]," in *Transactions of the Second Session of the International Congress of Orientalists*, London, September 1874, (Nendeln: Kraus Reprint, [1876] 1968), 177-204.

[52] Edmund Craster, *History of the Bodleian Library 1845-1945* (Oxford: Clarendon Press, 1952), 104.

[53] Chaudhuri, *Scholar Extraordinary,* 218, without mentioning a source; the same passage is quoted in Peter Sutcliffe, *Oxford University Press: An Informal History* (Oxford: Clarendon Press, 1978), 47 and V. H. H. Green, *Oxford Common Room: A Study of Lincoln College and Mark Pattison* (London: Edward Arnold, 1957), 219. K. A. Manley, "Max Müller and the Bodleian Sub-Librarianship, 1865," *Library History* 5 (1979), 33-47, at 34, note 4, refers to Bodleian Library, MS Pattison 130: Mark Pattison's diary, 7 December 1860.

[54] Schuyler, Jr., "Max Muller's Service to Science."

[55] N. N., "Appreciation of Max Muller," *New York Times* (1 December 1900) and Müller, *The Life and Letters of the Right Honourable Max Müller*, 2: 12.

[56] Ibid.

[57] Müller, *The Life and Letters of the Right Honourable Max Müller*, 2: 12.

[58] Chaudhuri, *Scholar Extraordinary*, 261.

The entrepreneurial and supervising aspects of Müller's work were probably seen as violating collegial standards. The autonomy of the individual scholar was still highly appreciated. Theodor Mommsen recommended that one should free Hermann Oldenberg, one of the contributors to the *Sacred Books of the East*, from his *Lohnschreiberei* (the fact that he has to produce for his living). In this context Mommsen spoke also about the big Müllerian factory.[59] Being part of a production process and being corrected by the editor-in-chief did not fit the scholarly ideal of the independent professor. This does not alter the fact that in many big projects in which Mommsen himself was also deeply involved low-paid "assistants" were needed. The emergence of "big science" and "big humanities" shows the emergence of a new type of scholar as entrepreneur and manager.

4   Conclusion

The above criticism of Müller shows that the persona of the scholar at the time implied an autonomous position as far as one's own work was concerned. Theodor Mommsen urged Friedrich Althoff – the highest ranking official in the Prussian Department of Education – to give Oldenberg a professorship in Germany. An academic of his standing should not be dependent on contractual work and be free to do his own research. Freedom and a certain degree of independence were seen as precious goods for a scholar. Especially in England, of course, some scholars had enough financial means to guarantee their independence and pursue their careers. In the obituary for his friend Arthur Penrhyn Stanley, Dean of Westminster, Müller wrote – with a slight touch of envy – that Stanley never had to make concessions, being financially independent. "He had not to push and to urge his claims himself or through others, and he thus remained a free man through life."[60]

The degree of independence of a British gentleman differed, of course, from that of a German professor, but both were able to pursue their academic interests – not bothered by the need for extra income. Scholars were also seen as owners of the outcomes of their work. They could take advice, no doubt, but they did not want their publications supervised and corrected by peers – let alone editors-in-chief. Scholars were ideally seen as colleagues. This changed

---

59   *Theodor Mommsen und Friedrich Althoff: Briefwechsel 1882-1903* [Correspondence Mommsen – Althoff 1882-1903], ed. Stefan Rebenich and Gisa Franke (Munich: Oldenburg, 2012), 200-201 and 207, letters of 23 January 1885 and 22 March 1885 ("grosse Müllersche Fabrikunternehmen"). I thank Bernhard Maier (Tübingen) for this reference.
60   F. Max Müller, *Biographical Essays* (London: Longmans, Green & Co, 1884), 131.

to a certain extent with the emergence of large-scale scholarship that called for more standardized procedures. Thus, the *Sacred Books of the East* marked a new stage in the emergence of structurally hierarchical relations within academia. Now "colleagues" had to be managed, and not only those in subordinate positions such as secretaries and other "assistants." It is evident that Müller had to work here with extreme caution, but "to push and to urge" was part of his persona as an entrepreneur-scholar. Till the present day this is an extremely sensitive issue among colleagues – even within modern universities where standards of output, efficiency, and competition prevail.

The flip-side of the emergence of bigger projects that could not be undertaken by a single scholar in his study was the need for cooperation and fundraising. Many times, Müller's charm, pleasant manners, hospitality, and even support were mentioned. Social qualities – if they can be summarized this way – became part of the ideal of the scholar. The "pushing and urging" could be experienced as manipulation and even exploitation, especially by younger aspiring scholars who needed money and a mentor and had not much of a position to negotiate. Here we can glimpse a sight of the modern manager–scholar who has to be able to raise funds and to "persuade" people.

What has disappeared – or at least is not that prominent any more – over the twentieth century is the combination of the persona of "the scholar" and that of what I have called the sage who provides moral guidance. Carl Sagan and some others may have had a certain amount of influence, but generally speaking the role of the sage seems to have been replaced by that of the intellectual who critically analyses societal and political issues. Scholarship as such has become a target of intellectual criticism. Concomitantly, we see the rise of alternative explanations of the world such as creationism and intelligent design, alternative procedures of healing, and even competing "science" that offers "counter-evidence" for the "alleged" process of global warming. Thus, the persona of the scholar is threatened because the authority of the professional as such is undermined in our mediatized world.

It is too early to jump to general conclusions about the usefulness of the concept of the scholarly persona. This chapter – just a rough sketch – has shown that it is not always easy to discern between various competing personae. One of the key issues here is how to link criticism of Müller to his various persona. Some critics detected moral flaws in his character, which are not clearly related to one particular persona. Other criticisms were directed to his scholarly work in general. Concerning Müller's own perception of his work as a scholar, it is remarkable how fiercely he defined his work as a science, which reaches results which are not the result of mere speculation or association, whereas older linguists, for instance, in his view just connected words of the basis of similarities without looking at the deeper roots of language families.

Müller was an Oriental scholar, a linguist, a sage, and a pioneering editor of a big series. Do these roles all qualify as a persona? Do they supplement each other, or is it better to look at how these personae qualify each other? I would suggest looking at frictions. In which respects are scholars criticized, for instance? Here we often see moral judgments and judgments concerning (lack of) skills and practiced values. In this chapter I stumbled on multiple personae such as the scholar–entrepreneur or the scholar–sage, which were connected, but at the same time distinguished, without being completely differentiated from one another at the time. The unbiased scholar could still provide wisdom to his audience. Even at the time this double role (if it was a double role) could lead to frictions, and some colleagues of Max Müller were quick to point out that his popular success with "young ladies" actually disqualified him as a serious scholar.

Bibliography

Alter, Stephen G. *William Dwight Whitney and the Science of Language*. Baltimore, MD: Johns Hopkins University Press, 2005.

Arnold, Matthew. *The Letters of Matthew Arnold,* 6 vols., edited by Cecil Y. Lang. Charlottesville, VA: University Press of Virginia, 1996-2001.

Bloch, R. Howard. *God's Plagiarist: Being an Account of the Fabulous Industry and Irregular Commerce of the Abbé Migne*. Chicago, IL: University of Chicago Press, 1994.

Chaudhuri, Nirad C. *Scholar Extraordinary: The Life of Professor the Rt. Hon. Friedrich Max Müller P. C.* Delhi: Oxford University Press, 1974.

Collini, Stefan, Donald Winch, and John Burrow. *That Noble Science of Politics: A Study in Nineteenth-Century Intellectual History*. Cambridge: Cambridge University Press, 1983.

Conway, Moncure D. *Autobiography: Memories and Experiences of Moncure Daniel Conway*, 2 vols. London: Cassell, 1904.

Craster, Edmund. *History of the Bodleian Library 1845-1945*. Oxford: Clarendon Press, 1952.

Daston, Lorraine and H. Otto Sibum. "Introduction: Scientific Personae and Their Histories." *Science in Context* 16 (2003): 1-8.

de Solla Price, Derek J. *Little Science, Big Science … and Beyond*. New York, NY: Columbia Press, [1963] 1986.

de Saussure, Ferdinand. *Cours de linguistique générale*. Paris: Payot, [1916] 1980.

de Saussure, Ferdinand. *Course in General Linguistics*. Translated by Roy Harris. London: Duckworth, 1983.

de Saussure, Ferdinand. *Writings in General Linguistics*. Oxford: Oxford University Press, 2006.

Green, Thomas J. *Religion for a Secular Age: Max Müller, Swami Vivekananda and Vedānta*. Farnham: Ashgate, 2016.

Green, V. H. H. *Oxford Common Room: A Study of Lincoln College and Mark Pattison*. London: Edward Arnold, 1957.

Holloway, John. *The Victorian Sage: Studies in Argument*. London: MacMillan, 1953.

Manley, K. A. "Max Müller and the Bodleian Sub-Librarianship, 1865." *Library History* 5 (1979): 33-47.

Molendijk, Arie L. "'To Unite Religion against all Irreligion': The 1893 World Parliament of Religions." *Journal for the History of Modern Theology* 18 (2011): 228-250.

Molendijk, Arie L. *Friedrich Max Müller and the Sacred Books of the East*. Oxford: Oxford University Press, 2016.

Molendijk, Arie L. "The First Conferences on the History of Religions: Religious Dialogue versus Scholarly Study." *NTT: Journal for Theology and the Study of Religion* 72 (2018): 211-224.

Müller, F. Max. "Buddhism." In Müller, *Chips from a German Workshop*, vol. 1, 182-231. London: Longmans, Green & Co, 1867.

Müller, F. Max. *Introduction to the Science of Religion*. London: Longmans, Green & Co, 1873.

Müller, F. Max. *Lectures on the Science of Language*, 2 vols., 7th ed. London: Longmans, Green & Co, 1873.

Müller, F. Max. "Address [to the Aryan Section]." In *Transactions of the Second Session of the International Congress of Orientalists*, London, September 1874. Nendeln: Kraus Reprint, [1876] 1968.

Müller, F. Max. *Biographical Essays*. London: Longmans, Green & Co, 1884.

Müller, F. Max. *Natural Religion*, Gifford Lectures Glasgow 1888. London: Longmans, Green, and Co, 1889.

Müller, F. Max. *Ramakrishna: His Life and Sayings*. London: Longmans, Green, and Co, 1898.

Müller, F. Max. *Auld Lang Syne*, 2 vols. London: Longmans & Green, 1898-1899.

Müller, F. Max. *The Question of Right between England and the Transvaal: Letters by the Right Hon. F. Max Müller with Rejoinders by Professor Theodor Mommsen*, Westminster: Imperial South African Association, 1900

Müller, F. Max. *My Autobiography: A Fragment*. London: Longmans, Green, and Co, 1901.

Müller, F. Max. *The Life and Letters of the Right Honourable Max Müller*, 2 vols., edited by [Georgina Müller]. London: Longmans, Green, and Co, 1902.

Müller, F. Max. *Thoughts on Life and Religion*, edited by [Georgina Müller]. London: Archibald Constable and Company, 1906.

N. N. "Prof. Max Mueller Dead." *New York Times* (29 October 1900).

N. N. "Max Mueller." *New York Times* (3 November 1900).

N. N. "Appreciation of Max Muller." *New York Times* (1 December 1900).

Paul, Herman. "What Is a Scholarly Persona? Ten Theses on Virtues, Skills, and Desires." *History and Theory* 53 (2014): 348-371.

Paul, Herman. "The Virtues and Vices of Albert Naudé: Toward a History of Scholarly Personae." *History of Humanities* 1 (2016), 327-338.

Planck, Max. *Scientific Autobiography and Other Papers* (1948). Translated by F. Gaynor. New York, NY: Philosophical Library, 1950.

Rebenich, Stefan and Gisa Franke, eds. *Theodor Mommsen und Friedrich Althoff: Briefwechsel 1882-1903*. Munich: Oldenburg, 2012.

Ritter, J., ed. *Historisches Wörterbuch der Philosophie*, vol. 4. Basel: Schwabe, 1976.

Schuyler, Jr., Montgomery. "Max Muller's Service to Science." *New York Times* (3 November 1900).

Sutcliffe, Peter. *Oxford University Press: An Informal History*. Oxford: Clarendon Press, 1978.

Thomas A. Sebeok, ed. *Portraits of Linguists: A Biographical Source Book for the History of Western Linguistics, 1746-1963*, 2 vols. Westport: Greenwood Press, [1966] 1976.

van den Bosch, Lourens P. *Friedrich Max Müller: A Life Devoted to the Humanities*. Leiden: Brill, 2002.

van der Veer, Peter. *Imperial Encounters: Religion and Modernity in India and Britain*. Princeton, NJ: Princeton University Press, 2001.

Vivekananda, Swami. "Ramakrishna: His Life and Sayings." In *The Complete Works of Swami Vivekananda*, 8 vols., 4: 409-421. Calcutta: Advaita Ashrama, 1973-1979.

von Harnack, Adolf. "Antrittsrede in der Preußischen Akademie der Wissenschaften." In *Adolf von Harnack als Zeitgenosse*, edited by Kurt Nowak, 2 vols, 1: 976-982. Berlin: Walter de Gruyter, 1996 .

Voigt, Johannes H. "Die Auseinandersetzung zwischen Theodor Mommsen und Max Müller über den Burenkrieg." *Geschichte in Wissenschaft und Unterricht* 17 (1966), 65-77.

CHAPTER 3

Epistemic Vice

Transgression in the Arabian Travels of Julius Euting

Henning Trüper

I

Virtue is usually understood to consist in a personal disposition, acquired and sustained over time, toward normatively sanctioned behavior. Such a disposition can become pertinent to epistemic work – the production of knowledge – when it ties together, within the medium of personhood, scholarly practice and other behavioral norms. As Lorraine Daston and Peter Galison have shown in their study of the meanings of "objectivity," nineteenth-century understandings of scientific method indeed entailed that the production of scholarly knowledge fully complied with a specific body of moral norms about virtuous character.[1] In a basic analysis then, for nineteenth-century scholars, methodology was to be understood through person-bound and person-making moral dispositions. The amalgam of methodological and moral norms was meant to be endowed with sovereign government over scientific practice. Knowledge and personae together thus hinged on practical normativity.

Granted, from a historical perspective it is inevitable to modify this basic analysis. Daston and Galison distinguish various stages of semantic change that pervaded the concept of objectivity itself. Broader study of relations between knowledge and virtue in European scholarship since the early modern period revealed a long and fractured history that undid much of the pretense to sovereignty in the compound of ethics and episteme that was the scholarly persona.[2] Moreover, even in the methodological discourse of nineteenth-century scholarship itself, a certain gap – at the very least a semantic one – stubbornly persisted between the spheres of the epistemic and the ethical. In the sources one can track the blurring of respective discursive patterns; but one can also, on occasion, see them separate and stand apart from each other. The

---

[1] Lorraine Daston and Peter Galison, *Objectivity* (New York, NY: Zone Books, 2007).
[2] Debate was above all instigated by Steven Shapin and Simon Schaffer, *Leviathan and the Air-Pump: Hobbes, Boyle, and the Experimental Life* (Princeton, NJ: Princeton University Press, 1985). Shapin has also continued the analysis into the twentieth century in his *The Scientific Life: A Moral History of a Late Modern Vocation* (Chicago, IL: University of Chicago Press, 2008).

compound of virtue and knowledge itself is not stable, but presents a case of historical dynamism, hardly surprising perhaps, given that virtue itself is a concept of permanent development. Fittingly, on the level of scholarly writing, referencing the embodiment of virtue in practice was a marker of the distinct temporality in which scholars framed their working lives.[3] It stands to reason that the presence of virtue in epistemic work had normative force over practice only at certain times, and was suspended at others. This would then seem to complicate the understanding of the historical efficacy of the underlying structural linkage between knowledge and virtue and to open a gap between the ethical and epistemic spheres.

In addition, the linkage of method and virtue contains another lacuna. The ethical discourse at hand privileges virtue over other discursive frameworks of ethical normativity, and virtue is bound up with personhood. Indeed, it was part of the promise of virtue ethics when it was re-formulated in the twentieth century – in a diverse array of interventions that prominently included the works of British philosophers G. E. M. Anscombe, Philippa Foot, and Bernard Williams, with Aristotle as a prime point of reference – that ethics might be released from the prison cell of the alternative of deontological versus consequentialist approaches. In addition, even circumvention of the Humean predicament of the naturalist fallacy – preventing conclusion from "is" to "ought" and vice versa – seemed to appear on the horizon. Virtue was to entail that individual moral decisions were secondary to acquired disposition, so that the facticity of lived life was foundational for the normativity informing ethical judgment. The ability of ethical judgment could be considered as part of acquired virtue. The notion that such judgment concerned artificially fragmented momentary events that could be held to deontological or consequentialist standards was to be discarded; as was the notion of the autonomy of normative discourse from the complexity of individual lives.

So why, if the approach aimed to overcome longstanding distinctions, did it open another gap? It would appear that virtue ethics tends to treat compliance and deviance differently, simply by slanting the analysis of normativity toward positive sanction. To be sure, the approach provided the mirror category of "vice" for a life lived wrongly, so that repeated transgression would eventually constitute a disposition toward the violation of norms. Nonetheless, in virtue ethics, vice and the theme of prohibitive rules and their violation become secondary concerns. The teleological orientation of the lived life toward a virtuous disposition assumes the role of a privileged source of moral ought. It might

---

3 As I have argued in *Topography of a Method: François Louis Ganshof and the Writing of History* (Tübingen: Mohr Siebeck, 2014).

seem that the history of scholarship provides a counter-example to this claim. As for instance William Clark and Martin Mulsow have shown, vice ethics were a prominent theme, and practical concern of early modern scholarship.[4] As Sari Kivistö has emphasized, such ethics favored those vices – in particular, the reckless pursuit of self-interest, and the hunger for fame – that were particularly apt at generating negative personae;[5] and yet by the nineteenth century this meticulously tended garden of moral topoi had all but disappeared. Ethical discourse had reverted to uncontrolled growth, and the asymmetry re-emerged. As a result, when studying the late modern period, it does not appear helpful to assume the existence of a teleology of vice equivalent to that of virtue. Modern vice, unlike virtue, appears to consist in a protracted series of aberrations rather than in the realization of an actual goal of life. As a consequence of this asymmetric structure, it would seem that such violations of rules that occur as random momentary events within an overall more virtuous context carry a different, presumably weaker, normative charge than those infractions that must be regarded as habitual. While certainly penal law is designed to accord to such notions, the overall language of normative morality does not always seem to function in this manner. Hence a gap opens between virtue and normativity: virtue is integrated into personhood in a way that vice is not, yet vice is still the target of norms. The bond that would tie methodological norms to personal dispositions, on the account that practical normativity is in some sense vested in such dispositions, thereby appears weakened.

In the present chapter, I seek to explore some of the implications of these problems for the history of scholarly personae.[6] Along the lines of a case study, I will seek to explore the relation of vice and persona in the production of scholarly knowledge. Considerable emphasis will be placed, in this undertaking, on the asymmetries that mark virtue and vice; and on the destabilizing effect of vice on virtuous personae. This emphasis responds, I think, to particularities of the history of Orientalism within the history of scholarship. Arguably more than scholars of other disciplines, Orientalists developed, and relied on, habits of transgression – specific epistemic vices – for their scholarly

---

4 William Clark, *Academic Charisma and the Origins of the Research University* (Chicago, IL: University of Chicago Press, 2006), here especially ch. 3-4; Martin Mulsow, *Die unanständige Gelehrtenrepublik: Wissen, Libertinage und Kommunikation in der Frühen Neuzeit* (Stuttgart: Metzler, 2007).

5 Sari Kivistö, *The Vices of Learning: Morality and Knowledge at Early Modern Universities* (Leiden: Brill, 2014).

6 Further developing an argument from my "Dispersed Personae: Subject Matters of Scholarly Biography in Nineteenth-Century Oriental Philology," *Asiatische Studien* 67 (2013), 1325-1360.

practice. In part, this tendency may have responded to the need to operate in contexts of moral heteronomy, where the rule systems scholars encountered were not of their own making and often only partially transparent to them. As I will seek to show, epistemic vice was intimately connected with modes of objectification, i.e. of constituting the objects of scholarly knowledge. Moreover, to the extent that scholarly personae as embodiments of virtue were required in the writing of Orientalist text, epistemic vice informed its own concealment. This type of vice thus provided a specific structure of reflective unreflexivity, as one might say. As a consequence, multiple forms and habits of transgression were inscribed into basic epistemic operations of Orientalism. These habits were not *merely* the result of outward impositions of, say, ideological constraints, such as European supremacism. Nor were they *simply* expressive of a desire for personal or imperial domination. Hopefully, then, the debate on Orientalism can be broadened in significant ways through attention on the interweaving of ethical norms and epistemic work and the problem of the asymmetry of virtuous and vicious scholarly personae.

II

The case is that of the travel diary of the German Orientalist Julius Euting (1839-1913) from his journey to "Inner Arabia" in 1883-1884. The voyage was undertaken on funding granted by wealthy aristocratic donors. Euting traveled together with a geographer, the Alsatian-born Frenchman Charles Huber (1837-1884), who had traversed the area before. Euting believed he required Huber's expertise and therefore extended his funding also to his companion, in spite of the fact that Huber had obtained money from the French government as well, which apparently, he neglected to tell Euting. Such duplicity in the context of a Franco–German scholarly rivalry was a bad omen.[7] It further complicated matters that Huber was murdered by Bedouins in July 1884, four months after he and Euting had parted company. Euting was apprehensive of voices in the French public that sought to blame him for Huber's death, although by July he had been traveling in Greece.[8] In any case, French authorities claimed ownership of the expedition's epigraphic finds. The most spectacular trophy had been the Old-Aramaic stele of Tayma, which had

---

7 As a particularly salient case study of Franco-German rivalry in this period, see Bénédicte Savoy, *Nofretete, eine deutsch-französische Affäre 1913-1931* (Cologne: Böhlau, 2011).
8 Euting to August Dillmann, 3 August 1884, Staatsbibliothek Berlin, Nachlass Dillmann [NL Dillmann], 80, fol. 8.

previously been "discovered" already by the British traveler Charles Doughty on his 1877 passage through the area, and also by Huber during his first Arabian voyage 1878-1882.[9] Euting insisted that he had purchased the stele from his own funds and agreed with Huber that it would be treated as his property. As his correspondence from the summer of 1884 suggests, he believed it would be expedited to Strasbourg.[10] Instead it was sent to, and remained in, Paris as a find of Huber's. Yet, Euting – perhaps less ingenuously than he later claimed – had transmitted his squeeze of the stele to his friend and Strasbourg colleague Theodor Nöldeke (1836-1930) already before Huber's death, and Nöldeke rushed to publish the inscription.[11] So the result was mixed, the priority of discovery split. Ernest Renan, then in charge of the collection of Semitic inscriptions for the *Académie des Inscriptions et Belles-Lettres*, the would-be dominant undertaking of international Semitic epigraphy, expressed his strong disapproval of the Germans' comportment.[12]

Published snippets from Huber's correspondence with the ministry of education in Paris suggest that Euting was rather profoundly mistaken about Huber's willingness to accept him as a travel companion.[13] Political ill feeling of the exiled Alsatian combined with personal antipathy for Euting's "enthusiasm," his naïve exuberance and lack of restraint. The letters also suggest that Huber was convinced he had managed to machinate Euting's departure from Arabia, by way of personal favor from the Amir of Ha'il, thus that he had dealt Euting a political defeat. Huber's travel diaries, which were published posthumously, did not make any mention of his companion.[14] The scholarly *personae*

---

9   As noted by Hélène Lozachmeur and Françoise Briquel-Chatonnet, "Charles Huber und Julius Euting in Arabien nach französischen, auch heute noch nicht veröffentlichten Dokumenten," *Anabases* 12 (2010), 195-200. On the textual corpus of European voyaging in Arabia, see Benjamin Reilly, "Arabian Travellers, 1800-1950: An Analytical Bibliography," *British Journal of Middle Eastern Studies* 43, no. 1 (2016), 71-93.
10 Euting to Dillmann, 16 July 1884, NL Dillmann, 80, fol. 6.
11 Theodor Nöldeke, "Altaramäische Inschriften aus Teimâ (Arabien)," *Sitzungsberichte der Königlich-Preußischen Akademie der Wissenschaften* 35 (1884), 813-820. The correspondence suggests that the inscription was published within days of the arrival of the squeezes in Strasbourg: Nöldeke to Dillmann, 25 June and 5 July 1884, NL Dillmann, 209, fols. 49-50.
12 Renan to Dillmann, 24 July 1884, NL Dillmann, 236, fols. 1-2. An early reconstruction of this conflict can already be found in David George Hogarth, *The Penetration of Arabia: A Record of the Development of Western Knowledge Concerning the Arabian Peninsula* (London: Lawrrence & Bullen, 1904), 281.
13 See Lozachmeur and Briquel-Chatonnet, "Huber und Euting."
14 On account of Huber's silence, the editors suggested that Euting would have to clarify on his own which of the epigraphic results were to be attributed to whom, see Charles Huber, *Journal d'un voyage en Arabie (1883-1884)* (Paris: Imprimerie Nationale, 1891), vii.

at hand therefore prominently participated in the vagaries of European national and imperial competition. Arguably, one can discern in this participation a first, systemic layer of transgression that thwarted the virtuous objectivity of any of the accounts given and invaded the actual published products of scholarly knowledge as well. The political constellation certainly favored, even legitimized, the vice of insincerity.

Euting had published the first portion of his account – which was expressly to make available to a "broader audience" a "readable description" of his "personal experiences [*Erlebnisse*], impressions and observations" – some twelve years after the conclusion of the journey.[15] The journey had led south from Damascus into the Najd and Tabuk regions in the central and northwestern Arabian Peninsula. His chief research interest had been the collection of Old-Semitic inscriptions, which were located mostly in the areas he visited last.[16] For the most part, therefore, the travel diary recorded quotidian events and covered secondary research interests in ethnographic observation, the study of Wahhabism, and the description of crafts and technology. After the first part of his revised diary had been published, Euting had never managed to bring the second part to print, in spite of the fact that the more substantive scholarly discoveries of his journey had taken place only toward its end. Even his retirement from the directorship of Strasbourg University Library had not helped the conclusion of the diary. When he died in January 1913, the task of the edition of the posthumous work passed to Enno Littmann (1875-1958), successor of Nöldeke in the Strasbourg chair of Semitics. Littmann swiftly, within roughly a year, managed to finalize the material; the second part appeared in the spring of 1914.[17]

For the analysis of the structure of habitual transgression, the vices, at the heart of the diary, this long-winded publication history provides additional complication. The structure in question is layered and the accumulation of layers was processual, so that posterior formations impinged on the previous ones. Different forms of the transformation of experience into written words and drawn images, and of these writings and drawings into printed matter, cannot be separated from the problem of transgression in travel; the journey, along with the persona it produced, was a "scene of writing"[18] (as well as a

---

15   Julius Euting, *Tagbuch einer Reise in Inner-Arabien: Erster Theil* (Leiden: Brill, 1896), vi.
16   Julius Euting, *Nabatäische Inschriften aus Arabien* (Berlin: Reimer, 1885).
17   Julius Euting, *Tagbuch einer Reise in Inner-Arabien: Zweiter Theil*, ed. Enno Littmann (Leiden: Brill, 1914), subsequent reference to the two parts of the diary in parentheses, as I and II, followed by page number.
18   Jacques Derrida, "Freud et la scène de l'écriture," in Derrida, *L'Ecriture et la différence* (Paris: Seuil, 1967), 293-340.

scene of drawing), and the persona was a soliloquizing actor on this scene. The inherent competition of divergent forms of representation, the visual aesthetics of the drawings and the poetics of the diary, further added layers of normatively prohibited infringement that must not be neglected if one wants to get a hold on the structure of transgression at hand. The diary and the events it narrated cannot be stably separated, and the writing participated in the vices that marked the journey itself.

III

Euting had left behind three types of manuscript source: firstly there were actual diaries, occasionally adorned with illustrations; secondly notebooks, which the author also used for small impromptu pencil drawings; and thirdly sketchbooks of panoramic format in which he inserted pencil drawings, often worked over with watercolors, of people, landscapes and townscapes.[19] The editorial difficulty was to make decisions on the combination of artwork and text; and then to produce a coherent narrative from the diary notes.

As for the first of these tasks, Littmann freely admitted to doctoring, in a decidedly unphilological manner, the text of the last two chapters, which Euting had not rewritten from the more restricted narrative format of the original diaries (II, X). In letter correspondence, Littmann even challenged Nöldeke to identify the passages he had made up in an exercise of stylistic mimicry.[20] To another mutual friend, just after Euting's demise, Littmann also mentioned that the transfer of the manuscripts of the deceased to the University Libraries of Strasbourg[21] and Tübingen, as decreed by Euting's will, only seemed possible after a vigorous purge. Everything that betrayed Euting's "weaknesses (great vanity, obscene things, relations with certain women)" had to be destroyed. "For posterity we have to preserve in purity the *good* Euting (and that was all in all the greatest part of his character [*Wesen*])."[22] The "good Euting," a typically virtuous scholarly persona, was also identical to the authorial voice of the 1896

---

19   Universitätsbibliothek Tübingen, Nachlass Julius Euting, Md 676, digitized: URL: <http://idb.ub.uni-tuebingen.de/diglit/Md676> (last accessed 28 January 2019).
20   Littmann to Nöldeke, 4 September 1913, Staatsbibliothek Berlin, Teilnachlass Nöldeke, NL 246.
21   Daniel Bornemann, "Les legs de Julius Euting ou l'organisation posthume d'un savoir," *La Revue de la BNU* 12 (2015), 30-41.
22   Littmann to Friedrich Veit, 24 February 1913, NL Littmann, K. 46, *An Veit* (orig. emphasis).

diary volume, which Littmann had read in his student days and later used as a model of diary writing during his own various journeys from 1899-1906 (II, VII). The 1896 tome had already shown "fully the amiable personality of the man who was in everything unvarnished [*ungeschminkt*], genuine and natural" (II, VIIf). Apparently, it did not occur to Littmann that these qualities stood in some contrast to the monumentalizing varnishing of the archival record.

Euting himself had already liberally reworked his own text. For instance, the scene of the travelers' arrival in Tayma reads in the original diary: "As soon as we had unloaded our luggage, once again all kinds of people poured into the café to see the Greenlanders; for quite in the manner of strange animals or Patagonians in a zoological garden, we were marveled at, and as Christians, to boot."[23] In the published version – edited by Littmann, but in this chapter still revised by Euting himself – the passage reads:

> As soon as our luggage had been moved into the house, everybody who felt entitled to do so – presumably because of their halfway decent clothing – poured in. Similar to the manner in which in Europe, in a zoological garden, one presents strange people, e.g. Patagonians or Tasmanians, we were marveled at as Nordic people [*Nordländer*], and Christians to boot, and all of it without risk or cost (II, 149).

One can see that Euting used the revision to intensify the derogatory character of the passage. The reference to the display of natives from portions of the globe remote from Europe alludes to the zoo as an allegory of sovereignty characterized by its command over both the spatially distant and the order of nature as such. The Patagonians had been assigned a particular role in the history of European exploration. Long into the eighteenth century their actual status as human beings and the question of whether they were actual giants had remained disputed.[24] Euting's reminiscence of this half-legendary nation suggests a playful contiguity with the historical semantics of the savage. The

---

23   Md 676-22, 3r.
24   See on this theme Jonathan Lamb, *Preserving the Self in the South Seas, 1680-1840* (Chicago, IL: University of Chicago Press, 2001). Also see the half-sentence in Kant's *Kritik der Urteilskraft*, AA 5, §67, p. 378, that marks the "New Hollanders" and "Patagonians" as exemplary of the lowest degree of humanity attainable; see further Gayatri Chakravorty Spivak's interptretation of this passage in *A Critique of Postcolonial Reason: Toward a History of the Vanishing Present* (Cambridge, MA: Harvard University Press, 1999), 26. See moreover the instructive discussion of the context in Reinhard M. Möller, "Die Feuerland-Episode in Georg Forsters 'Reise um die Welt' im Kontext einer anekdotischen Poetik der Interkulturalität," in *Georg Forster als interkultureller Autor*, ed. Stefan Greif and Michael Ewert (Kassel: Kassel University Press, 2014), 79-107.

seeming reversal – in the passage, Arabs regard the Europeans "as if" they were savages – seems like a perfect miniature illustration of the cultural-relativist perspective allegedly inherent, though historically stunted, in nineteenth-century Orientalism.[25] Yet, actually, the point of the passage lies elsewhere. The change from *Grönländer* (original diary), meaning Inuit, to *Nordländer* (published version) indicates that Euting did not seek to imply a relativist stance. It seems hard to deny that the passage primarily aims to produce a comical effect of mirror-image reversal; the sordid and unspeakably ignorant Arabs just have it all wrong. Euting's revisions are not merely transgressions against the integrity of his own notes, but constitutively bound up with the denigration of his Arab hosts. The pattern of transgression at hand concerned both local obligations and the long-established epistemic virtues of the genre of the travelogue, which since the enlightened era had dictated an appreciative representation of local standpoint.[26]

A striking example for the extent to which Euting's revisions transcended the original diary text concerns the passage about the "discovery" and first readings of the stele of Tayma on 17 February 1884 and subsequent days. Entirely without support of the original diary, Euting provides an account of events that gives him a degree of priority over Huber, who although he had seen the stone during his 1880 sojourn in Tayma allegedly admitted to Euting that he had not considered it significant. Euting also suggests that their agreement to send the stone to Germany was settled on site. Again, the original diary makes no mention of such an accord. Moreover, in the revised text Euting suppressed the information that he had not at first recognized the script on the stele as Aramaic. The original diary, by contrast, does not seem at all concerned with priority, property, or epistemic mastery, but repeatedly refers to the explorers as a unified agency of "we" (II, 157-61).[27] The making of scientific discoveries required forgery, the "counterfeit" of which Nietzsche spoke at length with regard to philological method. As James Porter has shown, this motif was intimately related to the falsification and imprecision of quotations in Wilamowitz's attack on Nietzsche.[28] "Bad philology" was hardly inconsequential, and it was so ubiquitous that it must be acknowledged as part and parcel

---

[25] The overall argument given by Suzanne Marchand in *German Orientalism in the Age of Empire: Race, Religion, Scholarship* (Cambridge: Cambridge University Press, 2009), particularly hinges on this idea as an organizing principle.

[26] As Jürgen Osterhammel, *Die Entzauberung Asiens: Europa und die asiatischen Reiche im 18. Jahrhundert* (Munich: C. H. Beck, 1998) has shown at great length.

[27] Md 676-22, 6v-11r.

[28] James I. Porter, "'Don't Quote Me on That!' Wilamowitz Contra Nietzsche in 1872 and 1873," *Journal of Nietzsche Studies* 42 (2011), 73-99.

of practice. In the revision of the diaries, both Littmann and Euting forsook the precepts of philological methodology.

It is then hardly surprising that similar patterns of deviance and inexactitude also mark the second editorial challenge Littmann faced, the combination of artwork and text. In principle, the publication followed the model of the first part, which had used drawings and black-and-white renderings of the watercolors as illustrations. Littmann was, however, perhaps more smitten with the drawings than their actual author. The second part therefore appears to contain a larger overall number of images, and it did not merely rely on the more worked out and larger-sized pictures in the sketchbooks, but also included a great number of the small, often very perfunctory pencil sketches from the notebooks. These sketches had to be adapted for publication, a process that entailed rather far-reaching graphic intrusions through which the drawings were modified in size and clarified in contour. For this work, Littmann enlisted the aid of an architect–archaeologist colleague from one of his own expeditions, Daniel Krencker (1874-1941). Krencker's modifications to the drawings of landscapes, figures, and scenes were often quite cavalier. For instance, in a set of pictures with which Euting illustrates some of his more outlandish manners of making squeezes of out-of-the-way inscriptions by hanging out of windows or climbing the stem of a palm tree, Krencker went so far as to broaden the frame and change the perspective of the images to make them appear more adroit.[29] Euting's drawings were in this case integrated with the actual text of the diary in a manner that could not be reproduced in print (Figs. 3.1-3.2).

For Littmann, there was no doubt that Euting's sensibility, his overall epistemic virtue as a traveler, was based on his graphic skills and on his ability to see in accordance with aesthetic frameworks that had normative as well as scientific significance:

> As a painter, he had also learned to observe. And with fine humor he knew how to take the things themselves and represent them as something different. It is precisely in this detailed description of life in Inner Arabia that the main value of the Diary probably resides. In addition there are also the many drawings and images from a country so far away (II, VIII).

Thus there was a direct convergence of writing skills, of the rendering of detail on the level of text, and of graphic representation. The aesthetic regimen of the gaze also enhanced Euting's ability as an epigrapher who was able to produce, next to the inevitable squeezes, exceptionally precise hand-drawn copies

---

29   Md 676-22, 51r, 52r and Euting, *Tagbuch II*, 228f.

FIGURE 3.1
Julius Euting, Original Diary, University of Tübingen Library, Md 676-22, 52r.

FIGURE 3.2
Julius Euting, *Tagbuch*, II, 229, detail: "Making a squeeze of an inscription."

of inscriptions.[30] Yet, as Krencker's adaptations indicate, the persona of the scholar with privileged eyesight – one of the key topoi of epistemic virtue in the nineteenth century[31] – also relied on a structure of counterfeit that dovetailed with the vice of bad philology.

IV

Euting himself also believed in the linkage of reason, writing, and draughtsmanship. During his sojourn in Ha'il he asked a local Arab to draw a map of rivers in the area, and regarded the result as a *Machwerk*, a job so lousy he saw fit to copy it into the published diary for demonstration (II, 21). Similarly, he included a few drawings of a local prince, *Mâgid*,[32] which Euting likewise considered inferior:

> Since I was unable to praise these efforts as hoped, but on the contrary assured him that in Europe one would at most slap a pupil around the head a few times for such a shameful daub, he admitted that this was also not yet the most perfect thing he was able to produce in the area of painting. This claim only prompted me to press him further until he wrested from himself the second work of art, with which I declared myself somewhat more satisfied:

FIGURE 3.3 Julius Euting, *Tagbuch*, II, 26, detail: "Drawing by the Prince Mâgid."

He was, I believe, quite pleased when the call for the general prayer sounded (II, 25f).

---

30 John F. Healey, "'Sicherheit des Auges': The Contribution to Epigraphy of Julius Euting (1839-1913)," in *Biblical and Near Eastern Essays: Studies in Honour of Kevin J. Cathcart*, ed. Carmel McCarthy and John F. Healey (London: Clark International, 2004), 313-330.
31 Daston and Galison, *Objectivity*, ch. 1-2.
32 Names for which I have preserved Euting's system of transcription appear in Italics (when outside of quotations).

Euting's own draughtsmanship therefore constituted in his mind a domain, not merely of aesthetic and epistemic skill, but of superiority. The practice of drawing was an arena of aesthetic competition; and in Euting's case, it was also one of provocation and manipulation.

A few days after the episode with *Mâgid*, Euting reworked a previous portrait sketch of another prince, *'Abd el-'Azîz* – who was an adolescent at the time and later, in 1897, became Amir – in watercolors and showed the result to the sitter:

> He did not seem entirely satisfied – who is entirely satisfied when one shows him his image? – To reassure himself, and to assuage female curiosity, he showed it around in the harem.
>
> Although he himself did not suffer from fear – unlike his relative *'Obeid*, who expected imminent and ineluctable calamity from the useless and sinful images – he appeared nonetheless distraught by the thought that this noble cousin and uncle of his could manipulate the *Emîr* to forge some kind of plot against him. He was visibly relieved when, before his own eyes, I pulled the leaf from the sketchbook and promised him that henceforth I would not talk about nor show this image to anyone in this country (II, 36f).

The relative here referred to, *Ḥamûd el-'Obeid*, was the Amir's cousin and a powerful senior courtier. The same evening the Amir, *Muḥammed ibn 'Abdallâh*, asked to see the sketchbook and showed interest specifically in the portraits and none in the landscapes, even though the latter genre was more tightly connected to European imperial pursuits, especially that of establishing the controlling and all-encompassing gaze of the European traveler.[33] Euting avers that he felt relieved about having removed the prince's image from his sketchbook (Fig. 3.4).[34] Yet after the departure from Ha'il, he pasted the portrait back into the book, and a line-drawn version is included in the print version of the diary as well. Promises made at the scene clearly failed to apply elsewhere. Significantly, however, Euting refrained from portraying the *'Emîr* himself. The overall competition, into which the Orientalist inserted his artwork on site, was crucially located in the context of life at court where one vied for proximity to the ruler with other notables. It was for this reason that Euting was particularly keen to assert his superiority over members of the Amir's entourage,

---

33 Following W. J. T. Mitchell (ed.), *Landscape and Power* (Chicago, IL: University of Chicago Press, 2002).

34 The portrait was later pasted back into one of the sketchbooks, Md 676-32, 30r.

FIGURE 3.4 Julius Euting, Original Sketchbook 6, University of Tübingen Library, Md 676-32, 30r: "Abdalaziz, Hâjel 29. Nov. 83, since 1897 Emîr of Hâjel."

a behavior which, at least according to his own account, he displayed far less in his dealings with commoners.

It may be worth adding that this type of competition also governed the behavior in such "courtly encounters"[35] in which the European visitor was not impressed with the overall courtly setting. Toward the beginning of the sojourn in Ha'il, Euting scorned the "few ridiculous European armchairs (thrones?) and gilded garden furniture" (1, 174) that supposedly constituted the splendor of the Rashidi court. This dismissive attitude, however, did not prevent him from adopting an unabashedly partisan stance in favor of the Rashidi when it came to prognosticating the political future of the Najd. He remained convinced that the Rashidi court would overcome their Saudi rivals, and he did not live to see the overwhelming victory, around 1920, of the Saudi family he had failed to visit. To be sure, for many years, favoring the Rashidis, who had received a greater number of European visitors, was topical for Orientalist scholarship. Yet, the partisanship of European travelers was precisely an effect of their integration into courtly life; and this type of life was traditionally at least interpretable as a structure of vice of such depth that it justified political revolution.

The theme of the forbidden depiction of humans continued to haunt Euting's long stay in Ha'il, which was, after all, the territory of the severe Wahhabi interpretation of Islam that had been topical in all European travelogues of Arabia since Jean Louis Burckhardt had provided extensive discussion of the

---

35   With the formula proposed by Sanjay Subrahmanyam, *Courtly Encounters: Translating Courtliness and Violence in Early Modern Eurasia* (Cambridge, MA: Harvard University Press, 2012).

then-still-novel sect in the 1810s.[36] Euting had set out on his journey with a vivid research interest in this religious movement and its concomitant political history, which notably included the decades-long rivalry of the Saudi and Rashidi families. When it came to adopting an Arab name for the purpose of having less explaining to do during the journey in those parts of the country not accustomed to Europeans, Euting started calling himself ʿAbd el-Wahhâb (I, 50), adopting the name of the father of Muḥammad ibn ʿAbd al-Wahhāb, the founder of the sect. Nonetheless, during the sojourn in Ha'il, he preferred run-ins with official religious sentiment over actual research. His chapter on Wahhabism for the most part merely summarized knowledge Carl Ritter had processed more than thirty years earlier, without ever setting foot on Arabian soil.[37] Euting's observations were diverted into portraits, which served as an instrument to provoke his hosts, rather than to represent scholarly knowledge. Accordingly, the drawings were perfectly public. On several occasions the sketchbooks were circulated among the courtiers, and in previous stages of the journey, among other classes of locals as well.

On 12 December 1883, a few days after the episode with ʿAbd el'Azîz, Ḥamûd el-ʿObeid explicitly reproached Euting that the drawing of human figures constituted a transgression against religious commandment. "When I responded: At home [*bei uns*] it is not a sin, he snapped at me: 'But you are not in your country here!'" (II, 55). The Amir, who was present, abstained from expressing an opinion, but somewhat later that evening, Huber requested – on behalf of the Amir, as he claimed – that Euting desist from creating further human portraits. Another five days later, however, the court's indomitable concern with visual representations of the human form resurged. The Amir asked Euting whether it was true that in Europe paper was used as currency, and if so, how it was possible that something so devoid of material value could serve this purpose. Euting responded with a short, improvised lecture on the nature of paper money as guaranteed by the political sovereign. Asked to produce such a piece of money, he recuperated a bill of 100 German Marks from his purse and began to explain the iconography. His interlocutors soon expressed particular curiosity about the nature of a pair of nude putto figures on the dorsal side of the bill:

---

36 Jean Louis Burckhardt, *Notes on the Bedouins and Wahábys* (London: Colburn & Bentley, 1830). The first European travelogue that mentioned the sect was Carsten Niebuhr's; see Giovanni Bonancina, *The Wahhabis Seen through European Eyes (1772-1830): Deists and Puritans of Islam* (Leiden: Brill, 2015).

37 Euting, *Tagbuch* I, ch. VII, which drew on Carl Ritter, *Allgemeine Erdkunde* XIII (= *Erdkunde Asiens* VIII, 1. Abt., Forts.) *Die Halbinsel Arabien* (Berlin: Reimer, 1847), 448-532.

I saved myself by resorting to the bold claim that these figures were djinns (genies). "What!! *that* is what Djinns look like? Come here everybody, now you can see djinns!" With exclamations like: mâ schâ 'llâh, and subḥḥâna 'llâh, or jâ sattâr ('God's wonders, nothing is going to happen?') they gave free rein to curiosity and secret shudder ... With feigned indolence, as if I disposed of the freshest and most reliable knowledge of djinn matters, I provided all information desired. Actually, the djinns were of course much larger, some even shockingly large, but here, because of the small size of the paper, one had only depicted the smallest ones, and in addition they had been selected from the harmless, even beneficial class. – My 100 bill I only received back after 3 or 4 days, for Ḥamûd el-'Obeid sent it over into his harem, and from there it circulated to Mâgid, 'Abd el'Azîz and so on: obviously they all wanted to revel in how much their women were scared by the display of djinns (II, 61f).

In this manner, through a parody of the circulation of currency, Euting had the better of his Wahhabi opponents, or so he claimed. The icon of the nude putto, to be sure, was itself a symbol of the comical, by virtue of its failure both to refer to and resemble anything real. Although in this episode, it was the Amir who asked the initial question, again it was actually the courtiers who were derided most for their credulity, their apparent inability to discern which European iconic signs were realist, because natural, and which were not. For the overall mode of visual representation in which Euting operated, this episode indicates that realism – if defined as unalloyed referentiality between the image and the entity depicted – was not a comprehensive norm for understanding the sign-system at hand. One also had to understand the distinctions between the imaginary and the real, and the natural and unnatural, as well as the inextricable intermingling of these categories in any European pictorial record. Although Euting's own images seemed straightforwardly referential representations, in fact they were part of a broader system whose other modes of non-referential, non-realist representation one needed to understand as well. Therefore, the Arabs at Ha'il, from Euting's point of view, were constitutively unable to understand what his sketchbooks actually showed, and their circulation primarily served his own amusement.

In order to grasp the non-referential charges of Euting's images, a sideglance to context is helpful. His journey almost overlapped with Christiaan Snouck Hurgronje's (1857-1936) sojourn in Mecca. Snouck, a Dutchman with ties to German scholarship (he had studied with Nöldeke) was a philologist with an affinity toward novel technologies of documentation. During the Meccan stay, he was the first to produce photographs of the city, notably the holy sites.

FIGURE 3.5   Julius Euting, Original Sketchbook 7, Md 676-33, 22v-23r, detail: The sandstone formation and proto-Arabic inscription site "Mahagge[h] 11 Feb. 84, from WNW."

When in the diplomatic mess after Huber's demise, the French consul in Jiddah intervened with the Ottoman government to obtain Snouck's premature departure from Mecca,[38] he left behind his camera so that a Meccan acquaintance could take pictures of the Hajj.[39] Although Euting was hardly any less practically inclined, he did not rely on photography during his own journeys. His activities as a draughtsman, in line with all contemporary visual art, were marked by tacit competition with the new technical medium of representation. For all their realism, his drawings of landscapes and technical devices displayed (Fig. 3.5), and indeed celebrated, not only the skill, but also the imprecision, of the hand.

This is perhaps most obvious in his renderings of the travel route in handdrawn maps that were inserted at the beginnings of the chapters (Fig. 3.6). These drawings failed to deploy any of the methods of mathematically guided representation that were well-established already in the eighteenth century. The blurred shapes of the watercolors functioned in a similar manner. They suggested the insufficiency of precise observation and the indispensability of the imagination in order to grasp the author's phenomenal experience. The colors as well as the pencil linings were applied sparingly. Especially in the panoramic landscapes, portions of the page were often left untouched. The ideal in these depictions was the spatial, three-dimensional illusion, the successful

---

38   The linkage was treated as common knowledge among Orientalists, see e.g. G. W. J. Drewes, "Christiaan Snouck Hurgronje," in: *Biografisch Woordenboek van Nederland*, URL: <http://resources.huygens.knaw.nl/bwn1880-2000/lemmata/bwn2/snouckc> (last accessed 28 January 2019).

39   Christiaan Snouck Hurgronje, *Mekka: Bilderatlas* (The Hague: Nijhoff, 1888).

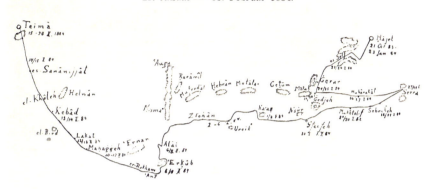

FIGURE 3.6 Julius Euting, Tagbuch, II, 107, detail: Beginning of Ch. X, "From Hâjel to Teimâ."

application of perspective. The concomitant questions of standpoint and foreshortening dictated the standard of exactitude of the shapes and indirectly the application of shadings and the decisions as to what had to be captured in greater or lesser detail. Photography, however, excelled precisely at perspective and precision. Euting's drawings competed with the new medium by way of evoking a mood of nostalgia, expressed through a touching dilettantism that supposedly eluded photography. The long delay of publication only enhanced this sense of pastness. This is an indicator that the outdated model of objectivity by dint of virtuous eyesight was not what was at stake in Euting's visual work.

Upon departure from Ha'il at the end of January, and again when the two scholars went their separate ways in late March, Huber used the frictions over the images against Euting. The French geographer eventually suggested that the Amir of Ha'il had ordered Euting's departure from the country altogether. While Euting's account is hardly reliable, it was not a mere fabrication either, as Huber's correspondence with his Paris sponsors indicates. When preparing the unrevised diaries for print, Littmann went out of his way to lend credence to Euting's perspective and to cast doubt on Huber's integrity. In this process, in square brackets he added a reference to another text, the Arabian travelogue by the Russian-German adventurer Eduard von Nolde (1849-1895). Unfamiliar with the details of Euting's and Huber's journey, and even their names – Euting remained unnamed, Huber consistently misspelled as "Hubert" – Nolde related with befuddlement the implausible story he had been told in Ha'il that Huber had been traveling with a "Prussian servant." Littmann concluded that this perception must have had its origin in what Huber had let on at court (II, 105).[40] At the time it was not clear – and it was in fact never entirely clarified, at least to European travelers – who had killed Huber, and why. Nolde could only register that the Amir of Ha'il denied any involvement. These assurances appeared somewhat doubtful since Nolde was also shown, at court, a signed portrait photograph of Huber that had allegedly been lifted from the latter's belongings after the murder (which however had taken place far from Ha'il, in the area of Medina). This image caused Nolde considerable unease:

> The fact that I was sent Hubert's portrait in and of itself did not need to mean a bad thing; yet, it appeared somewhat odd and, as my people thought, highly suspicious that in the portrait the neck of the unfortunate man had been scratched, even cut open, with a pointed instrument, clearly as a sign and note about the fact that his throat had been cut. This, however, subsequently raised the question of whether the mark was old or recent, and whether, if the latter, it was not meant to be a memento for me, or perhaps for all of us? Since I did not want to augment the concerns, which were already ample, I therefore declared the said neck mark, which I had attentively studied through the magnifying glass, as unconditionally old....[41]

This episode may have suggested to Nolde that the courtiers of Ha'il were capable of parodying the visual aesthetics of their European visitors, not only in the department of indexical realism, where the murder was repeated on the photograph; but also with regard to the manipulation of imagination, in which Nolde and his (native) servants were given a scare, quite in the manner in which, according to Euting, the 100 Marks had been used to frighten the princely womenfolk. As for the matter of dying, Nolde certainly did not require a memento; he committed suicide in London in 1895, before he had even seen the manuscript of his travelogue through print.[42]

Ironically, Nolde may have misunderstood the significance of the cut on Huber's neck. Euting, when he visited the private residence of a merchant, a Jewish convert to Islam who had moved to Ha'il years ago, had noted that the walls were covered in ornamental depictions, especially of animals but also human and various other kinds of figures: "The larger animals all had their necks cut

---

40   The reference is to Eduard von Nolde, *Reise nach Innerarabien, Kurdistan und Armenien 1892* (Braunschweig: Vieweg, 1895), 43.
41   Nolde, *Reise*, 45.
42   Ibid., introductory note by F. Andreae.

off, in order to dispel the imagination of animate nature, and therefore the sinful character of the representation" (1, 193). Years later, when Littmann returned to Euting's pioneering work on the proto-Arabic Thamudic inscriptions, he quoted this passage approvingly and submitted a number of analogous "mortifications," as he called them, in Thamudic rock graffiti as well as in Turkish shadow theater and Ancient Egyptian iconography.[43]

Among his various travel diaries – the collection at Tübingen holds thirty-six items unevenly devoted to a dozen or so journeys – it was only in the Central Arabian documents that Euting resorted with some consistency to the specific visual genre of portraiture, for which, as he admitted himself, he did not have much talent (1, 30). More specifically, this pursuit only marked his protracted courtly encounter on the road to and in Ha'il. There are no portraits in the visual record of the journey after Ha'il. The particular fate of Huber's photograph, as recounted by Nolde, and especially in light of the interpretation Euting might have offered of the cut across the image, suggests that portraiture not only constituted a deliberate act of transgression and provocation, but actually served to organize agency and personae in a specific way, by means of repeated transgression against a system of rules that was religious and "Oriental" and therefore begged Orientalist infringement. Portraiture created material objects that were representations of individuals, and more specifically, of individual heads. As the courtiers of Ha'il and Nolde understood, if perhaps in divergent fashion, what one did with these signifiers could be regarded as having repercussions on the signified, be it in terms of destruction or protection. There is, however, a question to be asked about the transgressive particularities of an Orientalism that collected heads, even if only in representation. It so happens that this question also provides a way of studying the problem of epistemic vice as a structure apart that poses a challenge to the homogeneity of the complex of Orientalism as a whole.

V

The literature on Orientalism has frequently emphasized the "fetishist" quality of European representations of the Oriental. The psychoanalytic bent of many of these discussions has been helpful for understanding the possibilities of projection and transference contained in the Orientalist positing of types of

---

43   Enno Littmann, *Thamūd und Ṣafā: Studien zur altnordarabischen Inschriftenkunde* (Leipzig: Brockhaus, 1940), 35.

object, and individuation within those types.[44] Nonetheless, it appears problematic that this reading method tends to pathologize the quotidian scholarly work of objectification in an undifferentiated manner. The inevitable ontological productivity of scholarship is then made to coincide neatly with a sexually grounded desire for domination and power that in addition is invested with unconditional primacy over knowledge.

Arguably, however, this type of manoeuver substitutes social for epistemic subalterns; and in and of itself, this substitution is a *non sequitur*. So, at this juncture the argument requires additional argumentation in order to lay out the specific manner in which epistemic objectification would translate into its social correlate. I contend that the search for such an argument leads into an impasse. One would be drawn into a notion of epistemic vice, that is to say, a disposition in the subject of knowledge to transgress against the norms of virtue that otherwise historically constituted the habitus of the method-abiding scholar.[45] Such a disposition, in order to be epistemic in character, would need to impinge on scholarly objectification. I believe that it is actually this type of disposition that makes objectification appear like, and potentially overlap with, fetishization. I will however argue that epistemic vice does not emerge out of the same root of sexualized power; but that in the ambit of philology, it emerges out of the problematic of semantics, of generating knowledge about linguistic meanings. In philology, epistemic vice – as a broadly formative force that generates a rich experiential and agential subject – aims at undermining the explication of meaning and works toward the absurd, rather than power.

It is significant, for instance, that Euting did not mark the political system of Bedouin rule as in any form desirable. Other explorers, by contrast, had fetishized the very polity they were visiting. British travelers Wilfrid and Anne Blunt, for example, had fantasized that they would die happily "even if we have our heads cut off in Ha'il," in exchange for the privilege of having beheld this

---

44 Foundational for this reading remains Homi K. Bhabha, "The Other Question: Stereotype, Discrimination, and the Discourse of Colonialism," in Bhabha, *The Location of Culture* (London: Routledge, 1994), 66-84.

45 Daston and Galison, *Objectivity*, remains to date the most comprehensive formulation of an account of epistemic virtues as historically malleable and as formative forces in the production and maintenance of scientific knowledge. The debate about the necessity of a scholarly "persona," composed from virtues, as a historical bridge across the ethics–epistemology divide, has developed rapidly in recent years: see Herman Paul, "What Is a Scholarly Persona? Ten Theses on Virtues, Skills, and Desires," *History and Theory* 53 (2014), 348-371. For a divergent usage that lays greater emphasis on performance, see Mineke Bosch, "Persona and the Performance of Identity: Parallel Developments in the Biographical Historiography of Science and Gender, and the Related Uses of Self Narrative," *L'Homme* 24, no. 2 (2013), 11-22. See also my own "Dispersed Personae."

ideal shepherd polity.[46] The motif of beheading, however, disposes of considerable fetishist legibility, as a stand-in, according to Freud, of castration.[47] Yet, this specific coupling of sublimated erotic desire and violence did not inform Euting's Orientalist perception. With amused disdain, but hardly with fascination, he included an account of a demonstration of swords during which Ḥamûd el-ʿObeid recounted stories of beheading (II, 67). Also, beyond the imagination of beheadings, Euting does not appear to have developed a consistent structure of eroticizing his Arabian encounters. Unlike in paradigmatic pictorial Orientalism, his visual work remained devoid of erotic motifs. As regards the narrative, the most pertinent passage concerns his interaction with a young woman in the village of *Kâf*, where in the beginning of the journey he was forced to wait for several weeks while Huber and the envoy of the Rashidi court that was to accompany them to Ha'il pursued business in Damascus. In *Kâf* the daughter of a local repeatedly proposed to Euting to marry her and bring her to Europe. Euting responded with objection after objection, but began to take a particular liking to the girl because she had a riposte to every argument. Subsequently, she had to depart because of a death in her family in a neighboring village. Euting ended the episode by wondering about the missed opportunity of this marital union, and by recalling other traveling Orientalists who had got married underway (I, 81f).[48] Whatever one makes of this episode, its erotic imagination does not quite appear to reproduce the familiar organization of sexual desire around stereotypes of the inaccessible veiled woman and the harem, the dominated exotic prostitute, or the oppressed Muslim woman to be salvaged by the enlightened modern European.

With greater justification one might perhaps argue that Euting invested some measure of fetishist projection in the firearms he was carrying. Admittedly, most of the considerable supply of weapons he transported into Arabia had been donated to him by the King of Württemberg and served as presents to the Amir of Ha'il (I, 182). Nonetheless, the overall arc of his account culminated in an episode of considerable, if blind, violence by use of firearms. As

---

46 Anne Blunt, *A Pilgrimage to Nejd, the Cradle of the Arab Race, a Visit to the Court of the Arab Emir, and 'Our Persian Campaign'* (London: John Murray, 1881), I, 208. See also Ali Behdad, *Belated Travelers: Orientalism in the Age of Colonial Dissolution* (Durham, NC: Duke University Press, 1994), ch. 5.

47 Sigmund Freud, "Beiträge zur Psychologie des Liebeslebens III: Das Tabu der Virginität" [1918], in Freud, *Gesammelte Werke*, 19 vols., ed. Anna Freud et al. (Frankfurt am Main: Fischer, 1972-1987), 12: 159-80, at 178; also idem, "Eine Beziehung zwischen einem Symbol und einem Symptom," in *Gesammelte Werke*, 10: 394f.

48 Md 676-19, 84v has an early, much shorter version of this episode under a different date (19 instead of 17 September).

I will argue, it is precisely the details of this episode that do not bear out a consistent analysis of the diary in terms of fetishism.

When Huber and Euting separated in March, Huber was to return to Ha'il by way of Tayma, where he would pick up the stones there acquired, and expedite them to Europe from Ha'il via Damascus. Euting, by contrast, was to travel from al-'Ulā to the Red Sea coast, to the small port town of Al Wajh, where he was to seek out a means to leave the Arabian Peninsula. This permitted him to conclude some further epigraphic work, which had been his main objective anyway. He does not seem to have regretted departing from Arabia on the proposed route, although the passage to Al Wajh was considered particularly dangerous because it involved the crossing of Bedouin territory that had not been subjected by the Amir of Ha'il. The court supposedly had some clout with the *Bélî* tribe, but none with the *Geheineh* who were assumed to be the deadly enemies of the *Bélî*. Forced to rely on an escort from the latter tribe, Euting was concerned about his security.

At the very beginning of the travel narrative, shortly after departing from Damascus, Euting recounts a holdup during which he was robbed of a handgun and a small sum of money (I, 4f). This "adventure" (his term) he recounted as a comical rather than a violent moment. Euting was duped by the robbers; the scene was presented as an initiation into Arabian customs, or more generally the customs that held beyond the borders of "the civilized world" (I, 39). A few days after the robbery, the local Druze sheikh restored the handgun and money to Euting (I, 18f). The narrative arc of the journey as a whole was one of the loss of naïveté and the acquisition of full self-sustenance. Euting was initially unable to fend off on his own the fleas that began to inhabit his clothing and the bedbugs that assaulted him at night (I, 11, 13); he required the aid of Ottoman soldiers to avert a swarm of hornets (I, 16); he resented the brutal treatment of the Arab and Druze rural population at the hands of the same soldiers (I, 14); he had to learn dromedary-riding (I, 31-7) and various kinds of table manners. The voyage was not merely an accidental string of happenstance events. Rather, Euting accumulated knowledge and thereby extended his agency. The plotline was one of maturation. The endpoint of this arc was reached precisely *en route* to Al Wajh, on the night of 30 March 1884, in a scene that mirrored the holdup at the beginning of the diary. Only, this time around, Euting and his hired escort snuck up on their pursuers at night and killed two of the presumptive assailants. Although this event was recounted in the unrevised portion of the diary, Littmann included Euting's two distinct reports about the shooting in full and without alteration, one shorter and composed briefly after the incident, the other longer and formulated later (II, 266-70).

The longer report, if read against Euting's intention, suggests that the incident was another result of the Orientalist's heedlessness, since he had ordered his four-man travel escort to make camp for the night even though they were apprehensive and wanted to continue to a more distant encampment of their tribe, the *Bélî*. Two of the escort, who as a precaution had decided to settle for the night at a short distance from the rest of the group, soon returned running as they had suddenly become aware of the presence, behind some brush, of a group of 10-12 other Bedouins, who had drawn their attention as they had lit a small fire, allegedly in order to light their antiquated matchlock rifles. Euting's group – he states that he ran ahead and was "in command" (II, 268) – immediately launched a preventive attack during which they fired blindly into the bushes. The fire was not returned. Euting's main escort, a young man named *Rḍejjân*, called out to the other group and inquired to what tribe they belonged, then went to meet them behind the bushes, from where he returned with the news that two men had been killed, one by a shot in the forehead, the other by a shot that had penetrated his shoulder and lung. Entirely on *Rḍejjân*'s authority, Euting claimed to know that he had himself killed the second victim, whereas the other one was, perhaps, *Rḍejjân*'s casualty, or else also his own. That they had prevented a potentially fatal ambush was not doubtful to Euting. Purportedly, the other group had left their camels further behind and had approached the German Orientalist's party stealthily. Nonetheless, all explanation of the event Euting provided remained hearsay. He never beheld his alleged assailants as his group departed in a hurry. With reference to the rest of the night as well as the following period, he concluded: "I would never have believed that when (– excepting, of course, war –) one has shot dead one or even two people one senses so little remorse afterwards and sleeps on it so well and superbly. Maybe, because I have not seen the corpses" (II, 269). The first report, by contrast, asserted: "Had a bit of a restless night ..." (II, 267).

In the days after Euting's exercise in the blind discharge of firearms, while his group was in the *Bélî* camp, the epigrapher learned further details about the incident. Unsettled by *Rḍejjân*'s comportment in the immediate aftermath of the shooting, Euting began to suspect that the other group had been in its majority *Bélî*, though it included a set of three "mean-looking" *Geheineh* with whom Euting's group had actually crossed paths a few days earlier. The alleged feud between the two tribes on which many of Euting's apprehensions and decisions in this portion of his voyage were based, thus dictated neither the attempted attack nor the responses to it. Euting's nervousness over the next days was in part the result of his realization that his escort was unreliable and that he did not fully understand the significance of tribal identities. In the *Bélî* camp he even encountered one of the *Bélî* members of the group of presumptive robbers, as well as the brother of the man he had killed, and he learned his victim's name, which he gave as *Sleimân ibn Selâmah*. Euting never even confirmed whether the victim was part of the *Geheineh* or *Bélî* tribes, an oversight that Littmann in a particularly crude intervention saw fit to correct in favor of the *Geheineh* theory (II, 270f). This meant that in the published account the tribal feud motif was of greater prominence than in the original diary. This motif, however, endowed Euting's act of violence with the meaning of a seamless interweaving with a profound local cultural pattern that he had come to know as a result of his scholarly observation of Bedouin affairs during the journey. It was therefore a matter of scholarly objectification that posited tribal identities in a specific way and then mobilized them in such a manner that local participants, including the Orientalist, were induced to act upon them.

In the original diary this process of objectification remained more ambiguous than its editor Littmann assumed, although the motif was undeniably present. For instance, on 4 April Euting noted that he was apprehensive of being pursued by *Geheineh* avengers; but his fears remained as unsubstantiated as before; and later that night he met yet another group of *Bélî* who turned out to have been among a party of assailants Huber had only narrowly been able to fight off a few days after he had parted from Euting and shortly before their accidental re-encounter in the fortress of *Madâin Ṣâliḥ* (or *el-Higr*) on 25 March (II, 254f).[49] In the diary entries, Euting recorded his unease, though he insisted once more on the imperturbable healthiness of his sleep: "I am only afraid the hoodlums will lie in wait for me somewhere along the way; on account of my firm sleep, I could easily fall prey to them."[50] He was unhappy to be stuck with the larger *Bélî* group for two full days and his escort for even longer. Although the Bedouins "celebrated" Euting "as a hero," on account of his "blind heroic feat" from the night before (or so he said), he expressed resentment about everything on site and heaped expletives on his hosts, whom he found a particularly beggarly, obtrusive, and unclean group. He especially resented the curiosity of the Bedouins: "Everything the filthy swine want to touch, every object passes from one filthy hand into the next."[51] In the entries for the following few days, until he reached Al Wajh on 6 April, Euting repeatedly used the same expletives. A particularly lengthy tirade provided a long list of complaints, among which the Bedouins' *Saugesang*, *Gleichheitsflegelei*, and

---

49 Md 676-22, 76r. Interestingly, in *Nabatäische Inschriften*, 3, Euting points out that his distrust of the *Bélî* had taken hold at this point already since the group whose guest he had become had assaulted the companion from whom he had just parted. Littmann does not take this passage into account.
50 Md 676-22, 73r.
51 Md 676-22, 73v.

Unlenksamkeit, that is to say, their "swine-chant" (which Littmann simply omitted from the list), their impudent tendency to treat Euting as an equal, and their obstinacy to command. Euting also complained that the Bedouins lacked a "sense of time," and he deplored their intransigent imprecision when asked for directions.

The passage culminated in a bizarre little poem, a sort of parodistic *Saugesang* on the part of Euting (which Littmann also excluded from publication):

Bedu Bedu ihr seid Säue	Bedu Bedu you are swine
Paviane Nashornthiere	baboons and horn-nosed beasts
die man nennt Rhinocerosse	whom one calls rhinoceroses
Crocodile & Vampyre	crocodiles & vampyres

Littmann, when adapting these portions of the diary, believed that the "good Euting" once again needed salvaging. He eliminated all instances of Euting's particularly offensive labeling of his Muslim hosts as "pigs" (he inserted less offensive expletives instead, e.g. *Lumpen*, "rascals") and he added softening passages: "This is how I then felt and thought about the Bedouins ... Later, when the anger had abated, I judged them more mildly again and did not conceal their good sides" (II, 279). This labor on the good Euting's equanimity obscured the profound unsettling of the discursive pattern of the diary that had been wrought by the author's recourse to blind violence. Euting's notions of his understanding of the rules of the game of Bedouin life was in fact shattered, even if he opted not to admit it. Interacting with the Bedouins was not a game, but life itself: Euting did not have a clue what was going on, and neither did anyone else involved. The verbal abuse of the Bedouins in this portion of the diary is also a sign of a loss of control over meaning. In this respect, the expletives, in their unspecified direction, are continuous with the blind violence of the nocturnal assault. In the writing of the diary, which occurred on site during the journey to Al Wajh (since the second report about the shooting is inserted only afterward), recourse to abusive humor constituted a distinct choice. In this choice the noticeably immature nature of Euting's invective is particularly striking. Apparently, the discourse of the travel diary, when it collapsed, broke down into the mere calling of names: crocodiles and vampires. The humor involved, however petty, marked the breakdown of the plotline, of the meaning of tribal identities and violence, and, since a string of names does not form a sentence, of actual syntax. This collapse did not follow any pre-given structure of objectified desire. Instead, it underpinned – forming an indispensable, if negative, backdrop to – the scholarly objectification of the Bedouin tribes that Euting as well as Littmann belabored in the diary.

VI

In this process of the loss of (the preconditions for) meaning, Euting insisted on an authorial voice that remained at least in control of laughter. The only derision he freely admitted having suffered was that on the part of unspeaking nature itself. An example of this occurred during the sojourn in Ha'il. While on a solitary hunt for ibexes, Euting caught sight of two specimens, at a mere sixty meters distance, but at the exact moment when he was pinned into a steep descent and could not reach for his rifle:

> Filled with greed and anger I had to watch as the rascals kept their complete calm; for they had immediately discerned my harmlessness. Just once, as they disappeared around the corner, they turned their heads toward me with their wretched beards! Did not the one damned creature [*Sakermenter*] even stick out his tongue and laugh at me to boot? *Hah! infamy!* (II, 78)

What on the surface appears to be an exercise in comical anthropomorphism also plays on the motif of the muteness of nature, the inability of the animal to deploy linguistic or quasi-linguistic signs. A first hunt had been undertaken a few days previously, under the guidance of a skilled local huntsman, the brother of one of the Ha'il courtiers, but the party had failed to spot any prey. Over the following days, Euting repeatedly went hiking in the mountains on his own, but when he encountered the animals on 29 December he was thwarted by the terrain. The Amir had already gifted him the skull of a "strong ibex whose horns measured 4½ spans in length" (II, 72, 97) on the evening of the first unsuccessful hunt. The practice of hunting, as a symbol of sovereignty over a territory, eluded Euting; instead the territory as well as the animals defied him. The only resort against this defiance was the comical.

In one of his denigratory anecdotes about *Ḥamûd el-ʿObeid*, Euting relates how the Rashidi prince demonstrates the use of swords, in front of his "amazed" infant son, by wildly brandishing about a weapon in a manner Euting finds laughable. "O Atta Troll!" (II, 67) he exclaims in the published version of the diary,[52] with reference to Heine's verse epic from the 1840s.[53] The reference to the mere title, and title character, of the poem is obscure because Heine's

---

52   See Md 676-21, 21r for the respective passage, in which the Heine reference is lacking.
53   Heinrich Heine, "Atta Troll: Ein Sommernachtstraum" (1843/1847), in Heine, *Historisch-kritische Gesamtausgabe der Werke*, 16 vols., ed. Manfred Winfuhr (Hamburg: Hoffmann & Campe, 1973-1997), 4: 7-87.

satire, written "in the fanciful dreamy manner of that romantic school in which I whiled away my happiest years of youth, and then wound up by thrashing the schoolmaster,"[54] is abundantly polysemic. Atta Troll, the escaped dancing bear who preaches to his offspring a revolutionary political doctrine of the profound equality of animals and humans, in Euting's specific reference might perhaps simply be taken to serve as a figure representing the ludicrousness of pious agitation. In the original as well as the published diary (II, 66), the anecdote is adorned with what the original version explicitly declares to be a "caricature" of Ḥamûd, the point at which Euting's staging of the comical meets with his courtly habit of portraiture (Fig. 3.7). The caricature is accompanied by a little verse of derisive poetry that emulates the rhymeless trochees of Heine's *Atta Troll*:

Und mit Staunen sehen's die Franken	And the Franks watch in amazement
wie der fromme Sohn des Wolfes	as the pious son of the wolf
lüstern fuchtelt mit dem Säbel	lustfully brandishes his saber
seltsam vor dem Feuerscheine.	oddly in the fiery glow.

The "Franks" in this instance (using the common retranslation of the Arabic term for "Europeans") are Euting and Huber; and the "lust" in the brandishing of the saber indicates the stories of beheading with which Ḥamûd, to Euting's distaste, adorned the demonstration. Indeed, it is the combination of piety and violence that Euting, who like so many Orientalists had in his youth abandoned the study of Lutheran theology, targets in this passage. However, he omitted the poem from the published version, as well as yet another use of *Sauhund* he had originally hurled at the Arab nobleman. Both were replaced with the reference to Heine, whose satire served as a subtler substitute. The reference in fact also explains the choice of meter in the *Bedu Bedu ihr seid Säue* poem; which suggests that *Atta Troll* formed something of a poetic background to this entire portion of Euting's journey.

Yet, arguably the reference marks a breach through which Heine's "ironic" polysemy invades Euting's text.[55] In Heine's poem the ursine revolutionary and prophet is a figure that satirizes not least the false promises of Jewish emancipation and the credulity with which they were met, while equality remained

---

54 Heinrich Heine, *Atta Troll*, trans. Herman Scheffauer (London: Sidgwick & Jackson, 1913), 30.
55 Heine, "Atta Troll," Paralipomena, 218, provides a hauntingly ironical characterization of the irony informing his authorial voice.

FIGURE 3.7   Julius Euting, Original Diary, University of Tübingen Library, Md. 676-21, 21r: Caricature of Ḥamûd el-ʿObeid.

constantly denied precisely by those who professed humanistic universalism.[56] The poem's authorial voice repeatedly professes such universalism, in the form of innate human rights, and then ironizes it. The rambling narrator also feigns to be the hunter of the escaped bear, even though he then hires a professional hunter who turns out to be one of the early undeads of German literature – on some level a symbol of the mindless political executioners of the counter-revolutionary politics of the period – to do the actual shooting. The narrator's journey is also one into the haplessness of German politics, in which Atta Troll is a stand-in for the intellectual obtuseness and impotence of German political thought and post-romantic political poetry.[57] The most prominent target of satire throughout the poem is Ferdinand Freiligrath's Orientalist and exoticist poem *Der Mohrenfürst* ("The Moor Prince"). Freiligrath had partly translated and subsequently emulated Victor Hugo's 1829 philhellenist cycle *Les Orientales*, a prime example of poetic Orientalism in pursuit of Ottoman themes. In *Mohrenführst*, Freiligrath sentimentalizes the fate of a fictitious enslaved African king, who is demoted from civilized humanity by symbols of his sensual and violent nature, while at the same time the poet does not find a word of overt criticism for the actual institution of slavery. Heine parodies with particular tenacity, in several passages of *Atta Troll*, the outré black-and-white color tropes of Freiligrath's composition. This finely wrought derision of the poetic fetishization of skin color underlines the impression that the underlying problem Heine skewers is that of the inconsistencies bedeviling modern manifestations of humanistic universalism.[58]

In eighteenth-century German literature, the dancing bear had enjoyed a specific literary career as a symbol of the courtier whose refined cultivation is a form of captivity. As Winfried Woesler has demonstrated, Heine was familiar with this meaning, although in his appropriation of the theme he transformed it almost beyond recognition.[59] Atta Troll, too, continues to express pride about his achievements in the art of dance, without recognizing the extent to which he is thereby exposed to the dominant forces. German revolutionary political thought, the culture of emancipated Jewry, Orientalist poetry, Swabian

---

56   Ibid., Caput VI, 27, in Scheffauer's translation: "Yea the very Jews shall win / All the rights of citizens, / By the law made equal with / Every other mammal free" (59).
57   On the meanings of the epos see still Winfried Woesler, *Heines Tanzbär: Historisch-literarische Untersuchungen zum "Atta Troll"* (Hamburg: Hoffmann & Campe, 1978).
58   The epilogue to Susanne Zantop's *Colonial Fantasies: Conquest, Family and Nation in Precolonial Germany 1770-1870* (Durham, NC: Duke University Press, 1997) makes a number of useful observations on Heine's subtle criticism of imperial imagination; as far as I see, this argument has not been raised with regard to *Atta Troll*.
59   Woesler, *Heines Tanzbär*, 139-177.

pietist poetry – everything remained in the orbit of power. Heine declared: "Dream of Summer night! Fantastic / Aimless is my song. Yes, aimless / E'en as Love, as all existence, / As creator and creation!"[60] Only this reckless affirmation of poetic autonomy – one of the aspects of romanticism Heine upheld – founded his claim to artistic sovereignty; but at the cost of steering poetic discourse toward absurdity.

Euting's exclamation of "O Atta Troll," and his almost nonsensical ditties, which bind the diary to Heine's epic, align his text with the poet's notion of "aimlessness" and open it up to the absurd. The meaning-giving structures of his text are such that they provide for their own depletion. Euting's diaries, in fact his entire journey, are always on the brink of mere "caprice."[61] It is also this caprice that forms the background to his sudden, "aimless" exercise of violence and his professed lack of remorse: the shooting of the alleged *Geheineh* Bedouins was yet another collapse of the meaning-giving structures of purpose and forward planning, of a kind with what had been written into the diary all along.

VII

In the collapse of meaning engineered through the diary, the embracing of vice – as a disposition toward transgression against norms – played a particular role. To the extent that the passing of the bounds of sense was part of Euting's and other Orientalists' epistemic work, vice assumed an actual epistemic character and entered into a function equivalent to the one enjoyed by virtue in other portions of scientific work. Recurrent transgression had a corrosive effect on semantics. Euting's repeated remarks on the soundness of his sleep indirectly address the question of guilt, the effect that his infractions had – and which he denied – on the integrity of his notion of self. This process was not merely a matter of dismounting a positive sense of one's own virtuousness, of accepting that one was not as morally good a person as one had pretended. Rather, transgression did not provide a stable frame for developing an alternative sense of integral selfhood. Euting's transgressions had an odd tendency to negate their seeming goals. Again and again, with undefeatable credulity, he accepted Huber's allegations about the disfavor of the Amir of Ha'il, which is all the more astounding since the Amir himself had warned Euting about his

---

60   Heine, "Atta Troll," Caput III, 17, here in the translation by Thomas S. Egan (London: Chapman & Hall, 1876), 9, which in this instance is closer to the original.
61   Ibid.

companion's malevolence (II, 104f). *Ḥamûd el-ʿObeid*, the imagined enemy at court, whom Euting consistently presented as the caricature of a religious fanatic and greedy hypocrite, actually berated the Rashidi representative at Tayma for not having been sufficiently hospitable to the European travelers (II, 255), factual evidence of the generous protection he offered to the expedition.[62] It is hard to avoid the conclusion that Euting simply desired for his actions at Ha'il to destroy his own position, his own agency, the efficacy of scholarly objectification, and ultimately his scholarly persona.

To the extent that there was to be a linkage between scholarly knowledge and the agency of the scholarly traveler, then, Euting's acquisition of knowledge in Arabia was characterized by this self-destructive pattern. There are certain things that the diary knows, but Euting himself, as the diary's unreliable narrator, does not. His chief tool for generating the respective narrative arc was to overstate the provocative character of his draughtsmanship. The structure of transgression that informed his pictorial work was therefore in the last instance directed against itself. Ultimately, the escalation of this structure led into the situation of absurdity that marked Euting's narrative of the voyage to Al Wajh: the one or two murders, perhaps, certainly committed, in reckless, yet self-defensive attack, in command, but guided by his escort, without ever seeing the victims, taking for granted his agency over the authority of a Bedouin he otherwise regarded as untrustworthy. The blindness with which he was struck during this nighttime scene negated the scholarly eye as the prime instance of objectification. Along the way, victims emerged.

It was this negation Littmann sought to conceal when he insisted on the salvaging of the good Euting, the virtuous image of the admired epigrapher and narrator. While this intention was informed by virtuous piety toward epistemic virtue, it nonetheless required embracing the vice of bad philology. As a result, the authorial voice of the diary became even less reliable. The virtuous image of the good Euting, in other words, did not merely negate the self-destructive structure of epistemic vice, but actually contributed to it; the relation was circular. This circularity was an integral feature of the writing practice, and of the textual form, of Orientalist knowledge. The scholarly persona, a representation of a scholarly subject, was then tied to virtue as much as vice, and thereby carried within itself its dissolution, its *Mortifikation*, the self-inflicted cut across its own neck.

---

62 It is worth mentioning Anne Blunt's enthusiastic portrayal of this member of the princely family, *Pilgrimage*, I, 228-230.

Bibliography

Behdad, Ali. *Belated Travelers: Orientalism in the Age of Colonial Dissolution*. Durham, NC: Duke University Press, 1994.

Bhabha, Homi K. "The Other Question: Stereotype, Discrimination, and the Discourse of Colonialism." In Bhabha, *The Location of Culture*, 66-84. London: Routledge, 1994.

Blunt, Anne. *A Pilgrimage to Nejd, the Cradle of the Arab Race, a Visit to the Court of the Arab Emir, and "Our Persian Campaign."* London: John Murray, 1881.

Bonancina, Giovanni. *The Wahhabis Seen through European Eyes (1772-1830): Deists and Puritans of Islam* Leiden: Brill, 2015.

Bornemann, Daniel. "Les legs de Julius Euting ou l'organisation posthume d'un savoir," *La Revue de la BNU* 12 (2015): 30-41.

Bosch, Mineke. "Persona and the Performance of Identity: Parallel Developments in the Biographical Historiography of Science and Gender, and the Related Uses of Self Narrative," *L'Homme* 24, no. 2 (2013): 11-22.

Burckhardt, Jean Louis. *Notes on the Bedouins and Wahábys*. London: Colburn & Bentley, 1830.

Clark, William. *Academic Charisma and the Origins of the Research University*. Chicago, IL: University of Chicago Press, 2006.

Daston, Lorraine and Peter Galison. *Objectivity*. New York, NY: Zone Books, 2007.

Derrida, Jacques. "Freud et la scène de l'écriture." In Derrida, Jacques. *L'Ecriture et la différence*, 293-340. Paris: Seuil, 1967.

Drewes, G. W. J. "Christiaan Snouck Hurgronje." In *Biografisch Woordenboek van Nederland*: <http://resources.huygens.knaw.nl/bwn1880-2000/lemmata/bwn2/snouckc> (last accessed 28 January 2019).

Euting, Julius. *Nabatäische Inschriften aus Arabien*. Berlin: Reimer, 1885.

Euting, Julius. *Tagbuch einer Reise in Inner-Arabien: Erster Theil*. Leiden: Brill, 1896.

Euting, Julius. *Tagbuch einer Reise in Inner-Arabien: Zweiter Theil*, edited by Enno Littmann. Leiden: Brill, 1914.

Freud, Sigmund. *Gesammelte Werke*, 19 vols., edited by Anna Freud et al. Frankfurt am Main: Fischer, 1972-1987.

Healey, John F. "'Sicherheit des Auges': The Contribution to Epigraphy of Julius Euting. 1839-1913)." In *Biblical and Near Eastern Essays: Studies in Honour of Kevin J. Cathcart*, edited by Carmel McCarthy and John F. Healey, 313-330. London: Clark International, 2004.

Heine, Heinrich. *Atta Troll*. Translated by Thomas S. Egan. London: Chapman & Hall, 1876.

Heine, Heinrich. *Atta Troll*. Translated by Herman Scheffauer. London: Sidgwick & Jackson, 1913.

Heine, Heinrich."Atta Troll: Ein Sommernachtstraum" (1843/1847). In Heine, *Historisch-kritische Gesamtausgabe der Werke*, 16 vols., edited by Manfred Winfuhr, 4: 7-87. Hamburg: Hoffmann & Campe, 1973-1997.

Hogarth, David George. *The Penetration of Arabia: A Record of the Development of Western Knowledge Concerning the Arabian Peninsula*. London: Lawrence & Bullen, 1904.

Huber, Charles. *Journal d'un voyage en Arabie (1883-1884)*. Paris: Imprimerie Nationale, 1891.

Kivistö, Sari. *The Vices of Learning: Morality and Knowledge at Early Modern Universities*. Leiden: Brill, 2014.

Lamb, Jonathan. *Preserving the Self in the South Seas, 1680-1840*. Chicago, IL: University of Chicago Press, 2001.

Littmann, Enno. *Thamūd und Ṣafā: Studien zur altnordarabischen Inschriftenkunde*. Leipzig: Brockhaus, 1940.

Lozachmeur, Hélène and Françoise Briquel-Chatonnet. "Charles Huber und Julius Euting in Arabien nach französischen, auch heute noch nicht veröffentlichten Dokumenten." *Anabases* 12 (2010): 195-200.

Marchand, Suzanne. *German Orientalism in the Age of Empire: Race, Religion, Scholarship*. Cambridge: Cambridge University Press, 2009.

Mitchell, W. J. T., ed. *Landscape and Power*. Chicago, IL: University of Chicago Press, 2002.

Möller, Reinhard M. "Die Feuerland-Episode in Georg Forsters 'Reise um die Welt' im Kontext einer anekdotischen Poetik der Interkulturalität." In *Georg Forster als interkultureller Autor*, edited by Stefan Greif and Michael Ewert, 79-107. Kassel: Kassel University Press, 2014.

Mulsow, Martin. *Die unanständige Gelehrtenrepublik: Wissen, Libertinage und Kommunikation in der Frühen Neuzeit*. Stuttgart: Metzler, 2007.

Nöldeke, Theodor. "Altaramäische Inschriften aus Teimâ (Arabien)." *Sitzungsberichte der Königlich-Preußischen Akademie der Wissenschaften* 35 (1884): 813-820.

Osterhammel, Jürgen. *Die Entzauberung Asiens: Europa und die asiatischen Reiche im 18. Jahrhundert*. Munich: C. H. Beck, 1998.

Paul, Herman. "What Is a Scholarly Persona? Ten Theses on Virtues, Skills, and Desires." *History and Theory* 53 (2014): 348-371.

Porter, James I. "'Don't Quote Me on That!' Wilamowitz Contra Nietzsche in 1872 and 1873." *Journal of Nietzsche Studies* 42 (2011), 73-99.

Reilly, Benjamin. "Arabian Travellers, 1800-1950: An Analytical Bibliography." *British Journal of Middle Eastern Studies* 43, no. 1 (2016): 71-93.

Ritter, Carl. *Allgemeine Erdkunde* XIII (= *Erdkunde Asiens* VIII, 1. Abt., Forts.) *Die Halbinsel Arabien*. Berlin: Reimer, 1847.

Savoy, Bénédicte. *Nofretete, eine deutsch-französische Affäre 1913-1931*. Cologne: Böhlau, 2011.

Shapin, Steven. *The Scientific Life: A Moral History of a Late Modern Vocation*. Chicago, IL: University of Chicago Press, 2008.

Shapin, Steven and Simon Schaffer. *Leviathan and the Air-Pump: Hobbes, Boyle, and the Experimental Life*. Princeton, NJ: Princeton University Press, 1985.

Snouck Hurgronje, Christiaan. *Mekka: Bilderatlas*. The Hague: Nijhoff, 1888.

Spivak, Gayatri Chakravorty. *A Critique of Postcolonial Reason: Toward a History of the Vanishing Present*. Cambridge, MA: Harvard University Press, 1999.

Subrahmanyam, Sanjay. *Courtly Encounters: Translating Courtliness and Violence in Early Modern Eurasia*. Cambridge, MA: Harvard University Press, 2012.

Trüper, Henning. "Dispersed Personae: Subject Matters of Scholarly Biography in Nineteenth-Century Oriental Philology." *Asiatische Studien* 67 (2013): 1325-1360.

Trüper, Henning. *Topography of a Method: François Louis Ganshof and the Writing of History*. Tübingen: Mohr Siebeck, 2014.

von Nolde, Eduard. *Reise nach Innerarabien, Kurdistan und Armenien 1892*. Braunschweig: Vieweg, 1895.

Woesler, Winfried. *Heines Tanzbär: Historisch-literarische Untersuchungen zum "Atta Troll"*. Hamburg: Hoffmann & Campe, 1978.

Zantop, Susanne. *Colonial Fantasies: Conquest, Family and Nation in Precolonial Germany 1770-1870*. Durham, NC: Duke University Press, 1997.

CHAPTER 4

German Indology Challenged

On the Dialectics of Armchair Philology, Fieldwork, and Indigenous Traditions in the Late Nineteenth Century

Pascale Rabault-Feuerhahn

1 Introduction

A spirit of discovery, hard-will and dedication to work are certainly the personality traits most frequently encountered in biographies of nineteenth-century European Oriental scholars. They are mostly praised for their tenacity and readiness to endure material sacrifices in order to reach their professional goals. At the beginning of the nineteenth-century, secular Oriental scholarship was still at its very start. Deciding to specialize in Oriental languages outside the framework of theological training and Biblical scholarship equalled an unpredictable bet on one's professional future. Moreover, some Oriental languages had just entered the framework of European scholarship: tools like grammars, dictionaries or textbooks were spare, if not completely missing. For this reason, the achievements of Orientalists forced the admiration of their biographers, and Oriental scholars often thought of themselves as adventurers of science, comparing their efforts in deciphering scriptures or understanding ancient texts with the physical challenges faced by colonial administrators in the field.[1]

The German born Iranologist and Indologist Martin Haug (1827-1876) is no exception to such biographical descriptions. In the various texts on his life and work, the celebration of the ethics of the Orientalist takes the shape of a true success story. Based on Haug's own accounts (written at the early ages of 25 and 32), his biographers particularly emphasise his social origins as the eldest son of a Swabian peasant and the fact that he had to overcome many obstacles to live his passion for learning and become an academic.[2] The extraordinary

---

[1] Pascale Rabault-Feuerhahn, "La philologie comme épopée: aspects de la tradition historiographique de l'indianisme en Allemagne au 19e siècle," *Histoire épistémologie langage* 33/2 (2011), 103-119.

[2] Theodor Benfey, *Geschichte der Sprachwissenschaft und orientalischen Philologie in Deutschland* (Munich: Cotta, 1869), 611, 614, 624, 633; Wilhelm Eilers, "Haug, Martin," in *Neue Deutsche Biographie*, vol. 8 (Berlin: Duncker & Humblot, 1969), 91-92; E. P. Evans, "Biographical Sketch,"

tenacity with which he fought against adversity and made his way to an academic career thus becomes a distinctive feature of his life.[3]

A major event in Martin Haug's biography was his appointment by the British government as a Superintendent of Sanskrit Studies in the Poona College, near Bombay, in 1858. This position, which he held from 1859 to 1866, made him one of the first German Indologists to go overseas: apart from missionaries, until late into the nineteenth-century German specialists of India were armchair philologists. This of course was largely due to the fact that Germany had neither colonies nor trading posts in India. Although they acknowledged that this situation made it more complicated to access Indian manuscripts and books printed in India, the vast majority of them claimed that strong philological skills mattered more than the direct contact with native speakers and indigenous commentary traditions. Their focus was on Sanskrit and on Indian antiquity. Their strictly textual and erudite approach was a proof that they were solely driven by scholarly interest and that their scholarship was more thoroughgoing than that of the British.

The paradoxical injunction to distinguish oneself as an outstanding scholar and at the same time to fit in within the system is a central issue in the building of academic careers. The proposition from the British government came at a time when Haug, who had obtained his doctorate in 1854, started to despair of ever obtaining a position at a German university. For this reason, his decision to accept the position in Poona can be interpreted as a strategy to beat his German colleagues on their own field by adopting a new perspective and accumulating a groundbreaking experience. Until now, Haug remains famous for having worked in close relationship with Parsee and Hindu scholars and having promoted and integrated their views into his own writings. This marked a great difference with the methods of his former professors and colleagues in Germany and ensured him a rare, if not unique knowledge.

Such a reading should not, however, overshadow the complexities of his trajectory. His correspondence shows evidence that he dreamt of going to India

---

in Martin Haug, *Essays on the Sacred Language, Writings and Religion of the Parsis*, ed. E. W. West (London: Trübner and Co., [1884] 2000), xvii-xxxi; E. Gaiser, "Martin Haug," *Bezzenbergers Beiträge zur Kunde der indogermanischen Sprachen* 1 (1877), 70-80; Julius Jolly, "Haug, Martin," in *Allgemeine Deutsche Biographie*, vol. 11 (Leipzig: Duncker & Humblot, 1880), 54-56; Ernst Trumpp, "Martin Haug," *Beilage zur Augsburger Allgemeinen Zeitung* 182 (1876). Haug's autobiographical account from 1859 reaches until the year 1854 and was extensively published by Friedrich Veit in: *Festschrift zur Erinnerung an die Haug-Feier in Ostdorf*, ed. Friedrich Veit, (Tübingen: Buchdruckerei von Gg. Schnürken, 1909). It is preceded by a biographical sketch by Veit himself. The main source for this text by Veit is another, even earlier autobiography by Haug from 1852: Veit, *Festschrift*, 1.

3 Gaiser, "Martin Haug," 70.

even before he was offered the opportunity to work at Poona. Besides, at the time when he accepted the British offer, he was still convinced of the superiority of European philological methods. Finally, after his return from India in 1866 he had to wait two more years before he obtained a professorship in Sanskrit at the University of Munich. Acknowledging these various facts and the tensions and contradictions in Haug's own attitudes allows one to draw a more complex picture of his trajectory than the mere success story of a self-made academic. It allows us to reflect on the changing and complex shaping of scholarly personae in the field of Indology at a time when this small, elitist discipline had growing international and intercultural implications.

By implication, the scholarly personae invoked in the subtitle of this chapter – the armchair philologist and the fieldworker – should be interpreted in ideal–typical manner as schematic models of how to be an Orientalist. Precisely because they were ideal-types, they were never fully embodied or lived out. Moreover, the case of Haug aptly illustrates that Orientalists did not simply replace the former with the latter. Exchanging personae was not a deliberate or one-directional process. And even if in the course of Haug's career some Orientalists became fieldworkers, armchair philologists did not disappear.

2   Becoming an Orientalist in Germany around 1850

While biographical sketches can often be little informed about the youth of the persons they are devoted to, in Martin Haug's case we possess accurate information about his early years thanks to his autobiographical texts and to the *Festschrift* published in his honour by Friedrich Veit in 1909. These texts provide rich and unique information on Haug's social, geographical and material condition in his youth.[4] They point to the obstacles that he had to overcome as the son of a Swabian peasant and to the outstanding intellectual skills and uncommon steadfastness that allowed him to succeed:

> What he became, he became by himself, by his own ability; few others deserve as much as him to be called the blacksmiths of their fortune … So Haug's scientific work bears the stamp of a profound nobility … From such a moral earnestness flowed … that independent spirit, who did not

---

[4] From an historiographical point of view, it is also interesting to confront Veit's text with that of Haug, since the latter was one of the main sources for the former.

bow to any authority and only recognized the truth as a higher judge over himself.[5]

Yet the rural family background of Haug did not imply that he was of modest extraction. As a matter of fact, he did not come from a poor family. His father was a rich, well-established farmer in Ostdorf, a village in Swabia. The financial difficulties Haug was confronted with were actually due to the fact that his parents expected him to take over the ruling of the farm and therefore refused to pay for his schooling.[6] Like most of the village's inhabitants, they considered intellectual activities as seeds for perversion and certainly not as a possible professional occupation. That he finally could make his way to an academic curriculum was due to both his extraordinary will and a series of fortunate encounters. This situation confirms the importance of combining macro- and microanalysis, social and personal factors, in the social history of science. It also invites us to consider the construction of Haug's academic career not only in terms of social climbing but also from the perspective of intellectual interests: how could a peasant's son in mid nineteenth-century rural Germany become interested in Oriental languages and decide to make it his life occupation?

Veit insists on the role of Haug's maternal uncle, a geometer and a man of great curiosity who liked to buy new agricultural tools as well as books on all sorts of subjects. He reportedly taught Haug how to read and write even before the latter went to school, and later paid for his schoolbooks. Haug also received the help of his school master who soon noticed his high capacities and convinced his father to let him become a "Schulincipient." Personal encounters and solidarities again played a decisive role in his first contact with classical and Oriental languages: as a child, he learnt Latin from a grammar offered to him by a boy who had abandoned school; Greek became accessible later, when he was about sixteen years old, thanks to a grammar his uncle gave him before dying; and finally a student in classical philology who had fallen ill and had to stay home agreed to teach him French and Hebrew.[7]

At about the same time, Haug was offered the opportunity to temporarily replace a school teacher and his salary allowed him to buy himself Wilhelm

---

5 Gaiser "Martin Haug," 75-76: "Was Haug geworden ist, ist er durch sich selbst, durch seine eigne Tüchtigkeit geworden; wie selten ein andrer darf er der Schmied seines Glücks genannt warden … So ist Haugs wissenschaftlichem Schaffen der Stempel eines tiefsittlichen Adels aufgedrückt … Aus solchem sittlichen Ernst floss … jener unabhängige Geist, der vor keiner Autorität sich beugte und nur die Wahrheit als höheren Richter über sich anerkannte."
6 Veit, *Festschrift*, 4.
7 Ibid., 6.

Gesenius' famous Hebrew dictionary (*Hebräisches und Chaldäisches Handwörterbuch über das alte Testament*, 1834). Soon after, in 1844, he successfully passed the *Lehrgehilfen-Examen* (examination to become a school assistant). Containing information about Haug's income and the price of the books he acquired, Haug's autobiography allows us to better evaluate the financial effort necessary to access erudite knowledge. Far from being anecdotal, the indications concerning the purchase of books provide also information on how specialized knowledge circulated, which books were available to the broader public and how in some cases they encouraged vocations. (Haug reportedly became aware of Franz Bopp's works thanks to an advertisement in the newspaper *Der schwäbische Merkur*).[8] At the time, Indological chairs existed at several German universities. But Indology was still a nascent and confidential discipline. The reading of the advertisement prompted Haug to buy Bopp's *Nalus, carmen sanscritum e Mahābhārato* (1819) and Friedrich Rosen's *Radices Sanscritae* (1827) and to start learning Sanskrit in 1844. As a matter of fact, Haug's interest in Oriental languages was growing broader: besides his teaching duties, he allegedly spent all his time trying to learn Hebrew, Arabic, Syriac, and Sanskrit. Although these achievements had already cost him enormous efforts and sacrifices, his self-taught knowledge in several Oriental languages led him to nurture higher ambitions than becoming a school teacher, and he started to consider applying for admission as a student of theology.

However, several obstacles hampered Haug's ambition: his tendency to spread out his higher goals and his knowledge put him at odds with the milieu of schoolteachers. Being also faced with his father's persistent refusal to financially support him, he opted for an easier way to enter university. Instead of taking the exam in theology, he went to Stuttgart to prepare the maturity exam, which qualified students to proceed to higher education at the Faculty of philology. Thus, at a time when theology offered the most opportunities to Orientalists, for Haug the surest way was paradoxically to make the detour via secular philology. The letter he wrote to Heinrich Ewald (1803-1875), the famous professor for Oriental languages, asking him for permission to attend his courses at the University of Tübingen, tells a lot about his early motivations:

> Since as yet I had never written to someone high-ranking, I appeal to your benevolent leniency, if I make mistakes of form, or if my language is not smooth and flowing enough. Surrounded with people prone to materialism and utilitarianism …, I had a strong desire, need even, for something better … In order to attain a deeper perception of the religious and

---

8   Ibid., 7.

philosophical ideas of the civilised peoples of the ancient world ... it was first and foremost necessary to further my knowledge of languages, which are like bridges in the kingdom of the mind ... And the wish to set foot in India or Persia either in full sun or under the silvery moonlight, to contemplate the ruins of an ancestral, noble and distant epoch, while looking for what could have been the original sense, this wish continues to arise growingly more acutely, at times even becoming a true obsession.[9]

While the awkwardness of expression and the almost naive way of presenting his motivations betray Haug's social origins, his letter also reveals his firm will. It can be read as an intimate testimony about the kind of dreamy, romantic, and ideal images that were associated with the Orient. This passage makes clear that Haug's motivation to study Oriental languages was due as much to fantasized representations as to his will to escape his trivial environment. Oriental scholarship appeared as way to elevate oneself and physically and mentally escape from reality into a distant space and time.[10]

At least Ewald seems to have been touched by Haug's sincerity and he accepted him as a student. Having passed his maturity exam, Haug managed to convince his father to let him go to university and give him some small financial help. However, in the meanwhile Ewald had left Tübingen. In the wake of the Revolution of 1848, he was allowed to return to Göttingen, from where he had been chased in 1837 because of his criticisms against the King's decision to abrogate the liberal Constitution. Ewald's departure was a cruel disappointment for Haug, who nevertheless had the possibility to follow the courses in Persian and Sanskrit of Ewald's successor Rudolf Roth (1821-1895).[11] Professional perspectives being very scarce in Oriental studies, he also matriculated as a student in classical philology. Apart from the small allowance from his father, his resources were a study grant from the philological faculty and private tuitions in Hebrew he gave to students of the Theological faculty.[12] After four years of hard labor and self-sacrifice, his material condition improved with an award of 44 Guilders for his doctoral dissertation in classical philology and

---

9   Haug to Ewald, 12 April 1847, in *Briefe an Ewald aus seinem Nachlass*, ed. Richard Fick and Götz von Selle (Göttingen: Vandenhoeck & Ruprecht, 1932), 26-27.
10 As had been the case with Sanskrit, Haug's knowledge depended on the books available in bookshops, since he had no access to academic libraries. His interest in Zoroastrianism had been raised by the works of Friedrich Nork (pseudonym of Josef Ferdinand Friedrich Korn, 1803-1850), like *Die Religion und Sprache der alten Perser* (1835) or *Brahminen und Rabbinen* (1837) which he found in a bookshop in Stuttgart at about the time of his letter to Ewald in Veit, *Festschrift*, 10.
11 Haug to Ewald, 16 June 1848, in Fick-Selle, *Briefe an Ewald*, 30.
12 Veit, *Festschrift*, 13.

subsequently a travel grant of 300 Guilders. Soon after, his father passed away and left him a significant legacy, allowing him to shift to Göttingen to follow Ewald's long-awaited courses. Ewald was very pleased to welcome such a motivated student and he offered him private courses in several Oriental languages: Hebrew, Arabic, Armenian, Turkish, and Chinese. In addition, Haug studied Sanskrit with Theodor Benfey, the famous Vedic scholar and specialist of Indo-European comparative grammar.[13]

Being in Göttingen meant a dramatic shift for Haug, who had never left Swabia before. It also gave him the opportunity to meet important representatives of his field, all the more so since in 1852 the city hosted the meeting of German philologists. In contact with this new environment, he began to consider an academic career, something that had been unthinkable for him until then despite his ambitious nature. But when he informed Rudolf Roth of his intention to obtain his "Habilitation," the latter categorically deterred him from embarking on an academic career. Instead, he advised him to take the final examination for school teachers.[14] Haug was convinced that Roth reacted this way because he considered that this was what a peasant son like him could at best aim at. Roth, on the contrary, claimed that he just felt it was his responsibility to warn Haug that becoming an Orientalist was a risky choice given that there existed only a few positions and that Haug could not rely on a solid family background.[15] He was also exasperated by Haug's lack of mastery of academic habitus.[16] As historians we are not able to decide on the real causes of Roth's reactions; however this episode reveals that, each in their own way, contemporary actors were acutely aware of the elitist dimension of the academic and especially Orientalist career. This awareness in turn increased their susceptibility. Becoming an Orientalist was, admittedly, a vocation. But hard work and self-sacrifice could not completely make up for problems of social legitimacy. Roth's reaction led Haug to look for another location at which to habilitate and this further delayed his entry into an academic career. It was also a major trig-

---

13   Ibid., 15. Haug retrospectively wrote to Ewald (16 April 1853) that he had learnt more in one year at Göttingen than he had in four and a half year at Tübingen (Fick-Selle, *Briefe an Ewald*, 31). On the role of Benfey and Ewald in Haug's intellectual formation, see Clarisse Herrenschmidt, "Once upon a time, Zoroaster," in *The Inconceivable Polytheism: Studies in Religious Historiography (History and Anthropology 1987/3)*, ed. Francis Schmidt, 209-238, esp. 221 sq.
14   Haug to Ewald, 2 June 1854, in Fick-Selle, *Briefe an Ewald*, 37-38.
15   Rudolf Roth, "Martin Haug," *Bezzenbergers Beiträge* (1877), 175-176, at 175.
16   Roth wrote to Ewald (29 November 1853): "There is no doubt that H(aug) possesses an iron will, a zeal for learning and a very unusual memory, but the right taste, and tact, even the necessary restraint still lacks him. If he gives me the opportunity, I will not fail to point out to him what he still seems to lack." Fick-Selle, *Briefe an Ewald*, 215.

ger for Haug's and Roth's subsequent fights, which got even worse when Haug started referring to the Indian grammatical and commentary tradition to criticize Roth's interpretations of the Veda and Avesta.

3 A German Indologist in India: Haug's Career and (Inter)National Scientific Policies

Haug finally habilitated in the Prussian city of Bonn in 1854, under the supervision of the Indologist Christian Lassen, who had been the first scholar to hold a chair of Indology in Germany in 1830. His essay on the Pahlavi language was an indirect but systematic criticism of Roth's interpretation of the Vedic and Avestic pantheon.[17] Although he was now integrated in academic life as a Privatdozent, in this foreign state his Swabian identity distinguished him from his colleagues, as the following anecdote about his classes shows: "Haug spoke of *Zoroaschter* and the *Aweschta* with such a charming Swabian accent. The people of Bonn loved to hear him talking, especially because it made them realize how *jebildet* [gebildet = educated] their own way of speaking was."[18]

Remarkably, while Haug's social origins had been a factor in his break-up with Roth, seen from other German states they had in common the same rural Swabian background and their accent was mocked alike. The Vedic scholar Theodor Benfey reproached Roth with the excessive lyrism of his translations of Vedic texts; he sarcastically accused him of transforming the Veda into "popular Swabian folksong."[19] Roth, for his part, tried to turn his rural origins into advantage and proudly claimed his origins, as reported by his biographer: "Once I complimented Roth for his expert translation of the various Indian expressions for milk, butter and cheese. He was very pleased and stroked his chin as he used to do and said: Yes, in Berlin they cannot do such a thing."[20]

But rurality was only a part of Roth's identity. He was foremost known as a precursor in Vedic studies and one of the leading scholars in Indology. By contrast, even after his death, Haug's whole professional trajectory continued to be related to his origins as a villager. For instance, the purpose of the *Festschrift* from 1909 is described as follows:

---

17   Martin Haug, *Ueber die Pehlewi-sprache und den Bundehesch* (Göttingen: Dieterichsche Buchhandlung, 1854). See Roth to Ewald, 20 June 1854, in Fick-Selle, *Briefe an Ewald*, 43-44.
18   Veit, *Festschrift*, 18-19.
19   Ernst Windisch, *Geschichte der Sanskritphilologie und indischen Altertumskunde*, vol. 1 (Strasbourg: K. J. Trübner, 1917), 262.
20   Richard Garbe, "Roth, (Walter) Rudolf (von)," in *Allgemeine Deutsche Biographie*, vol. 53 (Leipzig: Duncker & Humblot, 1907), 549-564, at 556.

On the one hand, to tell the peasants from Martin Haug's village of Ostdorf what one of them has achieved in the world, how he lived, loved and suffered; on the other hand, to draw the attention of his colleagues and friends from the later period on the special homeland in which his being was rooted.[21]

In this passage, Martin Haug's village origins are presented in a positive light, but also as a definitive line of demarcation between him and his fellow scholars. This way of presenting things is justified to the extent that the obstacles he encountered certainly forged his notoriously sensitive and determined character. But on the other hand, one should not overlook the other determinants of Haug's career and scientific personality: in particular, the growing internationalization of science around 1850.

Here again, individual trajectories and global dynamics are both at work and interact with each other in the construction of scholarly identities. The same year Haug arrived in Bonn, in 1854, Christian Bunsen (1791-1860), the famous mentor of Max Müller, resigned from his post as Prussian ambassador in London and settled in Heidelberg, where he wanted to continue his activity as a private writer. For his book series *Aegyptens Stelle in der Weltgeschichte* (*Egypt's Place in Universal History*, 5 vols., 1854-1857), he needed someone acquainted with the ancient Persian dialects. Haug, who could hardly make a living with his occupation as Privatdozent, was apparently recommended to him by Max Müller, the famous German Indologist working at Oxford (although it is not totally clear how Müller himself had heard of Haug). If Haug's path to an academic career was certainly not direct, his hiring by Bunsen in 1856 is another instance of the many personal encounters that gave him the financial means and social networks necessary for the pursuit of his purposes. Importantly, Bunsen soon sent him to Paris with the task of working on Persian manuscripts. Although Haug's biographers hardly insist on this episode, it gave him the opportunity to copy and study Oriental manuscripts from the rich collection of the Bibliothèque royale. For once, he was able to follow the usual path of the German aspiring Orientalists of his time, most of whom went to Paris and London in the course of their study.[22]

Working for Bunsen also put Haug in contact with new people, from a different social background. Due to his previous position as Prussian diplomat in

---

21 Veit, *Festschrift*, 2.
22 Pascale Rabault-Feuerhahn, "Paris, lieu fondateur et provisoire de l'indianisme allemand," in *Itinéraires orientalistes entre la France et l'Allemagne* (*Revue germanique internationale 7/2008*), ed. Pascale Rabault-Feuerhahn and Céline Trautmann-Waller, 139-156. In 1857, Bunsen sent Haug to London to study Palehvi manuscripts at the India House.

London, Bunsen had strong connections with British people. In Spring 1857 the British theologian Mark Pattison (1813-1884) came to visit him in Bonn. A former priest and tutor at Oxford, Pattison had resigned from his post in 1855 and he regularly went to Germany with the aim of developing international scholarly connections. Haug met him on this occasion and again six months later in London, when Bunsen sent him to England to study Pahlavi manuscripts at India House. On the same occasion, Haug became personally acquainted with Max Müller.[23] Pattison and Müller knew one another and they were both very involved in German–British academic relations. Pattison later became one of the most enthusiastic proponents of the Germanization of the British educational system, understood as a means of modernization and emancipation from the theological perspective.[24]

As for Max Müller, he played a pioneering and leading role in the presence of German Indologists in Great-Britain. For his big *Rig-Veda* edition (1849-1874), as well as for his edition of the *Sacred books of the East* (50 vols., 1879-1910) he had several German assistants. Not only was he convinced of the superiority of German philological methods, but he wanted to contribute to the development of German Indology, which enjoyed an increasingly international reputation thanks to the achievements in comparative linguistics and Vedic studies by scholars like Franz Bopp, Christian Lassen, Rudolf Roth, Theodor Benfey, Heinrich Ewald, and Albrecht Weber. The chairs of Indology that were created in Great Britain in the wake of the consolidation of the British power in India, were mostly held by German scholars (e.g., Theodor Goldstücker in London and Theodor Aufrecht in Edinburgh). Max Müller was a pivotal figure of this German milieu of British Indology.

In India itself, the educational landscape was undergoing dramatical changes. The British, who established their authority over the subcontinent, strove to westernize the Indian system of knowledge transmission. In 1854, Sir Charles Wood's educational despatch created a Department of Education in every Province, and in 1857, three universities were founded. In the traditional Indian system, Brahmanic schools (Gurukula) were financed by the "dakshina" charity paid by the kings to reward the wisdom of the Brahmans. Already in 1837, Mountstuart Elphinstone, the Governor of the Bombay Province, had established a Sanskrit College in Poona, known as "Hindoo College," in using the Dakshina Funds of the Peshwas (formerly the head ministers of the Maratha

---

23   Veit, *Festschrift*, 20.
24   H. S. Jones, "Pattison, Mark (1813-1884)," *Oxford Dictionary of National Biography*, online at <https://doi.org/10.1093/ref:odnb/21585> (last accessed 28 January 2019). In 1859 the British government entrusted him with the mission to report on continental education in Germany.

Kings). In 1842, an English school was added and in 1851 both institutions were merged and renamed "Poona College."[25] As a further step toward the modernization of the educational system, E. I. Howard, the director of Education of the Bombay Presidency, wished to entrust the direction of the Sanskrit curriculum at the Poona College to a European scholar. Pattison, whom he asked for advice, suggested Haug's name.[26]

Martin Haug's appointment in India can thus be interpreted as the meeting point of two concurrent trends in mid nineteenth-century British educational policy: westernization of the Indian educational system on the one side, the growing attention to German scholarship as a model on the other. The job offer came at a time (10 May 1858) when Bunsen started being disappointed by Haug's work.[27] The tensions with Bunsen and changes in his personal life (he was about to get married) led him to return to his job as *Privatdozent* in Bonn while waiting for the confirmation of these new perspectives. Because of a financial crisis in Bombay province, the confirmation came only in June 1859. Written during this long period of waiting, Haug's autobiography can be considered as a sign that Haug had the feeling of approaching a turn in his existence. As a matter of fact, his hiring in India meant not only a geographical displacement, but also a major shift in his self-understanding as a scholar: he who had to fight so strongly to be admitted into German academia, was suddenly hired as a representative of German scholarship. Even more ironically, he acquired this status precisely through breaking with the habitus of German (armchair) Indologists. In the context of the internationalisation of scientific life, the definition of the scholarly self went beyond questions of establishing one's disciplinary profile and of responding to the sociological characteristics of academics: national and cultural identities were also at stake.

Even if going to India singled him out from contemporary German Indologists, Haug hoped that it would help him to successfully insert himself into the German academic landscape afterwards. In fact, he did not only work for the British but was also endowed with a mission from the Prussian government. He wrote to Ewald:

---

25 R. N. Dandekar, "Ramakrishna Gopal Bhandarkar and the Academic Renaissance in Maharashtra," *Annals of the Bhandarkar Oriental Research Institute* 69(1988), 283-294, at 283-286.
26 Gaiser, "Martin Haug," 75 and E. J. Howard to Haug, 26 March 1859, in Veit, *Festschrift*, 85.
27 At that time, Haug was working on Bunsen's book *Vollständiges Bibelwerk für die Gemeinde* and, apparently, he did not meet as much with Bunsen's expectations as had been the case when he worked on Iranian and Indian subjects (Veit, *Festschrift*, 21).

> At the instigation of Bunsen ... I shall get an appointment as a Professor at a Prussian university with remuneration and directly be given leave for 4 to 5 years, if only I assume the obligation to buy Zend, Pehlewi, Pârsi and Buddhist texts for the Prussian government and to send substantial reports every year.[28]

At a time when collections of Oriental manuscripts were scarce in the German states, Haug's appointment at the Poona college became an issue of international competition. His personal interest and the interests of the British and the Prussian governments were intermingled. Although going to India was very uncommon for German Indologists, Haug's situation was part of a broader movement of German scholars working abroad at the service of foreign governments. Even before he was proposed the position at Poona, Haug already knew other scholars working for the British. One of them was Wilhelm Bleek, the famous specialist of African comparative linguistics and ethnology, who regularly participated in British expeditions, like the Niger expedition of 1854. The Bleek family lived in Bonn and supported Haug when he was habilitating there. From then on, Wilhelm Bleek and Haug remained close friends; Bleek wrote to Haug to share his adventures abroad and encouraged him to follow the same path.[29] Another close friend of Haug was Ernst Trumpp, a missionary who had been Haug's fellow student in Roth's courses. A few years before Haug, in 1854, he went to North Western India to study various Indian languages on the account of the English Ecclesiastical Mission Society. He was still there when Haug arrived at Poona.

In 1885, twenty years after Haug's return to Germany, Max Müller wrote to Friedrich Althoff, the Prussian Minister of Education, in support of the Indologist Richard Garbe, whom the Prussian Government wanted to send on a scientific mission to India:

> What German scholars can do in India has been proven by men like Haug, Bühler, Kielhorn, Thibaut, and others, who have succeeded in gaining employment in the English civil service. Unfortunately, such appointments are now harder to obtain than before, and it would therefore be all the more to be desired that Germany, and especially Prussia, which has

---

28 Haug to Ewald, 17 January 1859, in Fick-Selle, *Briefe an Ewald*, 62.
29 Haug to Ewald, 12 Juni 1854, ibid., 41-42. See also the correspondence between Haug and Bleek in Veit's *Festschrift*.

done so much for the study of Indian antiquity, now proves by a scientific mission led by itself the value it gives to scientific Indian studies.[30]

Georg Bühler, Franz Kielhorn and Georg Thibaut were hired in India shortly after Haug. The latter's approach did not serve as an example for the new generation of German Indologists, but also inspired a more systematic scientific policy on the part of Prussia. Before German unification as well as after, Prussia wished not to be outdone by England. Not only Haug, but also the Germans who succeeded him in the service of the British crown in India, had the task of collecting manuscripts for the benefit of the Prussian government: the Germans were well aware that access to primary sources remained their Achilles heel despite their philological advance.[31]

4 Western Armchair Indology Tested in the Field

At the time when he accepted Pattison's offer, Haug was convinced of the superiority of European scholarship over indigenous scholarly traditions. In the letters he sent to Ewald once he had reached India, he says how proud he feels to provide the Brahmans with new insights on Sanskrit culture and boasts that he has "exposed for the first time (to the brahmin) the historical origin of their caste." However, he was well aware from the start that he had things to learn from the contact with the pundits. Before he left, he was thrilled about having "the best opportunity to acquire a rare knowledge of Sanskrit literature along with great practical skills in Sanskrit and modern Persian (Bombay), and to become a connoisseur of the languages, literatures, customs and mores of the Orient."[32]

Furthermore, he realised that a gap existed between their understanding of the Avestic hymns and the Vedic rites and what European exegetes championed. To him, there was no doubt that the error was on the European side. This led him to try to conciliate Western philological analysis (whose rigorous, methodical nature he granted) and field observation. In the course of the years he spent in India, he developed close connections to Parsee and Hindu priests and scholars. He was the professor of Ramkrishna Gopal Bhandarkar (1837-

---

30   F. M. Müller to F. Althoff, 23 February 1885, Staatsbibliothek Berlin, Slg. Darmstaedter 2b1860, Müller, Frederick Max, Blatt 14-15.
31   In the same letter, Max Müller pointed to the fact that the authorization of the British government was required for acquiring manuscripts and ancient coins and that it was important "not to arouse the jealousy of English or Indian scholars."
32   Haug to Ewald, 17 January 1859, in Fick-Selle, *Briefe an Ewald*, 61.

1925), who later became the most famous Indologist in his country and the founder of the Bhandarkar Research Institute. Bhandarkar was both an Oriental scholar and a social reformer, a leader of the Prathna Samaj in Western India. For his endeavours he relied on Martin Haug's as well as Max Müller's views. Another important partner of Haug in India was Destur Hoshengji Jamaspji (1838-1908), a Parsee priest, with whom Haug later published several groundbreaking critical works and text editions in the field of Avestic studies: *An Old pahlavi Glossary* (1870), *Old Pahlavi Pazand Glossary* (1870), and *The Book of Arda Viraf* (1872). Haug also regularly gave conferences to a learned Parsee audience.

In combining both traditions, his aim was twofold: to reevaluate the status of indigenous commentaries and scholarly traditions, and, relatedly, to go beyond strictly textual philology and to leave space for an ethnographic approach taking into account contemporary practices. This endeavour culminated in the following episode:

> Last year already I enjoyed a rare opportunity (which until then had never arisen to any European), to gather information on sacrifices from a sacrifying priest (himself) … I made every effort to convince the priest to accomplish all the ceremonies of the soma sacrifice in my presence … In the shed next to my compound, he noiselessly built the required hearths and altars … The most important ceremonies were actually carried out: this lasted four days during which, sitting on my chair, I noted down everything that I deemed worthy of interest.[33]

The question of the status of indigenous knowledge and the credit it must be given, had been at the center of heated debates since the beginning of Indology in Europe. In Germany, Roth had decisively contributed to establishing an attitude of mistrust towards indigenous commentaries – even though earlier on, in the 1840s, he had planned to publish the *Rig-Veda* along with Sâyana's commentary. When this project failed and was taken up by Max Müller (the *Rig-Veda* Sanhita edition mentioned further above), Roth undertook to publish Yâska's Nirukta, a text including an etymological analysis of Vedic terms that enabled readers to better understand the hymns. However, in later works Roth was noticeably disdainful towards Indian science, notably Sâyana. One of his arguments was that there existed a temporal, geographical, and even ethnic gap between Sâyana and the Vedic Indians. Haug criticised Roth's views on the subject already before his departure for India. His critics became even harsher

---

33 Haug to Ewald, 10 May 1862, ibid., 80.

once he was in Poona, and they did not cease after his return to Europe in 1867 for reasons of health. His argumentation was opposed point by point to that of Roth: since Christian and Hindu civilisations had nothing in common, he said, modern Indians themselves were certainly more entitled to restore the right meaning of the Vedas than philologists from Europe.

Although Haug only related his ethnographic experience with the Vedic Sacrifice to Ewald, under the seal of confidentiality, this anecdote went around the community of German Indologists. Maybe it was betrayed by Georg Bühler (1837-1899), a German Indologist who arrived in India in 1863 as a Professor at the service of the British Government and with whom Haug did not get along very well. They were offended by Haug's participation in a sacrificial ritual, considering that it was a betrayal of Protestantism and the surest indicator of the devastating effect of the contact with modern India for the intellectual and spiritual well-being of Europeans. As a consequence, after his return to Germany, Haug had to thwart several maneuvers carried out by his colleagues, especially Albrecht Weber, the holder of the chair at Berlin and a close friend of Rudolf Roth and Otto von Boehtlingk, in order to prevent him from acceding to the *Ordinariat* that the University of Munich offered to him. In fact, a few years earlier, in 1864, Max Müller had published an anonymous review of Haug's translation of the *Aitareya Brahmana*, in which he defended Haug's work against the criticisms of Weber, Roth and Boehtlingk. Blaming them for not being able to accept other views than their own, he called them a "mutual praise society" and an "international sanscrit insurance company." This was the start of the famous, long lasting and violent feud between Müller on the one side and Weber, Roth, Boehtlingk, and Whitney on the other. In addition to his personal resentment against Müller, Whitney, who had been Roth's student at the same time as Haug, ferociously defended his former professor's point of view. A major issue in the quarrel was to determine who could legitimately be considered as a true representative of sound, solid German scholarship. As a disciple of Roth, Whitney considered himself a repository of the German scholarly tradition while, in his eyes, Müller, who had emigrated to England, had nothing more to do with it and was only a "humbug." Although Haug was not the direct target of the quarrel, his connections with native Indian scholars was likely interpreted as a step away from the German tradition.

From Haug's standpoint, it was clear that the opposition that he met at the hands of the discipline's masters concerning his nomination at Munich, was still related to the danger represented by the knowledge he had acquired in India. In a letter to Ewald, he gives thoughtful insight into the power relations at stake in Weber's attitude:

> However, I perfectly understand Albrecht Weber's opposition to my being recruited in a German university, namely one of the greatest ones, as is the case with Munich university. His Sanskrit-Dictatorship in Germany is now over. Thanks to the knowledge and viewpoints that I have acquired in India, and to my vast wealth of manuscripts …, I am truly in a position to make a firm and successful stand against Weber's monopoly.[34]

Haug was not wrong about his assets. After his return to Germany for reasons of health in 1866, he had to wait two more years before he was nominated at the University of Munich. His nomination was largely due to the fact that the Munich Library coveted the collection of Indian manuscripts he had acquired during his stay in India. With eight students in Vedic, seven in Zend and six in Pahlavi, among whom several came from other German states, according to his own count he had the largest number of advanced students in Indology throughout Germany.

Weber's and Roth's scholarly achievements had been major reasons for the international influence and reputation of German Indological scholarship. But in return, the internationalization of scientific activity (illustrated for instance by the creation of the International Congress of Orientalists in 1873) had direct implications on the definition and practice of Indological science in Germany itself. It is no coincidence that at the second session of the Congress, in 1874, Haug presented a paper "On the Interpretation of the Veda" which was a plea for the awareness of the native commentary tradition of India:

> Though the difficulties to be surmounted be far greater than most people think, there is, however, some hope that we may, in the end, by the application of all the helps that brahmanical scholarship, the still existing rites and comparative philology can afford, arrive at the sense which the rishis laid into their songs and prayers, opening fully up the rich mine of the most primitive thoughts of the whole Aryan race.[35]

Although at the same Congress Weber went to Haug in order to make peace with him, he was still far from admitting the legitimacy and relevance of Oriental scholarly traditions. Fifteen years later, commenting upon the 1889 session of the Congress held at Stockholm and Christiania, Weber sharply criticised

---

34 Haug to Ewald, 15 January 1868, ibid., 61.
35 [Martin] Haug, "On the Interpretation of the Veda," in *Report of the Proceedings of the Second International Congress of Orientalists held in London, 1874* (London: Trübner & Co., 1874), 24-27, at 27.

the presence of Oriental scholars, who in his eyes were not capable of producing any sound works. However, lines were moving by and by. In the same period (in the 1880s), Destur Hoshengji Jamaspji as well as Ramakrishna Gopal Bhandarkar (who had been Haug's surrogate at Poona while he was away collecting manuscripts) were both nominated Doctor honoris causa of German speaking universities (Göttingen and Vienna, respectively). Even if in his time Haug had been an isolated voice, his texts paved the way for a reappraisal of the Indian tradition by the next generation, incarnated by scholars like Richard Pischel, Karl Geldner, Alfred Hillebrandt, and Hermann Oldenberg. At the end of the century, German Indology was less than ever a homogeneous whole.

5 Conclusion

So, to what extent does the case of Haug allow us to say that nineteenth-century Orientalists tried to develop a new persona? Although Haug's travels to India and his experimentation with ethnographic methods were partly driven by a sense of dissatisfaction with European knowledge, including especially its philological methods, he did not intentionally try to exchange one model of how to be a scholar for another. To the contrary, the biographical perspective adopted in this chapter shows in some detail that Haug, at least initially, did what he could to conform to the philological persona cultivated by the German Orientalists whom he encountered in Göttingen and Bonn. He became a fieldworker of sorts only after circumstances – a vacant teaching position at Poona College – offered him an opportunity to exchange Germany for India. Processes of developing and adapting new personae are therefore seriously simplified if they are reduced to intentional projects.

Another cautionary lesson that can be drawn from this chapter is that different scholarly personae did not simply succeed each other. As evidenced by Haug's work on Vedic accentuation, taking into account the reality of the field, for instance by studying oral recitations, could have profound effects on exegetical practice. Also, in the late nineteenth century, more and more German Indologists – Georg Bühler, Hermann Jacobi, Richard Pischel – made part of their careers in India or went there for study or lecture trips. Crucially, however, these travels did not necessarily weaken the power of the armchair philologist. Indeed, as evidenced by Haug's own trajectory – his ambivalent relations with Destur Hoshengji Jamaspji in particular – the personae of the philologist and the fieldworker were not mutually exclusive. Neither did they chronologically succeed one another. If the case of Haug shows us anything, therefore, it is that the study of the scholarly personae benefits from taking into account the coexistence of personae, their overlap, as well as the conflicts that are possible between them at any given moment in history.

Bibliography

Benfey, Theodor. *Geschichte der Sprachwissenschaft und orientalischen Philologie in Deutschland*. Munich: Cotta, 1869.

Dandekar, R. N."Ramakrishna Gopal Bhandarkar and the Academic Renaissance in Maharashtra," *Annals of the Bhandarkar Oriental Research Institute* 69 (1988): 283-294.

Eilers, Wilhelm. "Haug, Martin.". In *Neue Deutsche Biographie*, vol. 8., 91-92. Berlin: Duncker & Humblot, 1969.

Evans, E. P. "Biographical Sketch." In Martin Haug. *Essays on the Sacred Language, Writings and Religion of the Parsis*, edited by E. W. West. London: Trübner and Co., [1884] 2000.

Fick, Richard and Götz von Selle (eds.). *Briefe an Ewald aus seinem Nachlass*. Göttingen: Vandenhoeck & Ruprecht, 1932.

Gaiser, E."Martin Haug." *Bezzenbergers Beiträge zur Kunde der indogermanischen Sprachen* 1 (1877): 70-80.

Garbe, Richard. "Roth, (Walter) Rudolf (von)." In *Allgemeine Deutsche Biographie*, vol. 53., 549-564. Leipzig: Duncker & Humblot, 1907.

Haug, Martin. *Ueber die Pehlewi-sprache und den Bundehesch*. Göttingen: Dieterichsche Buchhandlung, 1854.

Haug, Martin. "On the Interpretation of the Veda." In *Report of the Proceedings of the Second International Congress of Orientalists held in London, 1874*, 24-27. London: Trübner & Co., 1874.

Herrenschmidt, Clarisse. "Once upon a time, Zoroaster." In Francis Schmidt, ed. *The Inconceivable Polytheism: Studies in Religious Historiography* (*History and Anthropology 1987/3*), 209-238.

Jolly, Julius. "Haug, Martin." In *Allgemeine Deutsche Biographie*, vol. 11.,54-56. Leipzig: Duncker & Humblot, 1880.

Jones, H. S. "Pattison, Mark (1813-1884)." *Oxford Dictionary of National Biography*. online at <https://doi.org/10.1093/ref:odnb/21585> (last accessed 28 January 2019).

Rabault-Feuerhahn, Pascale. "Paris, lieu fondateur et provisoire de l'indianisme allemand." In Pascale Rabault-Feuerhahn and Céline Trautmann-Waller (eds.). *Itinéraires orientalistes entre la France et l'Allemagne* (*Revue germanique internationale 7/2008*), 139-156.

Rabault-Feuerhahn, Pascale. "La philologie comme épopée: aspects de la tradition historiographique de l'indianisme en Allemagne au 19e siècle." *Histoire épistémologie langage* 33/2 (2011): 103-119.

Roth, Rudolf. "Martin Haug." *Bezzenbergers Beiträge* (1877): 175-176.

Trumpp, Ernst. "Martin Haug." *Beilage zur Augsburger Allgemeinen Zeitung* 182 (1876).

Veit, Friedrich, ed., *Festschrift zur Erinnerung an die Haug-Feier in Ostdorf*. Tübingen: Buchdruckerei von Gg. Schnürken, 1909.

Windisch, Ernst. *Geschichte der Sanskritphilologie und indischen Altertumskunde*. Strasbourg: K. J. Trübner, 1917.

CHAPTER 5

Herbert Giles as Reviewer

T. H. Barrett

Herbert Allen Giles (1845-1935) was the second Professor of Chinese at Cambridge. His career – he replaced Sir Thomas Wade (1818-1895) in 1897 and retired at the age of eighty-five – spans the whole era of the emergence of the "professional Orientalist" persona. Yet, in the words of John Minford and Tong Man, his was "the persona of the literary amateur."[1] How does this persona of Giles compare with those of other Orientalist contemporaries, specifically in the area of reviewing? His younger contemporary Paul Pelliot (1878-1945) provides an illuminating point of contrast. Both were spirited – not to say aggressive – reviewers, but there the similarities cease. In examining the view Giles took of his work we have now not only his autobiography, published with annotation by Charles Aylmer, but also a manuscript catalogue of his personal library with annotations relating to reviewed copies, and it is these sources in particular that I have tried to deploy in answering this question.

Before turning to his case, however, it is worth perhaps providing some background on the emergence of the British study of China within the wider context of Orientalism. Though the ancient and medieval antecedents of Orientalism are well known, it is plain that a new impetus to the study of non-European languages was provided by the Reformation and the concomitant rise in study of the Bible. This of course affected Britain, but it must be said that the first English efforts to reach out beyond Europe linguistically towards East Asia at least were as much governed by the needs of trade and diplomacy, as this island nation sought to counterbalance economically and politically the perceived threat of the Counter-Reformation on the continent, as they were by Bible-centred piety, let alone intellectual curiosity.

This may seem an unnecessarily harsh verdict on the history of early Anglophone studies of China, but a wealth of scholarship both older and much more recent permits no other conclusion. From the sixteenth century onward there was a certain effort exerted to collect and translate into English accounts of East Asia published in other European languages, but demonstrably with an eye to emulating the commercial success of other nations rather than a pure

---

[1] John Minford and Tong Man, "Whose Strange Stories? P'u Sung-ling (1640-1715), Herbert Giles (1845-1935) and the *Liao-chai chih-yi*," *East Asian History* 17/18 (1999), 1-48, at 9, n. 13.

desire for knowledge, and even in the seventeenth century the Royal Society, far from being a body dedicated to the disinterested spirit of free enquiry, was likewise distinguished by its links with commerce.[2] It is true that the Chinese script did during the latter century stimulate a degree of speculation amongst a handful of learned men in England from Francis Bacon onward, but again the background to this speculation may be traced back to sixteenth century writings by non-British authors.[3] Actual linguistic contacts in Britain with native speakers remained fleeting and elementary, and such translations of Chinese materials as did begin to appear late in the century were indirect, drawing on earlier renderings into Latin by others.[4]

Further progress was, moreover, slow. The eighteenth century saw the partial translation directly into English of a Chinese novel, executed with the help of a speaker of Portuguese by an employee of the East India Company in Canton, but this was to remain for many years a distinct rarity: the pursuits of this man's successors seem to have remained largely the opposite of intellectual.[5] China is not absent from the English literature of the age, but it was a China chiefly perceived through the medium of sources both French and Catholic, and hence subject to considerable scepticism: Adam Smith's famous remark about having to depend for his view of China on "stupid and lying missionaries" aptly sums up the situation from the British perspective.[6] Using Catholic sources on China had in fact provoked unease from the early seventeenth century, and some had already gone on to voice the thought that Catholic success in China might be a prelude to reversing their recent failure in England.[7]

---

2   Donald F. Lach, *Asia in the Making of Europe, Volume I: The Century of Discovery* (Chicago, IL: University of Chicago Press, 1965), 209-215; note for example on p. 214 "Hakluyt was no cloistered scholar; in these years he was rapidly becoming one of the leaders in the organization of Eastern trade"; David. E. Mungello, *Curious Land: Jesuit Accommodation and the Origins of Sinology* (Honolulu, HI: University of Hawai'i Press, 1989), 37.

3   Mungello, *Curious Land*, 178-185, 190; Dinu Luca, *The Chinese Language in European Texts: The Early Period* (New York, NY: Palgrave Macmillan, 2016), 111.

4   Linda L. Barnes, *Needles, Herbs, Gods, and Ghosts* (Cambridge, MA: Harvard University Press, 2005), 75, 81-83; Matt Jenkinson, "Nathaniel Vincent and Confucius's 'Great Learning' in Restoration England," *Notes and Records of the Royal Society* 60 (2006), 35-47.

5   Peter Kitson, *Forging Romantic China: Sino-British Cultural Exchange 1760-1840* (Cambridge: Cambridge University Press, 2013), 33; Peter Quennell, ed., *Memoirs of William Hickey* (London: Routledge & Kegan Paul, 1975), 124-136.

6   David Martin Jones, *The Image of China in Western Social and Political Thought* (New York, NY: Palgrave, 2001), 32. Britain's ignorance in fact allowed some flexibility in the imaginative use of a notional "China," according to Paul Nash, "The Idea of China in British Literature, 1757 to 1785" (PhD thesis, University of Edinburgh, 2013).

7   Nicholas Koss, "Matteo Ricci on China via Samuel Purchas: Faithful Re-Presentation," in *Western Visions of the Far East in a Transpacific Age, 1522-1657*, ed. Christina H. Lee

Despite this, however, spiritual as opposed to commercial competition appears to have been pursued with conspicuously less vigor. Even in India, notwithstanding the success there of British trade, British Protestant missionary efforts were in the eighteenth century long preceded by those of Germans under Danish sponsorship, while the first Protestant missionary was eventually dispatched to China in 1807 only after an earlier expedition to the South Seas, chosen as a target on the optimistic assumption that less materialistically developed cultures would prove linguistically less challenging, ended in utter failure.[8] Inadequately funded by his missionary society, the China pioneer was eventually obliged to take up employment in Canton with the East India Company himself, with the result that by the time his translations of portions of the Bible in into Chinese had begun to appear, a fellow employee, more influenced by immediate diplomatic and commercial considerations, had in 1810 published the Chinese legal code in English translation.[9] Thereafter a certain amount of missionary Sinology was produced in the early to mid-nineteenth century.[10] "The two strands met in the case of the first British chair, that in Oxford, endowed in 1875 by a group of merchants trading with China specifically for the greatest British Sinologist of the nineteenth century, James Legge, much of whose career in China had been spent in the missionary field."[11] This statement is not strictly accurate in terms of chronology, since professorships had been founded earlier in London, but these chairs pursued only a markedly desultory existence well into the twentieth century.[12]

Such, then, were the roots of British Sinology. It is of course possible to point to one or two individuals before the collapse of British commercial interests in China in the middle of the twentieth century who came to the study of China out of a sense of intellectual adventure, but all in all such figures – or at least such figures as possessed enough curiosity to see them through the arduous

---

(Farnham: Ashgate, 2012), 85-100; Simon Kow, *China in Early Enlightenment Political Thought* (Abingdon: Routledge, 2017), 49.

8 Stephen Neill, *A History of Christian Missions*, 2nd ed. (London: Penguin Books, 1990), 194-200; Christopher A. Daily, *Robert Morrison and the Protestant Plan for China* (Hong Kong: Hong Kong University Press, 2013), 21-32.

9 Li Chen, *Chinese Law in Imperial Eyes: Sovereignty, Justice, and Transcultural Politics* (New York, NY: Columbia University Press, 2016), 69-111.

10 A. J. Arberry, *British Orientalists* (London: William Collins, 1943), 44-46.

11 Edmund Bosworth, ed., *A Century of British Orientalists, 1902-2001* (Oxford: Oxford University Press for the British Academy, 2001), 3 (editor's introduction).

12 The only connected narrative of this saga remains the opening remarks in Denis Twitchett, *Land Tenure and the Social order in T'ang and Sung China* (London: School of Oriental and African Studies, 1962), 1-12, though a forthcoming series of publications by Uganda Kwan is establishing a more detailed picture.

stage of language learning to the point of publishing original work – may be numbered on the fingers of two hands. The vast majority of Britons who learned Chinese did so out of immediate necessity, in the first instance with trade in mind – though this only required the rudiments of language, which soon became the province of local Chinese middlemen – and next of diplomacy, followed by the demands of Protestant missionary work, which was carried out by Britons after 1807 until 1949. When it was reluctantly conceded that Chinese was a language that might be taught in universities, those responsible were invariably ex-missionaries or ex-consuls or the like; only the rise of Hitler brought refugees with actual academic qualifications to the task. Some of the missionaries and diplomats turned out to scholars; most did not. Their competence mainly extended to translation, but not much beyond, though missionaries sometimes attempted to weigh up matters of religious import. Herbert Giles, however, learned his Chinese as a consular official.

Giles is primarily remembered today as a result of the use during the twentieth century in Anglophone Sinology and to some extent elsewhere of the Wade–Giles transcription of Chinese. This was not uncontested as the standard in his lifetime: the similar but distinct system used by the *Sacred Books of the East* series in Oxford was a rival at that point, but the use of the Wade system in pedagogy, and its subsequent incorporation in modified form by Giles into a dictionary that was the most comprehensive and up to date available in English for a generation, ensured its dominance until the rise of the Pinyin transcription used in China itself. Giles was not a great scholar, but he was prolific, and so affords the twenty-first century researcher plenty of opportunity to ponder the state of the study of China in his day in relation to other fields. Reviewing is one obvious area for investigation, though the careful reader of the following remarks will soon see that here the topic is touched on only in a quite preliminary way, and that much more extended research should be possible in the future.

The writing of critical evaluations of published academic work has long formed part of the professional activity of academics in the humanities and social sciences, so much so that by the mid-twentieth century we find it described as "the most common medium for prestige allocation," an essential component of collective academic strategies.[13] If one goes back half a century or so earlier than this, however, the various fields within Orientalism were not

---

13   C. Wright Mills, *The Sociological Imagination* (Oxford: Oxford University Press, 1959), 112. Mills (1916-1962) describes a stage in the development of his own field in which reputations were no longer built necessarily on published scholarship, but also on the building of what he describes as 'academic cliques' (107-113).

so heavily populated as to encourage collective strategies. What role did the book review then have in academic life? Can the academic book review be seen as a marker of professionalization?

In fact my choice of Herbert A. Giles as an exemplar of a British sinological reviewer of this period was based upon a reminiscence of reading the annotations to the unpublished typescript catalogue of his own library, which included instances wherein he referred to his published opinions of some of the works he owned, as well as adding some evaluations that do not seem to have appeared in print.[14] A closer reading of this document, however, points up the way in which first impressions can subsequently give way to much more problematic findings. The catalogue itself is not a straightforward document. It is undated, and is unfortunately not mentioned in its author's autobiography, which has been published with extensive annotation by Charles Aylmer. The autobiography itself in the judgment of its editor must have been prepared between 1918 and 1925; the latter date appears following the brief authorial Foreword.[15] Though for the purposes of the present investigation no attempt has been made to solve all the mysteries presented by the Giles catalogue, since it is only a few of his annotations that bear upon his attitudes as a reviewer, it would seem that it was kept up to date until about 1930, though some of the later entries may be by his son, Lionel (1875-1958), who is certainly responsible for at least one manuscript addition.[16] At least some of the annota-

---

14   The Cambridge booksellers W. Heffer & Son did publish a sales catalogue of Giles library in European languages after his death, but rather than an account of his library alone it was printed as a combined listing together with the books of William E. Soothill (1861-1935), who had been Professor of Chinese at Oxford, and of Soothill's son-in-law, the consular official and explorer Sir Alexander Hosie (1853-1925) – Hosie's wife Dorothea was some thirty-two years younger than her husband. The combining of these separate libraries, perhaps already undertaken for the Hosie and Soothill books before they reached Heffers, makes this catalogue difficult to use as a source on Giles alone, but reference to the catalogue numbers of items in this source that are mentioned here are added in any case below, preceded by the letter H.

15   See Charles Aylmer, "The Memoirs of H. A. Giles," *East Asian History* 13/14 (1997), 1-90, at 7, 8. Note that subsequently in this work he quotes the advice given him by Bernard Quaritch (1819-1899) to the effect that a catalogued library is worth twenty-five per cent more than an uncatalogued one, but does not mention his own books (17).

16   See the note on a work by "E. D. Edwards, D. Litt" in "Herbert Giles – catalogue of his library," MS Add 7982, University Library, Cambridge – below, "Giles catalogue" -- 32. On Lionel, see John Minford, "Lionel Giles: Sinology Old and New," *China Heritage Quarterly* 13 (2008), online at <http://www.chinaheritagequarterly.org/articles.php?searchterm=013_giles.inc&issue=013> (last accessed 28 January 2019). "Giles catalogue," Chinese section (following the main catalogue), 11, in describing a work translated and published in the *Bulletin of the School of Oriental and African Studies* 5 (1928-1930), 757-785, and subsequently commented on by Lionel in the next volume of the *Bulletin*, 633-640, by contrast

tions are wrong, and therefore plainly cannot be from the hand of Herbert Giles himself, given that they concern books he knew well. One cannot believe for example that someone who trenchantly exposed the mistakes of the missionary Timothy Richard (1845-1919) in translating the Buddhist text in Chinese known as the *Awakening of Faith* in 1907 would have subsequently attributed this translation to Sir Richard Carnac Temple (1850-1931), whose career of soldiering and anthropology in South Asia did not allow him an education in Chinese.[17] It is also conceivable but unlikely that a concordance to the *Laozi* published in 1921 would have been described by anyone who had opened it and looked at the contents as "LAO CHIEH LAO: LAO TZǓ (the old philosopher) explained by an old man, Ts'ai T'ing-kan," even if its author, a gallant Chinese Admiral, was indeed sixty at the time of its publication: the true meaning is "Laozi explained by Laozi," a good summary of an instance of what any concordance should do.[18]

But it is quite easy to spot the comments that can only have flowed from the pen of Herbert Giles, because Lionel's obituaries all agree that he was a gentle soul, whereas his father, though he could readily be charming enough face to face, was frequently quite the reverse, especially in writing. D. L. McMullen reports a Cambridge oral tradition suggesting that he used to chase prospective students away with a stick, though given that he was well into his eighties during the later years of his tenure of his professorship, perhaps he felt, even though he had had very few formal students, that he had done enough.[19] This pugnacious streak plainly extended to the private, unpublished remarks

---

simply notes the translation as being by "Miss E. D. Edwards." Edwards (1888-1957) was awarded her D. Litt.in 1931, according to W. Simon, "Obituary: Evangeline Dora Edwards," *Bulletin of the School of Oriental and African Studies* 21 (1958), 220-224.

17 "Giles catalogue," 4. For Timothy Richard and this text, see Francesca Tarocco, "Lost in Translation? The *Treatise on the Mahāyāna Awakening of Faith* (*Dasheng qixin lun*) and Its Modern Readings," *Bulletin of the School of Oriental and African Studies* 71 (2008), 323-343, at 334-336; for the Herbert Giles criticism of this translation, see Herbert Giles, *Adversaria Sinica* (Shanghai: Kelly and Walsh, 1914), 388 (H 786).

18 "Giles catalogue," Chinese section, 12. For a more accurate account of this pioneering concordance, see D. L. McMullen, *Concordances and Indexes to Chinese Texts* (San Francisco, CA: Chinese Materials Center, 1975), 8-9; Cai Tinggan (1861-1935) has an entry in Howard L. Boorman, *Biographical Dictionary of Republican China*, vol. 3 (New York, NY: Columbia University Press, 1971), 293a–295b. Of course, the Admiral may well have deliberately chosen a title conveying two different meanings.

19 Thus D. L. McMullen, in touching on Herbert Giles in "The Backhouse File: 'Glorious Veterans,' 'Sinologistes de Chambre,' and "Men of Science: Reflections on Professor Trevor Roper's Life of Sir Edmund Backhouse," *New Lugano Review* 1 (1979), 78-83. Cf. also Charles Aylmer's introduction to "The Memoirs of H. A. Giles," 6, where he is characterised as "a complex and contradictory person."

recorded in his library catalogue. To give one example, on the 1900 translation of R. K. Douglas (1838-1913) of the Chinese novel *The Fortunate Union* we read the manuscript comment "Only Ch. I published – fortunate-ly!"[20] Likewise we read on an offprint of a study by E. Denison Ross, "A Polyglot List of Birds in Turki, Manchu and Chinese" the comment "Packed with mistakes."[21] Such polemical remarks further extend to publications in Chinese, but only when they were produced by missionaries. Since Giles was the agnostic son of a clergyman who had been imprisoned for an infraction of ecclesiastical law and was furthermore obliged to make a living as a hack writer, this was a group that tended quite frequently to excite his irritation.[22] An 1890 Chinese version of the Gospel of Mark he records as "Griffith John's pretend translation with notes," while an 1887 New Testament is described as "Pretended translation by John Chalmers and Martin Schaub."[23] In two instances the annotation

[20] "Giles catalogue," 29, and note the strictures on Sir Robert's work in Aylmer, "Memoirs," 25 (on "a worthless and pretentious book") and 42. On the publications of Sir Robert Kennaway Douglas (1838-1913), one may consult Henri Cordier "Nécrologie: Robert Kennaway Douglas," *T'oung pao* 14 (1913), 287-290. Much has been written on *The Fortunate Union*, predominantly concerning the pioneering eighteenth and early nineteenth century translations into English, for example Kai-chong Cheung, "The *Haoqiu zhuan*, the First Chinese Novel Translated in Europe: With Special Reference to Percy's and Davis's Renditions," and James St. André, "Modern Translation Theory and Past Translation Practice: European Translations of the *Haoqiu zhuan*," in Leo Tak-hung Chan, ed., *One into Many: Translation and the Dissemination of Classical Chinese Literature* (Amsterdam: Rodopi, 2003), 29-37, 39-65, respectively.

[21] "Giles catalogue," 102. The offprint is listed as being from the *Memoirs of the Asiatic Society of Bengal* 2 (1909); it occupied pp. 253-340 and was reprinted separately in Calcutta by the Asiatic Society. Sir Edward Denison Ross (1871-1940) was the first Director of the School of Oriental and African Studies, University of London; obituaries by Sir Hamilton Gibb in the *Journal of the Royal Asiatic Society* 1 (1941), 49-52, and by Sir Ralph Turner in *Bulletin of the School of Oriental and African Studies* 10 (1942), 832-836, cover also his earlier career in India during which this work was produced (H 792).

[22] For the unfortunate ecclesiastical career of John Allen Giles (1808-1884), see John Minford and Tong Man, "Whose Strange Stories?" 2-3 (n. 2). For the conditions under which commercial writing was produced at this time in Britain, see Nigel Cross, *The Common Writer: Life in Nineteenth-Century Grub Street* (Cambridge: Cambridge University Press, 1988).

[23] "Giles catalogue," 15, 16 respectively. For what I take to be the translations concerned, see in the first case Hubert Spillett, *A Catalogue of Scriptures in the Languages of China and of the Republic of China* (London: British and Foreign Bible Society, 1975), 49, no. 241 and 51, no. 256, though the date of publication accords with neither; in the second case the reference seems to be to the item listed 39-40, no. 200, though again the date does not accord. Aylmer, "Memoirs," 29, shows that Giles published on Griffith John as a Bible translator in the missionary journal *The Chinese Recorder* 17 (1886), 260, after (as revealed at 23) touching generally on the topic of New Testament translation a few years earlier in the *China Review*; "Memoirs," 82, further places these remarks in a more general context by giving a brief account of the difficulties experienced by missionaries and indeed all Europeans in

provides precise references to the places in which Giles had published hostile reviews. The first concerns a 1913 partial rendering of the novel known later as *Monkey* or *Journey to the West*, namely Timothy Richard, *A Mission to Heaven*, to the catalogue entry on which is appended the manuscript annotation "For demolition of this Missionary Fraud, see *Adversaria Sinica*, pp. 387-426" – somewhat misleadingly, in that these two page numbers should be separated by a comma, not a hyphen. The second concerns the 1886 version of the course in Chinese by T. F. Wade and W. C. Hiller, *Tzŭ Êrh Chi: A Progressive Course in Colloquial Chinese*, the catalogue entry concerning which is followed by the sentence in manuscript "For demolition of the above, see *China Review*, vol. xvi, 248."

Both these reviewed works are dealt with also in his memoirs, in equally polemical terms, despite the fact that these remarks at least were clearly intended for wider circulation, if not formal publication.[24] Since the document in question in this case is designated 'Autobibliographical' at its start and seems to have been compiled in response to requests for some connected account of his numerous publications, it contains a great deal of further information on Giles as a reviewer, to say nothing of his reactions to reviews of his own work. The long span of literary activity it covers also gives a good if inevitably retrospective view of developments both in the career of its author and in the world in which he operated over more than half a century.

Giles had already started work before reaching China, publishing translations from Greek for a series edited by his father. But this seems to have reflected more than filial duty: he had evidently absorbed from his unfortunate father the imperative need to keep writing, and by 1871 was already producing critical remarks about missionary publications in a Shanghai newspaper, thereby incurring a warning from Sir Thomas Wade that he should "leave the missionaries alone" – an instruction which, needless to say, he ignored.[25] Unlike his father, he had not studied at any university, and had no formal academic qualifications, but a decent secondary education at Charterhouse, which before the Public Schools Act of 1868 had concentrated overwhelmingly

---

achieving even the beginnings of a good written style in Classical Chinese: here Giles cites his *Adversaria Sinica*, 379-381.

24 Wade's work with the assistance of the future Sir Walter Caine Hillier (1849-1927) is treated in Charles Aylmer, "Memoirs," 52-53; the second work by Richards to be savaged in print by Giles is noted on both 10 and 53, where it is described as "a scandalous exhibition of that dangerous mixture, zeal and ignorance." Sir Thomas Francis Wade, one time superior to Giles in China and his predecessor at Cambridge, is first touched upon in the "Memoirs" on 8; strictures on his command of Chinese follow also on 12 *et passim* (H 785, H 1408).

25 Aylmer, "Memoirs," 12-13.

on classical studies, had provided him with a certain basic scrupulousness concerning translation that found in China ample employment. Even today, for all the dictionaries and annotated translations produced over the past century and a half, Classical Chinese presents formidable problems, not simply to those educated outside China, but also for many native speakers of contemporary Chinese languages.[26] To be blunt, published mistranslations abound, and I am sure I have contributed my share. Reviewers who can offer improved translations thus provided and still provide a very necessary service to all their colleagues.

It is no wonder then that a keen eye for error kept Giles busy. Some of those attacked do seem to have fought back, and though in looking back he claims that he had made it his policy not to respond to such counter-attacks – even while he concedes "I have always carefully preserved press notices" – his own survey of his publications falsifies this assertion.[27] And there were plenty of outlets for his talents: in 1880, he claims, he "severed his connection with journalism," but perhaps this refers solely to newspapers, whereas on the China coast in the second half of the nineteenth century there were dozens of other periodicals that could provide a platform in English for the enthusiastic reviewer.[28] Many of these were often capable of adding Chinese characters to clarify matters of translation, and so afforded ample opportunity for vigorous debate on academic topics – while there were evidently not a few contributors besides Giles himself who were willing to plunge into controversy over things Chinese. This extraordinary hothouse for the first-hand study of China did produce along with a considerable amount of dross some truly remarkable work, most notably the early translations of James Legge (1815-1897), whose ultimate

---

26 For a good case study illustrating the difficulties encountered by translators into English and into Modern Standard Chinese of a short fourth century anecdote, see Rudolf Wagner, "Does This Make Sense? Reading Sinological Translations," in *Zurück zur Freude: Studien zur chinesischen Literatur und Lebenswelt und ihrer Rezeption in Ost und West: Festschrift für Wolfgang Kubin*, ed. Marc Hermann and Christian Schwermann, with Jari Grosse-Ruyken (Sankt Augustin: Steyler Verlag, 2007), 767-776. For the decline during the mid-twentieth century of a firm knowledge of Classical Chinese even in the few places where uninterrupted efforts were made to sustain it, see Frederick W. Mote, *China and the Vocation of History in the Twentieth Century: A Personal Memoir* (Princeton, NJ: Princeton University Press, 2010), 59-61.

27 Aylmer, "Memoirs," 14-15; cf. 36 for an example of a rejoinder and surrejoinder in a dispute between Sir James Haldane Stewart Lockhart (1858-1937) and himself.

28 Aylmer, "Memoirs," 22. For a listing of English-language publications that makes clear how many were active during the time that Giles was in China or thereafter, when he maintained his contacts in the area, see Kwang-Ching Liu, *Americans and Chinese: A Historical Essay and a Bibliography* (Cambridge, MA: Harvard University Press, 1963), 159-166.

colossal contribution to the Western understanding of the Chinese heritage has been justly honoured by a compendious study by Norman J. Girardot.[29]

The only conspicuously missing element was the presence of academics. Not a few of the participants in China coast scholarship were educated men, whether missionaries, consuls or other professionals, but they were not educators. The Orientalist persona was accordingly not conspicuous on the China Coast of the late nineteenth century; indeed, the meaning of 'Orientalist' was initially linked not to scholarship but to educational policy in colonial India, where a regard for local learning was so denominated in contrast to the demand that a purely British system of education should be imposed on all British subjects there.[30] The incorporation of Sinologists into the late nineteenth century Orientalist congresses of Europe brought them into the fold there, but in East Asia the institutions of higher learning that supported this development did not exist until the establishment of universities on the Western model in the early twentieth century. During that era, too, the handful of non-Chinese who pursued careers in Oriental studies in East Asia tended not to be run of the mill Western academics, but somewhat unusual individuals. The Estonian Baron Alexander von Staël-Holstein (1877-1937), who comes across as much as an aristocrat as a professor, affords a prominent example of this type.[31] Other visiting scholars of the Republican period in areas such as English language and literature might occasionally dabble in matters Chinese, but did not thereby assume an Orientalist persona at all: I. A. Richards (1893-1979), who published a study of Mencius, was one such visitor, but most steered well clear of Chinese interests in any case.[32] When Giles reached China there was perhaps a higher rate of involvement in studying China in the foreign community, but it was a study pursued erratically, if sometimes ardently, as an avocation by those with other reasons for being in the region. The missionary philologist Joseph Edkins (1823-1905) represents the type of learning that the young

---

29   On the overall environment in which Legge operated at this stage, see Norman J. Girardot, *The Victorian Translation of China: James Legge's Oriental Pilgrimage* (Berkeley, CA: University of California Press, 2002), 144-145. For studies of Legge providing a closer focus on translation matters, the many publications of Lauren F. Pfister should also be consulted.

30   For the shifting meaning of "Orientalism" in Britain, see Arberry, *British Orientalists*, 8; for the debate on India, see, *The Great Indian Education Debate: Documents Relating to the Orientalist-Anglicist Controversy, 1781-1843*, ed. Lynn Zastoupil and Martin Moir (Richmond: Curzon Press, 1999).

31   This is made clear by Wang Qilong and Deng Xiaoyong, *The Academic Knight Between East and West: A Biography of Alexander von Staël-Holstein* (Singapore: Gale Asia, 2014).

32   Rodney Koeneke, *Empires of the Mind: I. A. Richards and Basic English in China, 1929-1979* (Stanford, CA: Stanford University Press, 2004).

Giles would have encountered on his arrival in China.[33] Edkins seems to have preferred scholarly pursuits to venturing forth to convert the heathen on the streets of China's villages, but his status was always that of a minister of the gospel. Giles for his part arrived as and remained throughout his formative years in East Asia a consular official: the Orientalist persona was just not available to him as something to aspire to at this point.

Admittedly it would be unfair to damn the sometimes quite impressive though very uneven Anglophone scholarship of this time and place as solely amateur, especially when some contributors to the controversies of the age could clearly speak Chinese of some variety quite well. Others may have dealt with the locals through converts or compradors, but these local intermediaries were not subalterns in the same sense as in South Asia, in that the late Qing Chinese state, however beleaguered and however much subject to impatient ridicule and even contempt from foreigners, still had to be taken seriously. Nonetheless, the lack of any connection in China Coast sinological publications with institutions committed to carrying forward research and education on a continuing basis does deprive the undoubted erudition on display in these sources of any sense of goals to be achieved, or of any collective future to be worked towards.

But though the rumbustious sinological scene of the treaty ports, replete with the scholarly equivalents of the gunslingers of the contemporary Wild West, gave Giles ample opportunity to display his learning, he also had another card to play. As a published author even before he reached East Asia, he already had contacts with the insatiable metropolitan world of writing for mass (though not exactly popular) consumption in which his father labored. This meant that he was able to start producing work for the home market, with a collection of his earlier journalism appearing as a result of a period of leave in London in 1875.[34] After his return to China further articles and eventually books published in Britain followed, so that he was now rewarded by reviews of his work by literary figures of the day, including one of his 1888 *Chuang Tzŭ* by none other than Oscar Wilde (1854-1900), which Giles characterises as "written in his most racy style" – so stylishly written, in fact, that it was republished in 1997 as an independent slim volume.[35]

Yet despite this metropolitan literary success, his reviewing still continued unabated in the China coast press, where his linguistic expertise could be put

---

[33] Benjamin Penny, "More than One Adam? Revelation and Philology in Nineteenth-Century China," *Humanities Research* 14 (2007), 31-50.
[34] See Aylmer, "Memoirs," 16, for his *Chinese Sketches*.
[35] Oscar Wilde, *A Chinese Sage* (Dublin: Mermaid Turbulence, 1997), originally published in *The Speaker* (8 February 1890).

on display, even if echoes of his work there did on occasion reach Britain, or at least Oxford. Here Legge had become Professor of Chinese in 1876 and found himself in his work on the *Daode jing* bedevilled by voices from afar criticising his acceptance of the then current Chinese view of its authorship. In this assault on Legge's scholarship Giles was joined by another non-missionary reviewer in Shanghai, Thomas W. Kingsmill (1837-1910); the whole episode, which admirably illustrates the reviewing practices of this time and place, is well described in Norman Girardot's work on Legge, so a detailed account is not provided here.[36] Kingsmill and Giles do not seem to have collaborated under normal circumstances, but equally appear to have refrained – regardless of their common and apparently notorious pugnacity – from attacking each other, possibly (though this needs to be further documented) because they were both Freemasons.[37] But removal from the lively Chinese scene seems to have posed something of a problem for Giles after his resignation from the consular service in 1893, and subsequent permanent return to the United Kingdom, for he continued to send back reviews for printing in Hong Kong or Shanghai.[38]

One might have expected Giles to contribute to Britain's only established Orientalist serial of the nineteenth century, the *Journal of the Royal Asiatic Society*, which could print Chinese characters if necessary, but here there were evidently problems. Only from 1886 had the journal started to publish book notices, and indeed his own East Asian work was soon noted, but lengthier reviews discussing points of translation from Chinese appear to have remained beyond its scope for a good while longer.[39] Giles seems furthermore to have been put off by an unhelpful experience with the society, since in 1888 while back in Europe he had undertaken to correct the proofs of a Chinese library catalogue originally compiled for them by Henry F. Holt (d. u.), the former vice-consul who had served as a librarian, but though this was published in

---

36 Girardot, *Victorian Translation,* 425-446. Note James Legge, *Texts of Taoism,* vol. 1 (Oxford: Oxford University Press, 1891), 4, and cf. Aylmer, "Memoirs," 28-29.
37 See for a photograph of Kingsmill in Masonic garb Wolfgang Behr, "Kingsmill's *Shijing* 'Translations' into Sanskrit and the Idea of 'Congenial Languages' at the End of the Nineteenth Century" in *Sinologists as Translators in the Seventeenth to Nineteenth Centuries,* ed. Lawrence Wen-chi Wong and Bernhard Fuehrer (Hong Kong: Chinese University of Hong Kong, 2015), 307-354, 309; note also the reference to his disputatiousness in his obituary, also cited here, 308. For Giles as a freemason, see Aylmer, "Memoirs," 22.
38 For example, the review of Lockhart, mentioned above, note 16.
39 The new policy of providing "Notes of the Quarter" is introduced in *Journal of the Royal Asiatic Society* 18 (1886), 462; the work by Giles on the *Daode jing* in the *China Review* 16 (1886) of Hong Kong cited by Legge (see preceding note), is mentioned subsequently in this volume, 563.

1890 in the *Journal*, he had received neither thanks nor a copy of the work.[40] On top of this the Society had failed to order a copy of his 1892 dictionary, which prompted him to conclude that "the Society, nominally Asiatic, was really Indian in its sympathies, and had very rarely done anything for the advancement of Chinese studies."[41]

Though this situation changed after three decades, none of the reviews discussed so far appeared in Britain, and indeed after his favourite platform, the *China Review*, closed in 1901, he took the unusual step of cumulating his observations in short pieces separately published in Shanghai into one volume, under the series title *Adversaria Sinica*, thus effectively creating his own occasional periodical for reviewing purposes. Only in 1922 did the award of its triennial medal by the Royal Asiatic Society ensure that all was forgiven, if not forgotten, and in the following year he accepted an invitation from their journal to review *The Philosophy of Human Nature* by the missionary scholar J. Percy Bruce (1861-1934), after a few months earlier reviewing the pioneering sociological history of Chinese religion by Marcel Granet (1884-1940) for *Man*, the journal of the Royal Anthropological Institute.[42] But both these reviews are curiously muted, as if Giles did not know quite how to behave in print in such unfamiliar surroundings – the Bruce review quotes a substantial extract verbatim, perhaps feeling that anyone confronted with the author's rather odd translation choices would draw their own conclusions, while the review in *Man* misses entirely the originality of the analysis, affirming only "He has drawn upon the researches and translations of previous writers, marshalling lucidly facts already known, without adding any new ones."[43] The fact that Granet's *La Religion des Chinois* was in due course to be seen as so significant an advance that the distinguished social anthropologist Maurice Freedman (1920-1975) produced a full translation with an introduction – to say nothing of more recent renderings by others into Chinese, Japanese, and Indonesian – could not possibly be guessed at from the faint praise offered by Giles.[44]

Meanwhile, however, one last wrangle had taken place that had been published on the other side of the world. In 1917 the missionary scholar Samuel Couling (1859-1922) had printed in his *Encyclopedia Sinica* what must have been to its subject a most gratifying description of Giles as "one of the foremost of sinologues," noting "He has always been a keen controversialist, and has

---

40   Aylmer, "Memoirs," 31.
41   Ibid., 33.
42   Ibid., 71-72.
43   The reviews are in *Journal of the Royal Asiatic Society* 54 (1923), 103-104, and *Man* 82-83 (1922), 144 (H 388, 556).
44   Maurice Freedman, *The Religion of the Chinese People* (Oxford: Basil Blackwell, 1975).

dealt ruthlessly with all that he considered false scholarship in Chinese studies."[45] The following year a collective review of this reference work appeared in the *Bulletin of the School of Oriental Studies*, in which the entries on poetry (by Mrs. Couling) and painting (by Florence Ayscough) were treated by Arthur Waley (1889-1966), in his first publication as a reviewer.[46] The same issue of the *Bulletin* also contains some translations of prose and poetry by Waley, who had already published two groups of poems in the first issue of the new journal the year before.[47] But in 1918 he already published some remarks on the prosody of Chinese verse in the *Journal of the Royal Asiatic Society*, and in this piece he took Giles to task, among others, for some over-categorical statements on the topic.[48] A passing correction of Giles on prosody in fact appears in his first volume of his own translations in the same year, though this is balanced by a description of the older man's "wonderful dexterity" as a translator.[49] Yet this was but a mere cloud no bigger than a man's hand compared with the storm to come. The Giles "Memoirs" state that in 1918 Waley had responded politely enough in print to a review of these *170 Chinese Poems* by Giles in *The Cambridge Review*, but had revealed to him and all readers of that review that a Japanese scholar had backed his interpretation of a disputed passage and had been very critical of Giles as a translator.[50]

Giles had in fact opened his initial review of Waley civilly enough: "Mr. Arthur Waley may be congratulated upon the production of a very interesting

---

45 Samuel Couling, with an introduction by H. J. Lethbridge, *The Encyclopedia Sinica* (Hong Kong: Oxford University Press, 1983), 205. The introduction to this republication provides as much information as may readily be gleaned concerning Couling's career.

46 A. Waley, Z. L. Yih, and Sir Denison Ross, "*Encyclopedia Sinica,* by S. Couling," *Bulletin of the School of Oriental Studies* [1] (1918), 142-146, at 144-145. Ross must have come to know Waley during their overlap at the British Museum, Department of Prints and Drawings, at the start of the war; cf. Turner, "Obituary," 833. For Florence Ayscough (1875-1942), see Lindsay Shen, *Knowledge is Pleasure: Florence Ayscough in Shanghai* (Hong Kong: Hong Kong University Press, 2012). Couling had taken the very wise precaution of adding many corrections by Pelliot to the final pages of his work, 631-633, as well as soliciting an article from him (298-301), measures which do not seem to have been sufficient to attract a listing in the Walravens bibliography of his publications cited below, but at least forestalled an extended critical review.

47 For these translations as listed in a bibliography of Waley that, excluding only some short unsigned pieces and accidental omissions (see below), allows his career both as a translator and as a reviewer to be traced chronologically, see Francis A. Johns, *A Bibliography of Arthur Waley, Revised and Expanded* (London: Athlone Press, 1988), 77. The *Bulletin* piece of 1918 mentions a publication by Giles in passing, without comment.

48 See Arthur Waley, "Notes on Chinese Prosody," *Journal of the Royal Asiatic Society* 50 (1918), 249-261, at 255-256.

49 Arthur Waley, *170 Chinese Poems* (London: Constable, 1918), 11, 21.

50 Aylmer, "Memoirs," 60.

volume, which it is to be hoped will lead him on to further incursions into the illimitable field of Chinese literature. It may be said at once that the mere attempt to translate 170 Chinese poems is in itself no mean achievement." He then goes on to criticize the translation by Waley of one of the celebrated "Nineteen Old Poems," though to be honest, in the first case he raises, Waley is clearly right, and Giles is wrong.[51] The response in fact shows that at this point Waley was rather unsure of his understanding of the poem, but also that this was not going to stop him from driving home the one advantage he had over his moderately eminent Victorian critic: "SIR – In making his notes on my book Professor Giles should not have forgotten the possibility of alternative readings. Thus in l. 10 of the poem with which he deals he is translating a different text." In fact, it seems to have been the same text that Giles misunderstood. But Waley goes on:

> My interpretation both of the general meaning of the poem and of most of the passages disputed by the reviewer is confirmed by Mr. Katsura in his *Rekidai Kanshi Hy shaku*, which came into my hands after I had made my version. This Japanese scholar, by the way, complains in his introduction that on reading Professor Giles's "Chinese Literature," "Sono go-yaku no hanahada shiku ōki ni odorokeri," "I was amazed at the large number of mistranslations." But perhaps my reviewer would have a like opinion of Mr. Katsura's anthology.[52]

Waley must have known that this meant trouble, especially since he probably knew that Giles had no time for Japanese scholars anyhow.[53] Giles, to judge from his "Memoirs," thought that his 1905 publication on "Japan's Debt to China" had offended contemporary notions of Japanese uniqueness, but in any case his Royal Asiatic Society catalogue shows not the faintest compunction about misunderstanding the Japanese language anyhow. It is also significant that by contrast Waley's boss at the British Museum, Laurence Binyon (1869-1943), was in the habit of employing young educated Japanese at three shillings

---

51 Herbert Giles, "Chinese Poetry," *The Cambridge Review* 40, no. 986 (22 November 1918), 130-131 (cf. H. 897, "With a pencilled translation by Professor Giles").

52 Arthur Waley, "A Hundred and Seventy Chinese Poems," *The Cambridge Review* 40, no. 988 (6 December 1918), 162; the publishers of this periodical missed out one Japanese vowel with a macron above it, so the Japanese book title is somewhat mangled. This riposte by Waley is not listed in Johns, *Bibliography of Arthur Waley,* as far as I can see. The Japanese scholar Katsura Isoo 桂五十郎 (1868-1938) did publish a *Rekidai kanshi hyōshaku* 歷代漢詩評釈 [Chinese Poetry through the Ages, with Evaluations and Explanations] in 1910, but I have not had a copy to hand.

53 Aylmer, "Memoirs," 60, 45.

an hour to help out with reading East Asian texts, and no doubt this encouraged him to look to such assistance too.[54]

But although Lytton Strachey (1880-1932) had given a positive review to Giles in 1908, suggesting that Waley might have first heard good opinions of Chinese poetry from Bloomsbury acquaintances, allowing an "eminent Victorian" to go unchallenged would have assured him no credibility anywhere near Gordon Square. An old-fashioned sinological shootout was inevitable, and fortunately Samuel Couling had just started to publish in Hong Kong *The New China Review*, an ideal arena for this high noon duel. The scene unfolds in the Giles "Memoirs": first, in 1919, he sends off some translations with notes and alternative translations from Waley's *170 Chinese Poems*; in 1920 he adds another translation responding to one in Waley's 1919 *More Chinese Poems*; in May of that year he receives offprints of the first piece and sends one to Waley, who responds civilly; in July proofs of the second piece arrive, which when published "excited the anger of Mr. Waley so much that he rushed wildly into what he must have imagined would be a crusher for me. It was, in fact, an *imbelle telum*, and was easily disposed of in a reply by me." A further contribution from Waley "changed from defence to attack and tried to maul me" over a translation Giles had produced in 1884; naturally Giles responded, with – at least in his own retrospective – the implication "another one bites the dust."[55] This would have been premature: many years later, in 1970, Waley's friends posthumously published his second piece in an anthology of his work, with the passages from the work of Giles criticised therein, but without the response, thus promoting the immortality of the supposed victim: for posterity, Waley's Parthian shot "it is from a very glassy house indeed that my critic has hurled his courteous and learned stones" has thus become the last word on the matter.[56]

In 1922 it was Couling who actually died, and the *New China Review* went with him. Waley, however, still had the *Bulletin* at his disposal, and was therefore quick to follow up in 1922 with a couple of pages, published in Finsbury Circus but replete with Chinese characters, criticising another old Giles translation.[57] Further criticism of Giles may be found in the following year in Waley's

---

[54] Cf. my review of John Hatcher, *Laurence Binyon: Poet, Scholar of East and West, Bulletin of the School of Oriental and African Studies* 60 (1997), 398-399.

[55] Aylmer, "Memoirs," 60-63.

[56] Ivan Morris, ed., *Madly Singing in the Mountains: An Appreciation and Anthology of Arthur Waley* (London: George Allen & Unwin, 1970), 297-305, at 302; the earlier article on prosody that had criticised Giles also appears here, 284-294.

[57] Arthur Waley, "The Everlasting Wrong," *Bulletin of the School of Oriental Studies* 2 (1922), 343-344.

Introduction to the Study of Chinese Painting.[58] Unfortunately, the prolific Giles, though by no means a bad translator, had left plenty of hostages to fortune, and Waley if provoked, no doubt could have rounded up and butchered them all indefinitely at his leisure.[59] Rather than try to prolong the struggle, Giles had to content himself with one lengthy last review published in China in which he was able to use all his old skills on an unfortunate Japanese translator into English.[60]

In fact, he had long known that the game was up. His intellectual formation in the study of China went back after all to pre-academic times. These had existed in continental Europe itself long ago, at the very start of the nineteenth century, when, as Sir George Sansom (1883-1965) remarks of the warring scholars of this period "So frightful was the *Furor Sinologicus*, so violent were their quarrels and complaints, that they are said to have been more alarming to Napoleon than a charge of ten thousand Cossacks."[61] But in mainland Europe the establishment of professorships of Chinese in time quietened down the situation considerably, even if not without some bouts of atavistic behaviour, though the technical problems of producing specialist periodicals regularly incorporating Chinese characters delayed the arrival of the academic review in the field until much later.[62] Even so in 1890 the *T'oung pao* was launched, and from its start classic sinological reviews discussing translation problems in detail became possible in Europe.[63] In 1900 the establishment of a French academic institution in Hanoi meant that it was possible to set up another

---

58   Arthur Waley, *An Introduction to the Study of Chinese Painting* (London: Ernest Benn Limited, 1923), 185-186.
59   For an illuminating study of Giles as a translator that Charles Aylmer summarizes aptly as "a partial rehabilitation" ("Memoirs," 7), see David E. Pollard, "H. A. Giles and his Translations," in *Europe Studies China: Papers from an International Conference on the History of European Sinology,* ed. Ming Wilson and John Cayley, (London: Han-Shan Tang Books, 1995), 492-512, and note that this is based on prose translations by Giles – his belief that verse translations should be tortured into rhyme make his renditions of Chinese poetry all too easy a target.
60   Aylmer, "Memoirs," 77.
61   George Sansom, "Address Delivered by Sir George Sansom at the Annual Ceremony 1956," *Journal of Asian Studies* 24 (1965), 563-567, at 564. The main upholder of earlier traditions of combativeness into the latter part of the century was Stanislas Julien (1797-1873): note Girardot, *Victorian Translation*, 524-525 and n. 78, 715-716.
62   On this problem note Georg Lehner, *Der Druck chinesischen Zeichen in Europa: Entwicklungen im 19. Jahrhundert* (Wiesbaden: Harrasowitz, 2004).
63   Girardot, *Victorian Translation,* 460, sees this as the start of a new era of "French-Continental" dominance of the field; this may be somewhat unfair to Dutch sinology, which had already combined first-hand knowledge of Asia with a concern for academic professionalism.

periodical in East Asia, too, that was very different in its ethos from any of the China coast publications used by Giles.

It was in this organ that Pelliot was able to establish his reputation, and Giles readily acknowledged that in a collective environment, especially one that included East Asian scholars also, his French colleague was able to achieve far higher standards than a lone scholar stuck in Cambridge. He excuses his failure, pointed out as he says "very properly and justly" by Pelliot, to go back to original sources rather than just rely on later compilations by explaining "for the past twenty years I have had to work entirely single-handed, with no Chinese literate to help in hunting up phrases."[64] He was even happy to extend to the Frenchman's scholarship the term he usually reserved for his own reviews, namely "demolition."[65] And he must have known, too, that the prospects of the British ever setting up any similar institution to the French school in East Asia were absolutely nil. The University of Hong Kong came into being in his lifetime, but rather than risk allowing Chinese students to develop any dangerous ideas, it concentrated on STEM subjects (Science, Technology, Engineering and Medicine); when Chinese studies were introduced, the aim was again to shore up an adherence to traditional values amongst the colonial population rather than to educate any Europeans.[66]

Giles was the product of the heroic age of the study of China, an age when glorious and glorifying single combat was the norm, even if he was not without a degree of discretion.[67] Anyone who persisted in such an approach into the

---

[64] See in particular Giles, *Adversaria Sinica*, 389. Hartmut Walravens, *Paul Pelliot (1878-1945): His Life and Works – a Bibliography* (Bloomington, IN: Indiana University Research Institute for Inner Asian Studies, 2001), 1-21 shows that in less than ten years Pelliot, based in Hanoi, published almost one hundred reviews in the *Bulletin de l'Ecole française d'Extrême-Orient*. On Pelliot it is possible to consult *Paul Pelliot: de l'histoire à la légende*, ed. Jean-Pierre Drège and Michel Zink (Paris: Académie des Inscriptions et Belles-Lettres, 2013); especially relevant for this period is Yves Goudineau, "Paul Pelliot, franc-tireur de l'école Française d'extrême-orient," 21 Pelliot 28. I recall hearing in my youth the allegation relayed that Pelliot employed Vietnamese to hunt up his phrases, but the source of this rumour implied that this was down to jealousy and did not endorse the idea.

[65] Giles, *Adversaria Sinica*, 437.

[66] On the foundation of the University of Hong Kong, see Frank Welsh, *A History of Hong Kong* (London: HarperCollins, 1997), 355-359; for Chinese studies there, see the biographies of Chow Shouson (1861-1959) and Sir Cecil Clementi (1875-1947) in *Dictionary of Hong Kong Biography,* ed. May Holdsworth and Christopher Munn, (Hong Kong: Hong Kong University Press, 2012), 98, 104, respectively.

[67] Cf. Girardot, *Victorian Translation,* 382-394, on an episode of "Ritual Combat" and *Odium Sinologicum* concerning the supposed Babylonian connections of early China that Giles seems to have stayed out of, since it did not suit his own linguistic talents in reading Chinese.

twentieth century knew what the consequences would be: academic editors would not allow old-fashioned warriors to rant across their pages, and the only alternative was journals without Chinese characters or with rather limited circulations.[68] But this was not simply a matter of academic life reaching or at least striving for a more civilised tone. The use to which reviews were put had also changed. For, by contrast with Giles, Pelliot's reviews, if often equally heroic in spirit, actually presuppose a very different context, a context in which they will be read and learned from by students of Sinology in the French and other institutions in which they were then being trained – indeed, though the practice of reading old reviews is not currently encouraged by most teachers of Sinology, there is much that can be learned from such publications from the pen of a master like Pelliot even today. Giles, with his *ad hominem* flourishes, is not aiming at a student readership; sometimes his pieces come across as little more than self-assertion, even if his criticisms are often justified. A professional Orientalist may not have students, but surely his or her ambition was and is that they should write works from which others will learn. Indeed, the very idea of a journal run by educators such as the *T'oung pao* was of an ongoing, collaborative venture dedicated to the development of a field of study. Giles was never involved in such a project, and the journals in which he published for the greater part of his career were not run by academics either.

To some extent, it must be admitted, an Orientalist persona was at a certain point thrust upon him by posterity, a posterity which could point to the many academic distinctions conferred upon him and to his prizewinning compilations such as his *Chinese–English Dictionary* and his *Chinese Biographical Dictionary*.[69] These books have, however, not stood the test of time too well, and were arguably fortunate to benefit from the trend towards the comparative dominance of Anglophone publishing on China that asserted itself in the early twentieth century despite the technical superiority of contemporary French-language scholarship, which by contrast possibly saw its influence limited by its relative isolation from China's chaotic post-imperial progress.[70] A more considered judgment would be that by comparison with standards established

---

68 This was the fate of Erwin Ritter von Zach (1872-1942) at the hands of Pelliot in his role as editor of *T'oung pao*, see David B. Honey, *Incense at the Altar: Pioneering Sinologists and the Development of Classical Chinese Philology* (New Haven, CT: American Oriental Society, 2001), 80, 146-148.
69 Arberry, *British Orientalists*, 46.
70 This at any rate would seem to be the argument concerning academic Sinology in France during China's late imperial and Republican period propounded by Jean Chesneaux, "China in the Eyes of French Intellectuals," *East Asian History* 12 (1996), 51-64.

elsewhere the taint of amateurism took some time to be removed from British Sinology – until a point a few years after the death of Herbert Giles, in fact.[71]

But if Giles does not exhibit the persona of the professional Orientalist, at least he shows what it was not. For as noted at the outset, this essay agrees with John Minford and Tong Man that he was actually trying to be something other than an academic, because perhaps he saw that unless the study of the Chinese tradition gained more prestige in the wider intellectual life of his homeland it was unlikely that he would attract many students other than those with immediate practical purposes in learning the language for the furtherance of trade, diplomacy, or evangelism. Even if in our own retrospective view a somewhat inadequate professor is all he was, and his literary pretensions seem slightly absurd, his efforts as an author and as a reviewer do make sense.

Certainly a case can be made for seeing the changes in the appreciation in Chinese art and literature that took place in Britain (or at least in Bloomsbury) in the early part of the twentieth century as being sparked at least in part by his determined assault upon the literary world of the United Kingdom, even he was probably unaware of it at the time, and he probably would not have recognised the consequences as in any way congenial. For in fact though Ezra Pound (1885-1972) soon took a very different direction, his first contacts with Chinese poetry seem to have been through translations by Giles, while the career of Laurence Binyon (1869-1943) as a very influential interpreter of East Asian art was also substantially advanced through an early collaboration with Giles too.[72]

True, Giles perhaps did not advance his cause sufficiently through such opportunities for teaching as did present themselves. Plainly due to his shortcomings as a scholar he certainly had nothing to offer the most gifted potential student he probably ever met, the remarkable Russian V. M. Alekseev (1881-1951).[73] In fact he had but two students who made any academic impact. Ethel John Lindgren-Utsi (1905-1988) became an anthropologist of the Mongols, on whom she published, and with her second husband, Mikel Utsi, helped introduce reindeer to Scotland.[74] And his most notorious though unofficial student, Sir Edmund Trelawny Backhouse (1873-1944), the famous fraudster and forger, did help revise a small dictionary, with the future Sir Sidney Barton

---

71   Twitchett, *Land Tenure and the Social Order*, 10-12.
72   For Giles and Ezra Pound, see Anne Witchard, *Lao She in London* (Hong Kong: Hong Kong University Press, 2012), 41-42; for Binyon, see John Hatcher, *Laurence Binyon: Poet, Scholar of East and West* (Oxford: Clarendon Press, 1995), 168.
73   For Giles and Alekseev, see Christoph Harbsmeier, "Vasilii Mikhailovich Alekseev and Russian Sinology," *T'oung Pao* 97 (2011), 344-370, at 362.
74   Information courtesy of Lucy Cavendish College, Cambridge.

(1876-1946).[75] But as a model of persistence in adversity, a relentless advocate of the study of China at the university level who saw at that level virtually no rewards for his efforts, and understood well enough that the problem in fact lay with the indifference to alien cultures that pervaded and still pervades British society, his own inadequacies seem less important. Insofar as he knew what had to be done and knew the task was beyond his lone efforts, yet he carried on publishing even so, Herbert Allen Giles cannot be faulted.

And in truth, what had to be done remains a work very much in progress. While perhaps after their repeated skirmishes he tacitly ceded supremacy to Arthur Waley, Giles did live long enough to see selections from both their poetry translations published in China in 1934.[76] Together they had at least put the heritage of Chinese literature on the map in English. Yet their successors in the post-war period, men like A. C. Graham (1919-1991) and David Hawkes (1923-2009), though unlike them academically trained in Sinology, initially came to the study of East Asia through military language training during the Second World War, not through reading the publications of these pioneers. And despite the regular appearance of translations of contemporary Chinese literature from British publishers, this post-war generation of translators working with Classical Chinese have had no successors in the United Kingdom. In the Anglophone world it is principally translators in the United States that have promoted an understanding of China through its literary traditions. Though the foregoing remarks may have exposed some of his limitations, writing off Giles in his homeland is certainly still not something we can afford to do.

Bibliography

Arberry, A.J. *British Orientalists*. London: William Collins, 1943.

Aylmer, Charles. "The Memoirs of H. A. Giles," *East Asian History* 13/14 (1997): 1-90.

Barnes, Linda L. *Needles, Herbs, Gods, and Ghosts*. Cambridge, MA: Harvard University Press, 2005.

Barrett, T. H. "John Hatcher, Laurence Binyon: Poet, Scholar of East and West." *Bulletin of the School of Oriental and African Studies* 60 (1997): 398-399.

---

[75] Sir Walter Hillier, *An English-Chinese Dictionary of the Peking Colloquial,* new ed. (Shanghai: Kwang Hsüeh, and London: Kegan, Paul, Trench, Trübner, 1933) – the original preface, reproduced here, is dated 1918. Not all of the vocabulary of this dictionary was absorbed into later and larger works, like that of R. H. Mathews. For Giles and his view of Backhouse, see Aylmer, "Memoirs," 37-39.

[76] Johns, *Bibliography of Arthur Waley,* 48.

Behr, Wolfgang. "Kingsmill's *Shijing* 'Translations' into Sanskrit and the Idea of 'Congenial Languages' at the End of the Nineteenth Century." in *Sinologists as Translators in the Seventeenth to Nineteenth Centuries*, edited by Lawrence Wen-chi Wong and Bernhard Fuehrer. Hong Kong: Chinese University of Hong Kong, 2015, 307-354.

Boorman, Howard L. *Biographical Dictionary of Republican China*, vol. 3. New York, NY: Columbia University Press, 1971.

Bosworth, Edmund, ed. *A Century of British Orientalists, 1902-2001*. Oxford: Oxford University Press for the British Academy, 2001.

Chen, Li. *Chinese Law in Imperial Eyes: Sovereignty, Justice, and Transcultural Politics*. New York, NY: Columbia University Press, 2016.

Chesneaux, Jean. "China in the Eyes of French Intellectuals." *East Asian History* 12 (1996): 51-64.

Cheung, Kai-chong. "The *Haoqiu zhuan*, the First Chinese Novel Translated in Europe: With Special Reference to Percy's and Davis's Renditions." In *One into Many: Translation and the Dissemination of Classical Chinese Literature*, edited by Leo Tak-hung Chan, 29-37. Amsterdam: Rodopi, 2003.

Cordier, Henri. "Nécrologie: Robert Kennaway Douglas." *T'oung pao* 14 (1913): 287-290.

Cross, Nigel. *The Common Writer: Life in Nineteenth-Century Grub Street*. Cambridge: Cambridge University Press, 1988.

Couling, Samuel, with an introduction by H. J. Lethbridge. *The Encyclopedia Sinica*. Hong Kong: Oxford University Press, 1983.

Daily, Christopher A. *Robert Morrison and the Protestant Plan for China*. Hong Kong: Hong Kong University Press, 2013.

Drège, Jean-Pierre and Michel Zink (eds.). *Paul Pelliot: de l'histoire à la légende*. Paris: Académie des Inscriptions et Belles-Lettres, 2013.

Freedman, Maurice. *The Religion of the Chinese People*. Oxford: Basil Blackwell, 1975.

Gibb, Hamilton. "Edward Denison Ross, 1871-1940." *Journal of the Royal Asiatic Society* 1 (1941): 49-52.

Giles, Herbert. *Adversaria Sinica*. Shanghai: Kelly and Walsh, 1914.

Giles, Herbert. "Chinese Poetry." *The Cambridge Review* 40, no. 986 (22 November 1918): 130 Giles, Herbert 131.

Girardot, Norman J. *The Victorian Translation of China: James Legge's Oriental Pilgrimage*. Berkeley, CA: University of California Press, 2002.

Holdsworth, May and Christopher Munn (eds.). *Dictionary of Hong Kong Biography*. Hong Kong: Hong Kong University Press, 2012.

Harbsmeier, Christoph. "Vasilii Mikhailovich Alekseev and Russian Sinology." *T'oung Pao* 97 (2011), 344-370.

Hatcher, John. *Laurence Binyon: Poet, Scholar of East and West*. Oxford: Clarendon Press, 1995.

Honey, David B. *Incense at the Altar: Pioneering Sinologists and the Development of Classical Chinese Philology*. New Haven, CT: American Oriental Society, 2001.

Jenkinson, Matt. "Nathaniel Vincent and Confucius's 'Great Learning' in Restoration England." *Notes and Records of the Royal Society* 60 (2006): 35-47.

Johns, Francis A. *A Bibliography of Arthur Waley, Revised and Expanded*. London: Athlone Press, 1988.

Jones, David Martin. *The Image of China in Western Social and Political Thought*. New York, NY: Palgrave, 2001.

Kitson, Peter. *Forging Romantic China: Sino-British Cultural Exchange 1760-1840*. Cambridge: Cambridge University Press, 2013.

Koeneke, Rodney. *Empires of the Mind: I. A. Richards and Basic English in China, 1929-1979*. Stanford: Stanford University Press, 2004.

Koss, Nicholas. "Matteo Ricci on China via Samuel Purchas: Faithful Re-Presentation." In *Western Visions of the Far East in a Transpacific Age, 1522-1657*, edited by Christina H. Lee, 85-100. Farnham: Ashgate, 2012.

Kow, Simon. *China in Early Enlightenment Political Thought*. Abingdon: Routledge, 2017.

Lach, Donald F. *Asia in the Making of Europe, Volume I: The Century of Discovery*. Chicago: University of Chicago Press, 1965.

Legge, James. *Texts of Taoism*, vol. 1. Oxford: Oxford University Press, 1891.

Lehner, Georg. *Der Druck chinesischen Zeichen in Europa. Entwicklungen im 19. Jahrhundert*. Wiesbaden: Harrasowitz, 2004.

Liu, Kwang-Ching. *Americans and Chinese: A Historical Essay and a Bibliography*. Cambridge, MA: Harvard University Press, 1963.

Luca, Dinu. *The Chinese Language in European Texts: The Early Period*. New York, NY: Palgrave Macmillan, 2016.

McMullen, D. L. *Concordances and Indexes to Chinese Texts*. San Francisco, CA: Chinese Materials Center, 1975.

McMullen, D. L. "The Backhouse File: 'Glorious Veterans,' 'Sinologistes de Chambre,' and Men of Science: Reflections on Professor Trevor Roper's Life of Sir Edmund Backhouse," *New Lugano Review* 1 (1979): 78-83.

Mills, C. Wright. *The Sociological Imagination*. Oxford: Oxford University Press, 1959.

Minford, John. "Lionel Giles: Sinology Old and New." *China Heritage Quarterly* 13 (March, 2008), online at <http://www.chinaheritagequarterly.org/articles.php?searchterm=013_giles.inc&issue=013> (last accessed 28 January 2019).

Minford, John and Tong Man. "Whose Strange Stories? P'u Sung-ling (1640-1715), Herbert Giles (1845-1935) and the *Liao-chai chih-yi*." *East Asian History* 17/18 (1999): 1-48.

Morris, Ivan, ed. *Madly Singing in the Mountains: An Appreciation and Anthology of Arthur Waley*. London: George Allen & Unwin, 1970.

Mote, Frederick W. *China and the Vocation of History in the Twentieth Century: A Personal Memoir*. Princeton, NJ: Princeton University Press, 2010.

Mungello, David. E. *Curious Land: Jesuit Accommodation and the Origins of Sinology*. Honolulu, HI: University of Hawai'i Press, 1989.

Nash, Paul. "The Idea of China in British Literature, 1757 to 1785." PhD thesis, University of Edinburgh, 2013.

Neill, Stephen. *A History of Christian Missions*, 2nd ed. London: Penguin Books, 1990.

Penny, Benjamin. "More than One Adam? Revelation and Philology in Nineteenth-Century China." *Humanities Research* 14 (2007): 31-50.

Pollard, David E. "H. A. Giles and his Translations." In *Europe Studies China: Papers from an International Conference on the History of European Sinology,* edited by Ming Wilson and John Cayley, 492-512. London: Han-Shan Tang Books, 1995.

Quennell, Peter, ed. *Memoirs of William Hickey*. London: Routledge & Kegan Paul, 1975.

Sansom, George. "Address Delivered by Sir George Sansom at the Annual Ceremony 1956." *Journal of Asian Studies* 24 (1965): 563-567.

Shen, Lindsay. *Knowledge is Pleasure: Florence Ayscough in Shanghai*. Hong Kong: Hong Kong University Press, 2012.

Simon, W. "Obituary: Evangeline Dora Edwards." *Bulletin of the School of Oriental and African Studies* 21 (1958): 220-224.

Spillett, Hubert. *A Catalogue of Scriptures in the Languages of China and of the Republic of China*. London: British and Foreign Bible Society, 1975.

St. André, James, "Modern Translation Theory and Past Translation Practice: European Translations of the *Haoqiu zhuan*." In *One into Many: Translation and the Dissemination of Classical Chinese Literature*, edited by Leo Tak-hung Chan, 39-65. Amsterdam: Rodopi, 2003.

Tarocco, Francesca. "Lost in Translation? The *Treatise on the Mahāyāna Awakening of Faith* (*Dasheng qixin lun*) and Its Modern Readings." *Bulletin of the School of Oriental and African Studies* 71 (2008): 323-343.

Turner, Ralph. "Sir Edward Denison Ross." *Bulletin of the School of Oriental and African Studies* 10 (1942): 832-836.

Twitchett, Denis. *Land Tenure and the Social order in T'ang and Sung China*. London: School of Oriental and African Studies, 1962.

Wagner, Rudolf. "Does This Make Sense? Reading Sinological Translations." In *Zurück zur Freude: Studien zur chinesischen Literatur und Lebenswelt und ihrer Rezeption in Ost und West: Festschrift für Wolfgang Kubin*, edited by Marc Hermann and Christian Schwermann, with Jari Grosse-Ruyken. Sankt Augustin: Steyler Verlag, 2007, 767-776.

Waley, Arthur. *170 Chinese Poems*. London: Constable, 1918.

Waley, Arthur. "A Hundred and Seventy Chinese Poems." *The Cambridge Review* 40, no. 988 (6 December 1918): 162.

Waley, Arthur. "Notes on Chinese Prosody." *Journal of the Royal Asiatic Society* 50 (1918): 249-261.

Waley, Arthur. "The Everlasting Wrong." *Bulletin of the School of Oriental Studies* 2 (1922): 343-344.

Waley, Arthur. *An Introduction to the Study of Chinese Painting*. London: Ernest Benn Limited, 1923.

Waley, A., Z. L. Yih, and Sir Denison Ross. "*Encyclopedia Sinica*, by S. Couling." *Bulletin of the School of Oriental Studies* [1] (1918): 142-146.

Walravens, Hartmut. *Paul Pelliot (1878-1945): His Life and Works – a Bibliography*. Bloomington, IN: Indiana University Research Institute for Inner Asian Studies, 2001.

Welsh, Frank. *A History of Hong Kong*. London: HarperCollins, 1997.

Wang Qilong and Deng Xiaoyong. *The Academic Knight Between East and West: A Biography of Alexander von Staël-Holstein*. Singapore: Gale Asia, 2014.

Wilde, Oscar. *A Chinese Sage*. Dublin: Mermaid Turbulence, 1997.

Witchard, Anne. *Lao She in London*. Hong Kong: Hong Kong University Press, 2012.

Zastoupil, Lynn and Martin Moir (eds.). *The Great Indian Education Debate: Documents Relating to the Orientalist-Anglicist Controversy, 1781-1843*. Richmond: Curzon Press, 1999.

CHAPTER 6

Orientalism and the Study of Lived Religions

The Japanese Contribution to European Models of Scholarship on Japan around 1900

Hans Martin Krämer

1   Introduction: Religion and Japan within Orientalism

In the introduction to this volume, Ibrāhīm al-Yāziǧī is drawn upon to show the contrast between those Orientalists who "learned the [Arabic] language solely from books" and those who deemed it necessary to do fieldwork.[1] It is everything but self-explanatory that a "Lebanese philologist" is referred to matter-of-factly as on par with the lofty Leiden Orientalists, one of whom is the target of criticism. Rather, figures like al-Yāziǧī do not usually figure prominently in disciplinary histories, despite the fact that they were indeed part of the history of Orientalism. Only a few other cases have received prominent treatment such as those of Wang Tao, the interlocutor of the eminent sinologist James Legge, or R. G. Bhandarkar, the Indian scholar of Sanskrit studies, who was a frequent contributor to Orientalist congresses in Europe in the 1870s and 1880s.[2]

Before coming to the issue of the native contribution, however, let us dwell on the distinction between the two types of Orientalists referred to in the citation above, the book-learners and the fieldworkers. Religion, I will argue here, is especially salient in throwing further light on this distinction. As Suzanne Marchand has argued in her 2009 book on German Orientalism, religious texts were "central to the study of the Orient" in the nineteenth century, a tendency ultimately based on the dichotomous notion of an Eastern spiritual vs. a West-

---

1   Herman Paul, "Introduction: Scholarly Personae in the History of Orientalism, 1870-1930," in this volume, p. 1.
2   On Wang, see Paul A. Cohen, *Between Tradition and Modernity: Wang T'ao and Reform in Late Ch'ing China* (Cambridge, MA: Harvard University Press, 1987). On Bhandarkar, see Dermot Killingley, "R. G. Bhandarkar: The Basis of Theism and its Relation to the So-Called Revealed Religions (India, 1883): Introduction," in *Religious Dynamics under the Impact of Imperialism and Colonialism: A Sourcebook*, ed. Björn Bentlage, Marion Eggert, Hans Martin Krämer, and Stefan Reichmuth (Leiden: Brill, 2017), 415-418.

ern material world.[3] According to Marchand, this went hand in hand with a preference for ancient texts, so that "nineteenth-century academics in particular evinced little interest in the East's modern economic, military, or political conditions." Those were rather seen as concerns for "the journalist, official, or businessman."[4]

While evidence for this observation by Marchand may be found for all parts of Asian Studies, the question is whether dealing with religion really always meant dealing with ancient texts, in other words: whether there were not also, in Marchand's words, modern *religious* conditions. This becomes obvious once one turns to the anthropological study of religious practices based on fieldwork that became so important in the twentieth century, especially from the 1920s onwards. Yet, this does not mean that there had been no interest in contemporary Asian religions in nineteenth-century Europe. In this regard, the case of Japan is particularly instructive. While it could boast a number of ancient texts understood as relevant to religion (albeit not quite as ancient as India or China), it was also home to two "religions" (only identified as such in the nineteenth century) that offered interesting contrasts. To most European observers, one, Shintō, looked like a primitive animism, while the other, Buddhism, was a respectable book-based religion with a complex system of beliefs, practices, and ethics.[5]

All the same, Japan might be an outlier within the present volume. It was never regarded as the bearer of a great civilization, thus failing to attract the kind of fascination that especially India, but also China and the Near East exerted upon nineteenth-century European scholars. Mostly due to Japan's geographic position and the fact that the country was almost inaccessible until the 1850s, its study was also a latecomer within Orientalism. Indeed, it was not even always naturally included within that category. Although the *Congrès international des orientalistes*, first held in Paris in 1873, was founded by someone with a keen interest in Japan (Léon de Rosny – of him more later), the premier Orientalist journal in Germany, the *Zeitschrift der Deutschen Morgenländischen Gesellschaft* (ZMDG), founded in 1847, published next to nothing on Japan, "one of the less mature latecomers."[6] Indeed only three articles on Japan, one of which was a review, were ever published in the ZDMG until 1900.

---

3 Suzanne L. Marchand, *German Orientalism in the Age of Empire: Religion, Race, and Scholarship* (Cambridge: Cambridge University Press, 2009), xxvi.
4 Ibid.
5 On the question of what constituted a "religion" in modern Japan, see Jason Ānanda Josephson, *The Invention of Religion in Japan* (Chicago, IL: University of Chicago Press, 2012).
6 Markus Rüttermann, "Japanologie – Genese und Struktur," in *Grundriß der Japanologie*, ed. Klaus Kracht and Markus Rüttermann (Wiesbaden: Harrassowitz, 2001), 1-35, at 17.

The fact that Japan was a latecomer to Orientalism might have meant less interest in its ancient texts and a keener awareness of its present-day society and culture, and it may also be related to a specific configuration concerning ideal models of scholarship in the emerging field of Japanese studies around 1900. For the purposes of this chapter, I follow the concept of "scholarly personae" defined by Herman Paul as "models of abilities, attitudes, and dispositions that are regarded as crucial for the pursuit of scholarly study."[7] Although scholarly personae in this sense are "contested and unstable,"[8] they can be understood as ideal-types that inform how practitioners of a whole discipline or sub-discipline aspire to work at a given time. Our analytical gaze is thus directed away from the products of such scholarly work to the processes of scholarship, to non-discursive "styles of working."[9]

Reflecting on the concept of scholarly persona thus defined leads us to ask how research on Japan was pursued in the second half of the nineteenth century and how those engaged in research on Japan thought it should be pursued. It makes us aware of differences between the scholarly ideals upheld in Orientalism more broadly conceived and those in the new field of studies of Japan. The main concern of the present chapter is the question of whether there was an identifiable scholarly persona in the field of Japanese studies in the era of "high Orientalism" during the last decades of the nineteenth century.

It is possible, however, that while one can identify a persona, it may not necessarily have been scholarly in the narrow sense of the word. It appears that interest in Japan was rather satisfied by, in the words of Suzanne Marchand already quoted above, the journalists, officials, and businessmen, i.e. those who took care of the economy, military, and politics.[10] In the case of religion, we might expect another professional to intervene prominently, and that is, of course, the missionary. Given the historical dependence of the humanities on theology and the fact that many missionaries received higher education, there

---

7   Herman Paul, "What Is a Scholarly Persona? Ten Theses on Virtues, Skills, and Desires," *History and Theory* 53 (2014), 348-371, at 353.
8   Ibid., 365.
9   Ibid., 352, 370.
10 The prevalence of the academic amateur in the period when an academic discipline of Japanology had not yet emerged distinguishes the case of Japanese studies from the otherwise comparable case of Chinese studies. Referring to the existence of chairs for Chinese language at the Collège de France since 1814 and at the Écoles des langue orientales since 1843, the sinologist Robert Gassmann has stated: "The first stage of Sinology, the nineteenth century, is thus marked by a coexistence of the knowledge of China of the amateurs and professionals and academic Sinology." Robert H. Gassmann, "Sinologie, Chinakunde, Chinawissenschaft: Eine Standortbestimmung," *Asiatische Studien* 39 (1985), 147-168, at 153.

is an interesting extra degree of complexity to the case of the missionary, who might be less easy to disentangle from the role of the scholar than the "broad range of explorers, adventurers, and travelers" who authored much of nineteenth-century writing on Japanese religions.[11]

Ideal models of how to approach the study of Japan were also shaped by another decisive factor, however, and that is the native contribution already mentioned above. A sizable proportion of publications on Japanese religions in Western languages before 1920 was in fact authored by Japanese. Who were those Japanese, what were their agendas, and how did they influence European researchers, possibly even having an impact on forming ideal models of the study of Japanese religion in Europe? And how does their role square with what we think we know about the history of European Orientalism, i.e. processes of selfing and othering within European academia that presuppose a rather clear dividing line between "us" and "them"?

The first part of this chapter will be devoted to a rough sketch of European research on Japanese religion up to and around 1920. Who were the main protagonists? What were their major topics and approaches? What were their motives? Can we discern some kind of "persona" as a model or an ideal of how to approach the study of Japanese religion? In the second part, I will turn to the Japanese interlocutors of those European scholars, those Japanese who contributed to European knowledge by publishing in European languages or by being in close contact with European students of Japan. In concluding I will take up explicitly the question of the scholarly persona of studies on Japanese religion around 1900 between Orientalism, gentleman scholarship, and the Japanese impact.

2   Research on Japanese Religions in European Languages up to 1920

2.1   *History of Research on Japanese Religions up to the Middle of the Nineteenth Century*

The first systematic introduction to Europe of knowledge about Japan was through the hands of the Christian mission, mostly conducted by members of the Jesuit order, from the middle of the sixteenth century. Urs App has demonstrated just how influential and long-lived the body of information on Japan

---

[11]   Lawrence I. Conrad, "The Dervish's Disciple: On the Personality and Intellectual Milieu of the Young Ignaz Goldziher," *Journal of the Royal Asiatic Society of Great Britain and Ireland* 2 (1990), 225-266, at 265. Quoted in Paul, "Introduction," p. 10.

produced by the Jesuits was.[12] After this early impulse, no serious scholarship on Japan emerged until Engelbert Kaempfer, whose travels outside of Europe led him to Japan from 1690 to 1692, summarized the information he gathered during his stay there. In his posthumously published *The History of Japan* (1727), Kaempfer included a substantial chapter on religion, remarkable for its anti-Buddhist stance and its nuanced portrayal of Shinto.[13]

Kaempfer's book remained the most reliable source on Japan until the nineteenth century, when Philipp Franz von Siebold's *Nippon: Archiv zur Beschreibung Japans* (1832-1858) was published. Like Kaempfer, Siebold treated religion in a separate chapter, which showed little serious interest in Buddhism. Siebold's source of information were the Dutch "dissertations" written by his Japanese "students," just as in fact, Kaempfer had also had a Japanese informant (Imamura Gen'emon) for his chapter on religion.[14]

The main part of the religion chapter in Siebold's *Nippon* was penned by another collaborator of Siebold's, namely Johann Joseph Hoffmann, who became the first Professor for Chinese and Japanese Languages at Leiden University in 1855. More precisely, that chapter was a translation of a popular Japanese introduction to Buddhism from 1783 by Hoffmann, a translation that was richly annotated for the European reader based on other sources. It is especially because of these learned annotations that the eminent Japanese Buddhologist Sueki Fumihiko has characterized Hoffmann as having an "attitude that marks the beginning of a new Japanology which was to become determinative in Western academia."[15] This judgment is perhaps a bit premature: Hoffmann himself never published anything else on Japanese religions (or culture more

---

12   Urs App, *The Birth of Orientalism* (Philadelphia, PA: University of Pennsylvania Press, 2010).
13   Engelbert Kaempfer, *Werke,* vol. 1, no. 1, ed. Wolfgang Michel and Barend J. Terwiel (Munich: Iudicium, 2001), 172-206.
14   See Klaus Antoni, "Engelbert Kaempfers Werk als Quelle der Geschichte des edo-zeitlichen Shintō," *Nachrichten der Gesellschaft für Natur- und Völkerkunde Ostasiens* 161/162 (1997), 87-109.
15   "Er ist jedoch der erste gewesen, der den japanischen Buddhismus wissenschaftlich und philologisch studierte. Man kann zwischen Siebold und Hoffmann einen wichtigen methodologischen Wechsel feststellen. Siebolds Japanstudien basierten auf eigenen Erfahrungen und auf vielen Materialien, die er sich zuarbeiten ließ, ohne eigene Kenntnisse des Japanischen und der japanischen Originalquellen zu besitzen. Hoffmann hingegen begann seine Studien mit dem Erlernen der japanischen Sprache und mit philologischen Studien der japanischen Originalquellen. Seine Haltung markiert den Beginn einer neuen Japanologie, welche im westlichen Wissenschaftsbetrieb bestimmend wurde." Sueki Fumihiko, "Siebold, Hoffmann und die Japanischen Religionen," *Bochumer Jahrbuch zur Ostasienforschung* 26 (2002), 175-192, at 183-184.

broadly), but focused mostly on the Japanese language itself in subsequent years.[16]

2.2 Publications on Japanese Religions up to 1920

Indeed, publications on Japanese religion in European languages remained relatively rare. For this chapter, I have attempted to obtain an overall assessment of research on Japanese religions in the form of publications in German, French, or English from the time period between 1800 and 1920 by tapping into existing bibliographies, supplementing these with other publications I was aware of. This has yielded 47 monographs and 214 academic articles. Most of the latter were published in academic journals, but the results include everything that is at least three pages long and treats mainly Japanese religions as its subject. This count does not encompass chapters in travel reports or publications on, for instance, East Asian Buddhism that may also have a chapter on Japan. Also excluded were books or articles dealing only with Christianity in Japan, which I did not regard as Orientalist scholarship.

A review of this data shows that starting in the 1870s, in the case of articles, or in the 1880s, in the case of monographs, a small, but steady stream of publications averaging around five articles and one monograph a year were published. There is a slight surge around the Russo–Japanese War in 1904/05, which, according to Suzanne Marchand, "would mean big changes for orientalists,"[17] but no marked increase in volume during this period. An investigation of the list of works also yields that in many cases Japanese religion(s) was a passing interest; most authors only ever wrote one work on the subject. Only few authors stand out as showing a longer devotion to the topic of Japanese religions, and it is these individuals I now want to turn to, in rough chronological order (see Table 6.1).

It is remarkable that only the two oldest among these, publishing mainly in the 1860s and 1870s, were university-based Orientalists. These two were also the only ones who had never set foot on Japanese soil. All other major authors of works on Japanese religions up to the 1910s (with the sole exception of Karl Florenz, to be explained below) were non-academic professionals with the experience of extensive stays in Japan, not few of them spending their entire

---

16 Kiri Paramore disagrees with this in his assessment of Hoffmann, because he views Confucianism as a religion and points to how Hoffmann used the classic Confucian text *The Great Learning* (*Daxue*) as a primer for Japanese in his language classes at Leiden University. See Kiri Paramore, "Religion, Secularism and the Japanese Shaping of East Asian Studies," in *Religion and Orientalism in Asian Studies*, ed. Kiri Paramore (London: Bloomsbury, 2016), 129-143, at 132-133.

17 Marchand, *German Orientalism*, 214.

TABLE 6.1   Main authors of works on Japanese religions in European languages

Name	Life dates	Country	Occupation	in Japan
August Pfizmaier	1808-1887	Austria	scholar	–
Léon de Rosny	1837-1914	France	scholar	–
William George Aston	1841-1911	United Kingdom	diplomat	1864-1889
Ernest Satow	1843-1929	United Kingdom	diplomat	1862-1883
Marquis Lafayette Gordon	1843-1900	USA	missionary	1872-1899
Basil Hall Chamberlain	1850-1935	United Kingdom	language teacher	1873-1911
Arthur Lloyd	1852-1911	United Kingdom	missionary	1884-1911
Wilfrid Spinner	1854-1918	Switzerland	missionary	1885-1891
Percival Lowell	1855-1916	USA	businessman	1889-1893
Hermann ten Kate	1858-1931	Netherlands	physician	1898-1919
Carl Munzinger	1864-1937	Germany	missionary	1890-1895
Karl Florenz	1865-1939	Germany	scholar	1889-1914
Emil Schiller	1865-1945	Germany	missionary	1895-1931
Hans Haas	1868-1934	Germany	missionary	1898-1909
Johannes Martin Ostwald	1870–?	Germany	missionary	1903-1908
Johannes Witte	1877-1945	Germany	missionary	1910-1911

professional career there. Missionaries were conspicuous among them, and all of them started writing on Japan only after they had entered the country. In the following section, I will introduce the most influential of these authors in some more depth, dividing them into four groups: the early pioneers, consular personnel, teacher-scholars, and missionaries.

2.3   *Individual Biographies*

2.3.1   Early Pioneers: August Pfizmaier (1808-1887) and Léon de Rosny
Markus Rüttermann, who has attempted to exhaustively describe the "genesis and structure" of Japanese studies, has claimed that August Pfizmaier "marks the beginning of Japanology,"[18] the latter being defined by Rüttermann as a "cultural science asking for and explaining meaning" that "makes visible the self-articulation of Japanese culture within the sign systems of a non-Japanese audience." The crucial characteristic of Japanology is its "independent access

---

18   Rüttermann, "Japanologie," 16.

to the source language."[19] Therefore, Kaempfer and Siebold, who only had indirect access to Japanese sources through their native informants, are disqualified by Rüttermann's criteria.

Pfizmaier, in contrast, was a linguistic genius, who, as an autodidact, came to be able to understand and translate a number of non-European languages. His official title at the University of Vienna from 1843 onwards was "Dozent der chinesischen, türkischen, arabischen und persischen Sprache und Literatur" (Lecturer in Chinese, Turkish, Arabic, and Persian Language and Literature). He never went to a country where any of these languages were spoken by the native population but managed to master them at such a level that his translations are still in use today, at least in the case of Japanese. Pfizmaier devoted considerable energy to translating Japanese literature, and this included a number of premodern literary works such as Buddhist folk tales and Shintō myths. He never authored any analysis or synthesis of Japanese religion, however, but stayed within the perimeter of literary translations throughout his life.

This is in stark contrast to Léon de Rosny, the only other major author in Table 6.1 to have been an academy-based Orientalist. Somewhat similar to Pfizmaier, de Rosny was multitalented and divided his career between original-language based research on East Asia, especially Japan, and the ancient civilizations of Central and South America. He did both without ever leaving Europe – Josephson calls him an "armchair ethnographer."[20] In 1868, he became the first chair of Japanese, a position created for him, at the École des langues orientales in Paris, and in 1886, he became a professor for Far Eastern Religions at the École pratique des hautes études.

As the first Frenchman to study Japan in a scholarly way, it is not surprising that his early focus was on the language, producing textbooks and other introductory material. From the 1870s onwards, however, he increasingly turned to the study of Japanese religion and wrote several pioneering works in the field, both on Buddhism and Shintō.[21] This change of course may be traced back to de Rosny's encounter with a group of Japanese Buddhist priests traveling to Paris in 1872. As de Rosny's first shorter publications on Buddhism from the 1870s show, his view of Japanese religions was deeply shaped by this encounter:

19 Ibid., 16-19.
20 Josephson, *Invention*, 192.
21 De Rosny produced five monographs on Buddhism and Shintō between 1880 and 1891. Strangely, Rüttermann dismisses de Rosny as a proper Japanologist, arguing that he was merely "a language teacher … who did not choose the scientific path in dealing with Japan" (Rüttermann, "Japanologie," 17).

his agenda closely follows that of his reform Buddhist interlocutors from Japan.[22]

Neither de Rosny, nor the Leiden chairholder in Japanese, Hoffmann, nor Pfizmaier, who was not even given a professorial position, had any students desiring to follow in their footsteps, and thus no one continued their work based in the academy. Instead, the much later first generation of Japanologists who actually had chairs devoted to that subject in the strict sense had all been trained in Sinology, notably Karl Florenz and Serge Elisséeff.[23] In the meantime, the study of Japanese religions was for several decades dominated by amateur professionals, whose shared characteristic is that they wrote after having traveled to Japan, in fact mostly while they were in Japan.

2.3.2   Consular Personnel: William George Aston and Ernest Satow

This group is exemplified by two British diplomats who spent much, if not most, of their adult life in Japan. Ernest Satow arrived in Japan in the tumultuous period between the opening of the country (in 1854) and the establishment of the modern government (in 1868) at the age of 19 and went on to stay for twenty-one years, later returning as ambassador for another five years. William George Aston came to Japan shortly after Satow at the age of 23, staying on for twenty-five years. Both Satow and Aston worked for the consular service of the British legation in Japan. The British foreign service had by the 1860s concluded that in order to formulate a British Japan policy, deeper knowledge about Japan would be indispensable, and this meant not only a thorough training in the language but even research into Japanese history, culture, and society. This was the thinking of Consul General Harry Smith Parkes (1828-1885; in office 1865-1883), who provided his consular staff with ample spare time and encouraged them in their scholarly pursuits.[24]

Together with Basil Hall Chamberlain, to be treated shortly, Satow and Aston dominated English scholarship on Japan in general, not just religion, until the 1900s, as is immediately apparent when one looks at issues of the

---

22   See his "Les religions et le néo-bouddhisme au Japon," in *Mémoires du congrès international des orientalistes, première session, Paris, 1873*, vol. 1 (Paris: Vie Bouchard Huzard, 1874), 142-150.

23   See Paramore, "Religion," 131-133. Elisséeff had studied Chinese and Japanese at the Seminar for Oriental Studies in Berlin, before doing degree work at the University of Tokyo. He later became professor of Far Eastern Studies at Harvard and the supervisor of the thesis of Edwin O. Reischauer, who himself went on to supervise the doctoral theses of almost the entire first postwar generation of U.S. Japanologists.

24   Ōta Yūzō, *B. H. Chenbaren: Nichiō-kan no ōfuku undō ni ikita sekaijin* [B. H. Chamberlain: A Cosmopolitan Who Lived Moving between Japan and Europe] (Tokyo: Riburopōto, 1990), 102-104.

Transactions of the Asiatic Society of Japan (TASJ, published since 1874). Satow was also a member of the council of the Asiatic Society in Japan, publisher of the TASJ, when it was founded in 1872. His superior Parkes was one of the two vice presidents of the same society.[25] While Satow and Aston frequently dealt with history and literature, their work on Japan included, crucially, religion.

The depth of Aston's erudition is attested to by the fact that his translation of the *Nihongi*, the second oldest extant Japanese book dating from 720 CE and of tremendous interest for any historical study of Japan, is even today still the standard English translation that students of Japanese history turn to when making use of that seminal work of Japanese literary history. Yet neither Satow nor Aston ever won any formal acknowledgment by the academy, remaining scholarly amateurs throughout their lives.

2.3.3 Teacher–scholars: Basil Hall Chamberlain and Karl Florenz

In contrast, Basil Hall Chamberlain and Karl Florenz were attached to the academy, albeit in a somewhat roundabout way. They both started out in Japan as language teachers in Tokyo. Chamberlain arrived in Japan shortly after Satow and Aston, in 1873. Although he was to become close friends with Satow, he did not work as a member of the British legation, but rather came as an employee of the Japanese government, first teaching English at the Imperial Japanese Naval Academy from 1874 to 1882. Later, he became a professor of Japanese at Tokyo Imperial University at a time when all professors there were non-Japanese, even in subjects such as Japanese language and literature. He stayed in this post until 1911, when most of the other foreign professors had long been replaced by Japanese colleagues.

Different from Chamberlain, Florenz undertook rigorous academic training with leading Orientalists before coming to Japan.[26] Although the main focus during his years at Leipzig University was Sanskrit (he completed his studies with a thesis on the Vedas in 1885), he also studied Sinology and learned Japanese, initially in Leipzig, later (from 1887 to 1888) at the newly founded Seminar for Oriental Languages in Berlin. Florenz went to Japan in 1888 with the explicit aim of deepening his studies of Chinese and Japanese language and culture, in preparation for a later academic position in Orientalism. At first

---

25   Ōta, *B. H. Chenbaren*, 102.
26   Biographical data for Florenz was culled from the following two publications: Masako Satō, *Karl Florenz in Japan: Auf den Spuren einer vergessenen Quelle der modernen japanischen Geistesgeschichte und Poetik* (Hamburg: Gesellschaft für Natur- und Völkerkunde Ostasiens, 1995), 132-177; Michael Wachutka, *Historical Reality or Metaphoric Expression? Culturally Formed Contrasts in Karl Florenz' and Iida Takesato's Interpretations of Japanese Mythology* (Münster: LIT, 2001), 51-67.

unemployed, he became a lecturer in German language and literature at Tokyo Imperial University in 1889, but was quickly promoted to professor in 1891, a position he held until 1914. In contrast to his Tokyo Imperial University colleague Chamberlain, however, Florenz saw his academic efforts in studying Japan rewarded by being picked up for a chair in Japanology in Hamburg, in fact the first of its kind in Europe, in 1914. He would remain there until 1935.

Both Chamberlain and Florenz were better known for their works on Japan generally and on Japanese literature, but both contributed to the study of Japanese religions through their translations of classical texts. Chamberlain authored a translation of the *Kojiki* in 1882, the oldest Japanese book containing the founding myths as written down in 712 CE. Florenz also translated parts of the *Kojiki*, published in 1919 under the title *Die historischen Quellen der Shinto-Religion: Aus dem Altjapanischen und Chinesischen übersetzt und erklärt* (The Historical Sources of the Shintō Religion: Translated from the Old Japanese and Chinese and Explained).

Both Chamberlain and Florenz, like Satow and Aston before them, centered their academic pursuits on philological studies of ancient texts, which in all four cases were of Shintō provenance. While this focus on textual studies makes them adhere rather closely to the scholarly persona of the classical detached European Orientalist, all four of them did so while based in Japan for very long sojourns. And, surrounded by the living religions of Japan, none of them dealt exclusively with ancient texts. As early as 1875, Satow authored an article on current attempts to establish what is today called "Restoration Shintō" in TASJ, Chamberlain in 1893 wrote "Notes on Some Minor Japanese Religious Practices" for the *Journal of the Anthropological Institute*, and Aston in 1906 penned an article entitled "Ancestor Worship in Japan" for the anthropological journal *Man*. Florenz was known for his interest in Shintō not only as revealed through ancient texts, but its practiced rituals; he published a series of articles on "Ancient Japanese Rituals" in TASJ around 1900, collected utensils used in such rituals,[27] and contributed an extensive treatment of present-day Shintō to a volume on Japan in the series *Contemporary Culture*.[28]

2.3.4 Missionaries: Hans Haas

Another group of individuals was equally active in scholarship on Japan from an early point in time, in fact, soon after the opening of the country. In the

---

27 Wachutka, *Historical Reality*, 60.
28 Karl Florenz, "Die Religionen der Japaner, 1. Der Shintoismus," in *Kultur der Gegenwart: Ihre Entwicklung und ihre Ziele, Teil 1, Abteilung 3, 1: Die Orientalischen Religionen*, ed. Paul Hinneberg (Berlin: Teubner, 1906), 164-220.

context of the topic at hand – the study of Japanese religions – this group, that of the missionaries, is perhaps the most important. The first president of the Asiatic Society of Japan, James C. Hepburn (1815-1911) and one of the two founding vice-presidents, Samuel Robbins Brown (1810-1880), were missionaries.[29] As can be gleaned from Table 6.1, however, it was missionaries from the German-speaking countries who were to become most active in scholarship of Japanese religions a few years later, and it is one of them I will turn my attention to in this section.

Like his Swiss and German colleagues listed in Table 6.1, Hans Haas was a missionary for the Deutsche Ostasien-Mission (DOAM). Unlike the diplomat-type professionals then, he therefore had a fixed tenure in Japan, being sent there for a limited time by his mission center in Southern Germany. Haas published widely on all Japanese religions. He is perhaps best known today for his works on the history of Christianity in Japan; but even excluding those, his oeuvre is rather remarkable, spanning six books on Japanese Buddhism published between 1904 and 1912 as well as 28 articles on Shintō, Buddhism, and New Religions, published between 1899, the year after his arrival in Japan, and 1917.[30] Although he also dealt with Japanese religions historically, a clear focus of his work was on the contemporary religious scene. In this, Haas, who claimed for himself the positionality of Religious Studies, was somewhat unusual for a Christian missionary.

Haas is also special among the group of missionaries active in scholarly pursuits of Japanese religions in that he became a professor upon returning to Germany, albeit not in Japanese studies, but rather in religious studies (within a Faculty of Theology), at Leipzig University in 1915. Haas had been particularly active academically, serving as an editor for the journal *Zeitschrift für Missionskunde und Religionswissenschaft* (Journal of Missionary Science and Religious Studies) between 1910 and 1931 and the book series *Mitteilungen der Deutschen Gesellschaft für Natur- und Völkerkunde Ostasiens* (Communications of the German Society for the Study of the Nature and People of East Asia) between 1900 and 1909.[31]

Of the authors of works on Japanese religions treated so far, only Pfizmaier and de Rosny were "armchair Japanologists" conforming to a conventional model of Orientalists, epitomized in the field of Asian religions by Max Müller who, like Pfizmaier and de Rosny, never left Europe. Indeed, the important

---

29 Ōta, *B. H. Chenbaren*, 101.
30 Including other subjects than Japanese religion, Haas published no fewer than 161 books and articles in his lifetime. See Clara Böhme, "Hans Haas – Ein (fast) vergessener Religionswissenschaftler" (BA thesis, Göttingen University, 2012), vi-x.
31 Böhme, *Hans Haas*, 5.

aspect of this in the light of the concept of scholarly persona may be that this lack of experience was not due to a lack of opportunity but rather because they never even thought it worthwhile to leave the ivory tower, nor would it have been appreciated by their colleagues. Experience of living abroad was not among the skills expected from an Orientalist, nor was curiosity about the actual living cultures studied among the virtues embodied in the scholarly persona of the classical mid-nineteenth-century European Orientalist.[32] A good illustration of this is that Müller's competitor for the Boden Professorship of Sanskrit at the University of Oxford, Monier Williams (later Monier Monier-Williams), albeit successful in defeating Müller in the 1860 election, was widely considered to be the inferior scholar. In contrast to Müller, Williams did not restrict his notion of scholarship to pure philology but, for instance, founded the Indian Institute at Oxford with the pragmatic idea that "it would propagate a general knowledge of India among Oxford's ordinary students some of whom might go on to exercise control over India's destiny in Parliament."[33] More importantly, Williams had not only been born in India, but spent considerable time traveling there and injected insights from his time spent on the ground in his published work. None of this kept a majority of Sanskrit scholars – although not a majority of those eligible for voting, which included a large number of conservative clergymen – from clearly siding with Müller in 1860, who was seen to have the better qualifications for the post,[34] being more closely in line with the scholarly persona of the Orientalist.

It is interesting to note that the ideal of armchair philology slowly came under attack by the second half of the nineteenth century, although perhaps mainly from outside the academy. There is the prominent case of the personal encounter between Max Müller and Henry Steel Olcott (1832-1907), president of the Theosophical Society, who challenged Müller in person on the subject of Buddhism in 1888.[35] Olcott, who had by this time written several books on Buddhism, took exception to Müller's detached approach to that religion:

---

32   On the function of skills and virtues within the concept of scholarly persona, see Paul, "What Is a Scholarly Persona?," 357-360.

33   Gillian Evison, "The Orientalist, His Institute and the Empire: The Rise and Subsequent Decline of Oxford University's Indian Institute" (Oxford: Oxford University, Bodleian Library, 2004), 4, online at <https://www.bodleian.ox.ac.uk/__data/assets/pdf_file/0009/27774/indianinstitutehistory.pdf> (last accessed 28 January 2019).

34   Ibid., 3.

35   Donald S. Lopez Jr., *Buddhism and Science: A Guide for the Perplexed* (Chicago, IL: University of Chicago Press, 2008), 154-159.

I see this greatest pupil of that pioneer genius, E. Burnouf, sitting there and giving me his authoritative advice to turn from the evil course of Theosophy into the hard and rocky path of official scholarship, and be happy to lie down in a thistle-bed prepared by Orientalists for their common use … The Professor, finding me so self-opinionated and indisposed to desert my true colors, said we had better change the subject. We did, but not for long, for we came back to it, and we finally agreed to disagree, parting in all courtesy, and, on my part, with regret that so great a mind could not have taken in that splendid teaching of the Sages about man and his powers, which is of all in the world the most satisfying to the reason and most consoling to the heart.[36]

Although Olcott here represents the (non-academic) position of a believer in Buddhism, he also criticizes the scholarly attitude of "the Professor" on his "hard and rocky path of official scholarship." Indeed Olcott, who had moved to India in 1879, which he called his home until his death in 1907, sarcastically remarks on the setting of his meeting: "We sat alone in his fine library room, well lighted by windows looking out on one of those emerald, velvety lawns so peculiar in moist England; the walls of the chamber covered with bookcases filled with the best works of ancient and modern writers," thus implicitly denigrating Müller's style of approach to Buddhism from his secluded library in Oxford.[37]

Müller's, Pfizmaier's, and de Rosny's attitude stands in stark contrast to virtually the entire first generation of Japan scholars in the narrower sense. The scholarly persona formed by this group of people, in the sense of what came to be expected from someone qualified to write about Japanese religions, excluded anyone who had never encountered Japan through personal experience. Sometimes this was even articulated explicitly as in Hans Haas's praise for Rudolf Lange for his entry on Japanese religions in the third edition of Pierre Daniel Chantepie de la Saussaye's *Lehrbuch der Religionsgeschichte* (published in 1905), which he found to be "at this time certainly without parallel." One of the reasons Haas gave why Lange's work was so good was because the latter "knows the thought and life of the [Japanese] people not only from its writings but also from his own multi-year stay in the country."[38] In other words, intimate

---

36 From Olcott's published diary, quoted ibid., 157.
37 Ibid.
38 Hans Haas, "Die Japaner in der neuesten (3.) Auflage der Religionsgeschichte von Chantepie de la Saussaye," *Zeitschrift für Missionskunde und Religionswissenschaft* 20 (1905), 359-367, at 359.

knowledge of the contemporary field was considered an important asset by the most prolific European scholar on Japanese religions in the 1900s.

3 Role of Japanese Scholars in Agenda Setting

3.1 The Impact of Japanese Scholars on European Knowledge of Japanese Religion

The description so far of the field of research on Japanese religions in European languages around 1900 has been rather one-sided. This is because no fewer than fifteen of the 47 monographs written in European languages between 1850 and 1920 were in fact penned by Japanese authors. The same holds true for twenty of the 214 scholarly articles. Without exception, these texts were written by stakeholders, i.e. representatives of religious groups, usually Shintō priests or Buddhist priests. As I will be able to show in the following for a few instances of Buddhist authors, this did not diminish the scholarly value of those texts in the eyes of European scholars, who relied on the kind of insider information only Japanese informants could give. The focus of the following investigation will again eventually be on the question of scholarly personae: did Japanese scholars follow the lead of their European counterparts in forming their ideals of professional academic life or did they position themselves according to other criteria? Did the presence of Japanese colleagues influence scholarly ideals on the European side?

European scholarship on Buddhism antedates the interventions by Japanese Buddhists by several decades. Before 1860, several monographs treating Buddhism as a *sui generis* phenomenon were published,[39] and all of these early works published before 1860 rely on philological groundwork (Eugène Burnouf [1801-1852] and Félix Nève [1816-1893] were professors of Sanskrit, Robert Spence Hardy [1803-1868] translated from Sinhalese).[40] In a sense, they all took their cue from the "Sketch of Buddhism, Derived from the Bauddha Scriptures of Nipá," which Brian Houghton Hodgson had published in the *Transactions of*

---

39 Chiefly Eugène Burnouf, *Introduction à l'histoire du bouddhisme indien*, vol. 1 (Paris: Imprimerie royale, 1844); Félix Nève, *Le bouddhisme, son fondateur, et ses écritures* (Paris: Charles Douniol, 1853); R. Spence Hardy, *Manual of Buddhism in Its Modern Development* (London: Williams and Norgate, 1853); Charles Schoebel, *Le Bouddha et le bouddhisme* (Paris: Benjamin Duprat, 1857).

40 Charles Schoebel (1813-1888), who was a professor of ancient languages but probably did not read an Asian language at the time of the publication of his work, seems to be the exception to the rule. He described his book on Buddha and Buddhism as "plutôt un tableau général qu'une histoire détaillée".

the Royal Asiatic Society of Great Britain and Ireland in 1829, possibly the first attempt to describe Buddhism as a general phenomenon based on source reading. It was also Hodgson, a colonial administrator in India and Nepal, who supplied the European scholars with source documents on Buddhism in Tibetan, Pali, and Sanskrit, most notably Eugène Burnouf in Paris.

While Burnouf as well as some other scholars around 1850 also took up texts from the Northern branch of Buddhism, this had not yet been conceptualized as Mahāyāna in Europe. Similarly, it took until the early 1870s for Japanese Buddhism to become an object of inquiry in Europe. The earliest explicit account in English of a specific Japanese sect of Buddhism is probably the two-page "A Brief Account of 'Shinshiu'" written in 1879 by Akamatsu Renjō (1841-1919) of the True Pure Land Sect (Jōdo Shinshū, or just Shinshū). It was published well hidden in a Japanese Buddhist journal that did not otherwise carry English-language articles,[41] but it was reprinted in full length in several general-interest books on Japan in the early 1880s,[42] and also later drawn upon by Paul Carus for his popular *Gospel of Buddha*.[43] The reason why the Shinshū drew the attention of laymen was simple. In the words of the British naval architect and long-time Japan resident James Reed:

> But here, in the Shin-shu (Shin-sect), we not only have the doctrine of a saviour taught, but with it the old Christian doctrine of justification by faith likewise – but by faith, not in Jesus, but in Amita Buddha ... He is the god of the paradise of the west, and in reality, although seldom in as many words, they worship him as Almighty God is worshipped by others. It is this Amita Buddha in whom the Shin Buddhists especially put their trust; and although ancient Buddhism seems to know of no sin-atoning power, they do not admit this, but trust in him for eternal salvation.[44]

---

41 *Kōryū zasshi*, appendix to vol. 1 (1879).
42 The earliest were Edward James Reed, *Japan: Its History, Traditions, and Religions: With the Narrative of a Visit in 1879*, vol. 1 (London: John Murray, 1880), 84-86 and William Gray Dixon, *The Land of the Morning: An Account of Japan and Its People, Based on a Four Years' Residence in that Country, Including Travels into the Remotest Part of the Enterior* (Edinburgh: James Gemmell, 1882), 512-514. Reed had in fact asked Akamatsu, who, due to his good English-language skills, was well acquainted with a number of Christian missionaries, to write this brief summary for him when he was travelling through Japan to collect material for his book. See Notto Thelle, *Buddhism and Christianity in Japan: From Conflict to Dialogue, 1854-1899* (Honolulu, HI: University of Hawai'i Press, 1987), 85.
43 Paul Carus, *The Gospel of Buddha: Compiled from Ancient Records* (Chicago, IL: Open Court, 1894). Carus, whose book went through at least nine editions, made use of Akamatsu's "Brief Account" for gospel no. 83 (see pp. 183-185, 240, 242).
44 Reed, *Japan*, vol. 1, 83. Next to Shinshū, only the Nichiren Sect is treated in some depth by Reed. See ibid., 79-99.

In other words, although Buddhism generally frequently appeared to Western observers as atheistic and based on radically different principles than Christianity, Shinshū, in which "Buddhism would seem to have been so utterly reformed as to lose many of its most distinctive features,"[45] allowed those same observers to make the case for a religious universalism, highlighting the alleged parallels between Christianity and Shin Buddhism, a strategy not alien to that employed by Japanese Shin Buddhist priests themselves.

Several younger True Pure Land Sect co-religionists of Akamatsu were to continue his pioneering work of introducing Japanese Buddhism to Europe in European languages. Foremost among these was priest Nanjō Bun'yū (1849-1927), who was sent to England along with his colleague Kasawara Kenju (1852-1883) by his head temple in 1876. After studying English in London for a while, they made their way, letter of introduction in hand, to Max Müller in Oxford who agreed to tutor them in Sanskrit, beginning in 1879. Nanjō was at that time thirty years old and had taught at his sect's Kyoto academy, the Takakura Gakuryō, since 1871. Nanjō became immersed in European Orientalism rather thoroughly: not only did he become a member of the Royal Asiatic Society in London,[46] but he also published important contributions to the field. Before returning to Japan in 1884 – Kasawara had to leave England prematurely and died in Japan in 1883 – Nanjō compiled a catalogue of all works contained in the standard Chinese Buddhist canon, published in 1883 as *Chinese Translation of Buddhist Tripitaka, the Sacred Canon of the Buddhist in China* (Oxford: Clarendon Press). It was widely cited in the following years in Orientalist scholarship,[47] and was enthusiastically lauded by Müller in a biographical sketch of Nanjō he published in 1898.[48]

Shortly after returning to Japan, Nanjō published another work in English, which also proved to be influential. This was a translation of an overview of the

---

45   Dixon, *The Land*, 514.
46   Friedrich Max Müller, *Chips from a German Workshop*, vol. 2 (London: Longmans, Green and Co., 1904), 201.
47   Examples that show the broad range of works, both academic and more popular, drawing upon Nanjō's catalogue include: Sylvain Lévi's introduction to Edouard Specht, "Deux traductions chinoises du Miliñdapanho," in *Transactions of the Ninth International Congress of Orientalists*, vol. 1, ed. E. Delmar Morgan (London: International Congress of Orientalists, 1893), 518-529, at 519; Louis de la Vallée Poussin, "Les conciles bouddiques," *Muséon* 3-4 (1905), 214-323; Albert J. Edmunds, *Buddhist and Christian Gospels* (Philadelphia, PA: Innes & Sons, 1908); Timothy Richard, *The New Testament of Higher Buddhism* (Edinburgh: T. & T. Clark, 1910); Ebbe Tuneld, *Recherches sur la valeur des traditions bouddiques Palie et non-Palie* (Lund: P. Lindstedt, 1915); Rudolf Hoernle, *Manuscript Remains of Buddhist Literature Found in Eastern Turkestan* (Oxford: Clarendon Press, 1916).
48   Müller, *Chips from a German Workshop*, vol. 2, 187.

twelve main sects of Japanese Buddhism that was being written in the original while Nanjō was working on the translation, i.e. the original and translation were written simultaneously. Nanjō's English version was published in Tokyo in 1886 as *A Short History of the Twelve Japanese Buddhist Sects*. Again, this work was widely cited, prominent examples being Basil Hall Chamberlain's bestselling *Things Japanese* (1890) and the second edition of Pierre Daniel Chantepie de la Saussaye's popular *Lehrbuch der Religionsgeschichte* (Textbook of Religious History, 1897).

Another True Pure Land priest active in Europe was Fujishima Ryōon (1852-1918), who traveled to France in 1882. Together with his brother in faith Fujieda Takutsū, Fujishima studied under Sylvain Lévi (1863-1935), in charge of Sanskrit Language and Literature at the University of Paris (Sorbonne) from 1889 to 1894 and as Chair for Sanskrit Language and Literature at the Collège de France from 1894 onwards.[49] Although the Japanese came as students to Lévi, Fujishima was in fact eleven years older than Lévi, who reminisced that it was this encounter that turned his studies in the direction of Buddhism (he had hitherto mainly studied languages as such and theater),[50] similar to the way de Rosny had been prompted to modify his research agenda after meeting Japanese Buddhists in 1872. The encounter with Fujishima and Fujieda also made Lévi realize the importance of supplementing the study of Buddhism through Sanskrit and Pali sources by adding Chinese sources.[51]

Fujishima became an active publishing scholar in France and published a partial French translation of the seventh-century Chinese travel diary *Nanhai jigui neifa chuan* (An Account of Buddhist Practices Sent from the Southern Seas) in the *Journal Asiatique* in 1889.[52] Furthermore, in the same year, Fujishima produced a French version of the same book Nanjō had translated three years earlier, now entitled *Le Bouddhisme japonais: Doctrines et histoire des douzes grandes sectes bouddhiques du Japon*. This was published with a Paris publishing house (Maisonneuve et Ch. Leclerc), which guaranteed the work some wider circulation in Europe. While the book on the twelve sects mainly focused on the history of those sects, Fujishima also attempted to enlighten the European readership with an article on "L'état actuel du Bouddhisme japonais" in 1901.

---

49   This was the chair previously held by Sylvestre de Sacy (1758-1838), Eugène Burnouf, and Philippe-Édouard Foucaux (1811-1894).
50   His doctoral thesis in 1890 was entitled *Le théâtre indien*.
51   Maejima Shinji, *Indogaku no akebono* (Tokyo: Sekai seiten kankō kyōkai, 1985), 136.
52   Ryauon Fujishima, "Deux chapitres extraits des Mémoires d'I-Tsing sur son voyage dans l'Inde," *Journal Asiatique* 8 (1888), 412-439.

The transition of Buddhology in Japan from a field of isolated pioneers to a discipline firmly entrenched in academic institutions is marked most clearly by the figure of Takakusu Junjirō (1866-1945), who also put out more specialized publications in Orientalism in European languages than any of his countrymen during the 1890s.[53] Although Takakusu was never initiated into the priesthood, he received his higher education at the college of the Honganji branch of the True Pure Land Sect (today's Ryūkoku University) and became an active lay member of that denomination, participating in its teetotalist movement and founding the monthly magazine *Hanseikai zasshi*, aimed at social reform, in 1887. When Takakusu went to Europe, he first sought out Max Müller, like his predecessor Nanjō had done. After graduating from Oxford University in 1894, Takakusu stayed in Europe, deepening his study of Sanskrit and Pali with teachers in Berlin, Leipzig (Ernst Windisch), Kiel (Hermann Oldenberg; Paul Deussen), and Paris (Sylvain Lévi). Takakusu translated several voluminous texts of ancient Chinese Buddhism into English, foremost among which was the *Nanhai jigui neifa chuan*,[54] which had earlier been partially translated by Fujishima Ryōon. While Takakusu also authored several papers for the *Journal of the Royal Asiatic Society*, perhaps his most lasting achievement in a European language was that he was chosen by Max Müller to translate a part of volume 49 of the *Sacred Books of the East* project, which occupied most of Müller's scholarly attention during the last years of his life.

3.2 Ideals of Scholarship among the First Generation of Japanese Scholars of Religion

The long stay in Europe, the time of apprenticeship with a well-known European master of Sanskrit or Pali, and the experience of having performed at European Orientalist congresses and published in European-language journals functioned as something of a rite of passage for the founding generation of Buddhist Studies in Japan. All of the individuals mentioned in this section went on to become leading scholars in this field. Foremost among them was Nanjō, who was awarded the first Doctor of Philosophy in modern Japan in 1889. In 1901, he became a professor at Shinshū University (the predecessor of today's Ōtani University), but was soon promoted to university president, in

---

53 The biography of Takakusu was reconstructed according to Orion Klautau, *Kindai Nihon shisōshi toshite no bukkyō shigaku* [Buddhist Historiography as Modern Japanese Intellectual History] (Kyoto: Hōzōkan, 2012), 121-124, and Takagai Shunshi, *Takakusu Junjirō sensei den* [A Biography of Prof. Takakusu Junjirō] (Tokyo: Ōzorasha, 1993), 27-34.

54 I-Tsing, *A Record of the Buddhist Religion as Practised in India and the Malay Archipelago (A.D. 671-695)*. trans. J. Takakusu with a Letter from the Right Hon. Professor F. Max Müller (Oxford: Clarendon Press, 1896).

which post he served from 1903 to 1923. He published over 20 books in the last three decades of his life; a collection of selected works (published between 2001 and 2003) encompasses ten volumes.

Fujishima remained closer to his sect and traditional sectarian scholarship, immersing himself in educating future priests (and also making himself a name as an "aggressive anti-Christian propagator").[55] He published relatively little after returning to Japan in 1890 except for an anti-Christian treatise and a book on the relationship between religion and the state; a two-volume collection of his writings was also published in 1920, shortly after his death.

Takakusu Junjirō became professor of Sanskrit Studies at Japan's premier university, Tokyo Imperial University, in 1899, shortly after that chair had been established in 1897. Takakusu remained at Tokyo Imperial University until 1927, after which he served as president of the private Buddhist institution Tōyō University. From 1923, Takakusu was chief editor of the most important editorial project in modern Buddhism: the 88-volume edition of the Chinese Buddhist canon (*Taishō shinshū daizōkyō*), first published in 1932.

How did these Japanese scholars portray themselves, what were their (implicit) ideals for their (new) profession? We can gain a glimpse of the answer to this question by taking a look at the "Short Account of the Life of Bunyiu Nanjio, by Himself," which was published by Max Müller in his *Chips from a German Workshop* in 1894.[56] Nanjō here offers a strangely impersonal account, giving only the barest bones of biographical data, including almost none about his personal life. Instead, he focuses on how he ascetically devoted one-hundred percent of his life to scholarship in the service of his temple. A typical passage reads:

> In my 34th year, 1882, I became a member of the Royal Asiatic Society in London. I discovered a palm-leaf MS. of the Saddharmapundarika at the British Museum, and partly copied, partly collated it.[57]

In this account, even life-changing personal messages bear the same weight as philological accomplishments:

---

55 Thelle, *Buddhism*, 131.
56 Volume 2 of *Chips from a German Workshop* originally came out in 1876, but the chapter on Nanjō was not added by Müller until he published a revised edition of the work in 1894.
57 Friedrich Max Müller, "A Short Account of the Life of Bunyiu Nanjio, by Himself," in *Chips from a German Workshop*, vol. 2, 190-204, at 201.

> On the 16th day of July, 1883, Kenjiu Kasawara died, in his 32nd year, in Tokio. This sad news reached me in September.
>
> On the 19th October, my real father died in his 67th year in Kioto. This sad news reached me in December.
>
> In my 36th year, 1884, I collated my copy of the Saddharmapundarika with the MS. lent to me by Mr. Watters, the British Consul at Formosa. This collation was finished in January last.[58]

In his own memoirs, published in Japanese in 1927, Nanjō describes how his and Kasawara's life in Oxford centered entirely around work on Sanskrit sutras they had procured from Japan, supervised by Müller:

> I definitively remember it to have been towards the end of December 1879, while Kasawara was on leave in London for some reason, that a letter from Dr. M. [i.e. Müller] addressed to me arrived. It stated: "I have borrowed the Sanskrit manuscript of the Longer Sukhāvatīvyūha Sūtra, which you have been burning for for such a long time, from the Asia Society in London, so come over immediately." Hence, rejoicing from the bottom of my heart, I visited the professor's home, returned carefully carrying the manuscript with me, and pored over it, immersed in my dictionary ... When Kasawara returned, we copied it, for several days almost forgetting to either sleep or eat.[59]

After recounting how he and Kasawara spent 1881 hunting for manuscripts in Berlin, Belgium, Paris, Oxford, and Cambridge, frantically copying anything they could find, Nanjō concludes:

> When I look back at it today, I have never been as tense as back then. It was a literal case of "no sleep and no rest" and an immersion where we entirely forgot to sleep or eat. Especially Kasawara was stubborn in his single-mindedness, which sometimes troubled even me.[60]

Nanjō here implicitly connects Kasawara's work ethic with his premature death from tuberculosis less than two years later. A similar move may be detected in Müller's obituary for Kasawara, published in *The Times*:

---

58 Müller, "A Short Account," 202. The passage is here cited without any omission.
59 Nanjō Bun'yū, *Kaikyūroku* (Tokyo: Daiyūkaku, 1927), 150-151.
60 Ibid., 162.

Kasawara's life at Oxford was very monotonous. He allowed himself no pleasures of any kind, and took little exercise; he did not smoke, or drink, or read novels or newspapers. He worked on day after day, often for weeks seeing no one and talking to no one but me and his fellow-worker, Mr. Bunyiu Nanjio.[61]

Yet, despite lamenting Kasawara's death, both Nanjō and Müller, who lauds the two Japanese Buddhists' devotion to "hard honest work," are not critical of Kasawara's attitude, but rather affirmative: indeed, part of the attitude of the Japanese visitors seems to have been a conscious emulation of the (idealized) life of their teachers, foremost among them Max Müller, merely pushed to further extremes by the ascetic ideals about work the Buddhist priests brought with them to Europe.

Despite this quasi-religious attitude towards work, these clerics displayed no difficulties whatsoever in adapting to the demands of the secularist ideal of scholarship then current in Europe.[62] There is a striking absence of references to religion other than as an object of scholarly study in the ego documents produced by these Buddhist priests. No rituals, acts of devotion or personal worship are ever mentioned, and there is hardly any mention of Christianity, let alone other religions. The only exception to this observation found in Europe before the turn of the century is a ceremony conducted by two priests also from the Jōdo Shinshū, in the Musée Guimet in Paris in 1891. They staged an elaborate celebration of the *hōonkō*, the ritual for the death day of Shinran (1173-1262), the founder of their sect, made possible because Émile Guimet (1836-1918), who had established the museum, had brought with him a number of ritual implements from his visit to Japan in 1877.[63]

Yet, this event remained singular. Even outside of Oxford, Nanjō gave scholarly talks on Buddhism, but never engaged in religious activities or proselytization. This inner separation between their religionist and their scholarly selves likely predated their coming to Europe, as it may be found in the Japanese ideal of the "scholar monk" (*gakusō*). Nominally Japanese Buddhist priests were assigned a temple where they would have to fulfill parish duties, but it is almost a trope in (auto)biographies of scholar monks how they managed to evade those responsibilities in favor of a life devoted to pure scholarship, to be

---

61   Friedrich Max Müller, "Kenjin [sic!] Kasawara," *The Times* (25 September 1883).
62   On this challenge, see also the contribution by Holger Gzella to this volume.
63   L. C., "Un office bouddhique au Musée Guimet," *Revue de l'histoire des religions* 23 (1891), 212-217.

found in Nanjō's memoirs as well.[64] In other words, there was a tradition within Japanese Buddhism to adopt a distance from the ritual life of one's faith once one had decided upon the path of scholarship. While this scholarship remained in the service of religion and may thus not be called secular, in the actual practice the quotidian conduct of these scholar monks differed vastly from their temple priest peers, and this attitude was reinforced in the encounter with European Orientalism.

Speaking generally about the decades surrounding the turn of the twentieth century, Japanese scholars increasingly interacted with their European peers on a level playing field. They kept up to date on developments in the European scholarly world by spending longer times abroad, often paid for by the Japanese government or, in the case of Buddhist priests, by their sponsoring head temple. They published in European languages and they attended Orientalist congresses in Europe and North America.

In analyzing this increasing contact, Kiri Paramore has gone so far as to speak of a "Japanese manipulation of late-nineteenth early-twentieth-century European academia."[65] Certainly, the impact of Japanese scholarship was tremendous. Paramore's harsh wording, however, might obscure another layer to this impact, and that is the collaboration of Japanese scholars with European Japanologists. Less evident in the case of amateur scholars such as Satow and Aston, the question of indigenous help nonetheless comes up in the case of the professional Japanologists Chamberlain and Florenz. Chamberlain resorted to Japanese help in the typical form of the native informant such as when he presented his well-received "Suggestions for a Japanese Rendering of the Psalms" in elegant ancient Japanese style in the TASJ in 1880.[66] Karl Florenz closely followed (and openly acknowledged) the work of the scholar of classical Japanese Iida Takesato (1828-1900).[67] Iida never published anything in a European language, yet he was no mere native informant, being a senior university professor with a vibrant academic life in Japanese. Florenz would not have been able to put together his erudite annotated translation of the ancient Japanese classics without the help of a Japanese scholar such as Iida.

---

64 Nanjō, *Kaikyūroku*, 28-40. For another vivid illustration of the same phenomenon, see Murakami Mamoru, *Shimaji Mokurai den: Ken o taishita itan no hijiri* (Kyoto: Minerva Shobō, 2011), 84-85.
65 Paramore, "Religion," 134.
66 Ōta, *B. H. Chenbaren*, 118.
67 Wachutka, *Historical Reality*, 67-81.

4 Conclusion: Scholarly Personae in the Field of Japanese Religions

Understanding scholarly personae as ideal types and thus ignoring individual differences, three such personae can be identified in the material presented above. The first type is that of the classical mid-nineteenth century Orientalist, exemplified by Max Müller in the broader field of Religious Studies and by August Pfizmaier and Léon de Rosny in the narrower field of Japanese Religions. These scholars of Asia worked while based in Europe, indeed never even aspired to leave Europe to witness Asia first-hand. Their attention was to the (ancient) texts, and in their most extreme incarnation, they even viewed non-textual knowledge of the cultures they studied as a detraction from the (much more important) textual knowledge – a kind of modern *sola scriptura* principle.

The second type of persona is that of the Japanese scholar of Buddhism. The ideal model of this type was set by the early Europe travelers such as Akamatsu Renjō, Nanjō Bun'yū, and Kasawara Kenju. While this model was to some degree an emulation of that of the classical European Orientalist, several differences stand out. First, the fact that they had to travel abroad and spend several years in Europe for part of their training means a marked departure from the pure armchair model. Next, all of these scholars were Buddhist priests. In fact, Japanese scholarship on Japanese religions remained firmly in the hands of religionists until after the Second World War, even outside the narrower field of Buddhist Studies. This is certainly true for Western-language publications of Japanese scholars of Japanese religions, where the only standard overview at least until the 1970s was the 1930 textbook *History of Japanese Religion* (reprinted in 1963) by Anesaki Masaharu, who was an active lay member of the Jōdo Shinshū.[68] Thirdly, although this may have been partly due to the influence of the model of the classical European Orientalist, the devotion of the Japanese scholars of Japanese religion to their object of study was to have an ascetic quality, a devotion that is apparent in Nanjō's reminiscences about his life in Oxford, quoted above, and one that apparently cost his colleague Kasawara his health and life in 1883. Insofar as these three points became expectations of successful scholars in the field, one is justified to view them as constitutive of a scholarly persona in the narrow sense.

---

68   Hans Martin Krämer, *Shimaji Mokurai and the Reconception of Religion and the Secular* (Honolulu, HI: University of Hawai'i Press, 2015), 143. On Anesaki, see also Jun'ichi Isomae, "The Discursive Position of Religious Studies in Japan: Masaharu Anesaki and the Origins of Religious Studies," *Method and Theory in the Study of Religion* 14 (2002), 21-46.

Such a persona is also discernible in the third group, although it is not as clear whether one should refer to it as a "scholarly" persona: the revered European pioneers of the field of Japanese studies mostly stood outside of the academy, and all of them had first-hand knowledge of the country, its culture, and its language from the direct experience of living there for several years, often decades. As "Japan hands," they had gained a deep understanding of the country from immersion within it, while textual study followed upon making oneself familiar with contemporary life in Japan, and much scholarship on Japan, including Japanese religions, focused on contemporary society. Examples for the latter have already been given, and many more could be given by less prolific authors than those treated above.[69] This persona formed a relatively homogeneous ideal for practitioners of Japanese studies, who even in an age long before transport to East Asia became convenient were definitely expected to spend a longer stretch in Japan.

Another characteristic of Japanese studies scholars already in the period under consideration is that they were expected to deal with their Japanese peers as equals, to take Japanese scholarship seriously and include Japanese colleagues in their scholarly network. This may simply have been a necessity because of the vigorous injection by Japanese individuals into scholarly debates as they were conducted in European languages. It is here that the burgeoning scholarly persona of the Japanese studies practitioner took its most obvious departure from classical Orientalism. Quite different from the Saidian stereotype of the Orientalist construction of the Oriental, these (new) Orientalists had a deep appreciation of their Asian peers and close working relationships with them. Despite the quite different backgrounds of the early Japan scholars, as recounted above in the three categories of consular personnel, teacher–scholars, and missionaries, it is here that they all easily agreed and that it becomes clear how they contributed to one distinct persona.

Incidentally, while there is some evidence that this tendency could also be seen in subfields such as history,[70] it may be a peculiar trait of the subfield of

---

69 Some examples include: Alexander von Knobloch, "Die Begraebnisgebraeuche der Shintoisten" (Funerary Rites of the Shintoists) (1874); Wilfrid Spinner, "Leichenverbrennung in Tokyo" (Burning of Dead Bodies in Tokyo) (1889/92); D.G. Greene, "The Remmon Kyo Kwai" (1901); Emil Schiller, "Kriegsgebete bei den Shintotempeln Japans" (War Prayers at Japan's Shinto Temples) (1915); Johannes Witte, "Eine Schinto-Professur in Tokyo" (A Shinto Professorship in Tokyo) (1919).

70 Compare the example of Asakawa Kan'ichi (1873-1948), who taught history at Yale University from 1910 to 1945 and laid the groundwork for the study of medieval Japanese history in the United States, mainly through his pathbreaking monograph *The Documents of Iriki: Illustrative of the Development of the Feudal Institutions of Japan* (New Haven, CT: Yale University Press, 1929).

religion, where scholarly interest was matched on the Japanese side by a stake in the religious field itself, clearly observable in the substantial number of Buddhist (and also Shintō) priests engaged in academic pursuits in English, French, and German. Even those Japanese scholars who did not publish in European languages were not treated as native informants, but frequently taken seriously as peers of equal stature, offering a perspective on the object of inquiry that was unavailable to the outside observer, but nonetheless deemed necessary. As Michael Wachutka has put it, summarizing his study in contrasts of Karl Florenz and Iida Takesato:

> Karl Florenz, holder of the first independent chair of Japanology, therefore could lay through his pioneering research – based on the "etic" academic traditions and ideals of nineteenth-century Europe, as well as on the "emic" findings of native Japanese scholars such as Iida Takesato – the foundation for the establishment and institutionalization of a critical "modern Japanology."[71]

In other words, a combination of factors – the late opening of the country, the lack of academic positions in the discipline, the competition of Japanese scholars from early on – created a fairly distinct model of scholarly selfhood quite incompatible with the armchair Orientalist model of the earlier nineteenth century. And even when the study of Japan outside Japan slowly became increasingly professionalized by the expansion of Japanese studies at universities – during the Second World War in the U.S., since the 1960s in Europe – this model proved quite tenacious. Even today, the amount of one's professional life spent in Japan remains an important criterion for assessing colleagues in the field.

Bibliography

Antoni, Klaus. "Engelbert Kaempfers Werk als Quelle der Geschichte des edo-zeitlichen Shintō." *Nachrichten der Gesellschaft für Natur- und Völkerkunde Ostasiens* 161/162 (1997): 87-109.

App, Urs. *The Birth of Orientalism*. Philadelphia, PA: University of Pennsylvania Press, 2010.

Asakawa Kan'ichi. *The Documents of Iriki: Illustrative of the Development of the Feudal Institutions of Japan*. New Haven, CT: Yale University Press, 1929.

---

71 Wachutka, *Historical Reality*, 167.

Cohen, Paul A. *Between Tradition and Modernity: Wang T'ao and Reform in Late Ch'ing China.* Cambridge, MA: Harvard University Press 1987.

Böhme, Clara. "Hans Haas – Ein (fast) vergessener Religionswissenschaftler" (BA thesis, Göttingen University, 2012.

Burnouf, Eugène. *Introduction à l'histoire du bouddhisme indien*, vol. 1. Paris: Imprimerie royale, 1844.

Carus, Paul. *The Gospel of Buddha: Compiled from Ancient Records.* Chicago, IL: Open Court, 1894.

de la Vallée Poussin, Louis. "Les conciles bouddiques." *Muséon* 3-4 (1905): 214-323.

de Rosny, Léon. "Les religions et le néo-bouddhisme au Japon." In *Mémoires du congrès international des orientalistes, première session, Paris, 1873*, vol. 1., 142-150. Paris: Vie Bouchard Huzard, 1874.

Dixon, William Gray. *The Land of the Morning: An Account of Japan and Its People, Based on a Four Years' Residence in that Country, Including Travels into the Remotest Part of the Enterior.* Edinburgh: James Gemmell, 1882.

Edmunds, Albert J. *Buddhist and Christian Gospels.* Philadelphia, PA: Innes & Sons, 1908.

Evison, Gillian. "The Orientalist, His Institute and the Empire: The Rise and Subsequent Decline of Oxford University's Indian Institute." Oxford: Oxford University, Bodleian Library, 2004), 4, online at <https://www.bodleian.ox.ac.uk/__data/assets/pdf_file/0009/27774/indianinstitutehistory.pdf> (last accessed 28 January 2019).

Florenz, Karl. "Die Religionen der Japaner, 1. Der Shintoismus." In *Kultur der Gegenwart: Ihre Entwicklung und ihre Ziele, Teil 1, Abteilung 3, 1: Die Orientalischen Religionen*, edited by Paul Hinneberg, 164-220. Berlin: Teubner, 1906.

Fujishima Ryauon. "Deux chapitres extraits des Mémoires d'I-Tsing sur son voyage dans l'Inde." *Journal Asiatique* 8 (1888): 412-439.

Gassmann, Robert H. "Sinologie, Chinakunde, Chinawissenschaft. Eine Standortbestimmung." *Asiatische Studien* 39 (1985): 147-168.

Haas, Hans. "Die Japaner in der neuesten (3.) Auflage der Religionsgeschichte von Chantepie de la Saussaye." *Zeitschrift für Missionskunde und Religionswissenschaft* 20 (1905): 359-367.

Hardy, R. Spence. *Manual of Buddhism in its Modern Development.* London: Williams and Norgate, 1853.

Hoernle, Rudolf. *Manuscript Remains of Buddhist Literature Found in Eastern Turkestan.* Oxford: Clarendon Press, 1916.

I-Tsing. *A Record of the Buddhist Religion as Practised in India and the Malay Archipelago (A.D. 671-695).* Translated by J. Takakusu with a Letter from the Right Hon. Professor F. Max Müller. Oxford: Clarendon Press, 1896.

Josephson, Jason Ānanda. *The Invention of Religion in Japan.* Chicago, IL: University of Chicago Press, 2012.

Jun'ichi Isomae. "The Discursive Position of Religious Studies in Japan: Masaharu Anesaki and the Origins of Religious Studies." *Method and Theory in the Study of Religion* 14. (2002): 21-46.

Kaempfer, Engelbert. *Werke.* vol. 1/1: *Heutiges Japan,* edited by Wolfgang Michel and Barend J. Terwiel. Munich: Iudicium, 2001.

Killingley, Dermot. "R. G. Bhandarkar: The Basis of Theism and its Relation to the So-Called Revealed Religions (India, 1883): Introduction." In *Religious Dynamics under the Impact of Imperialism and Colonialism: A Sourcebook*, edited by Björn Bentlage, Marion Eggert, Hans Martin Krämer and Stefan Reichmuth, 415-418. Leiden: Brill, 2017.

Klautau, Orion. *Kindai Nihon shisōshi toshite no bukkyō shigaku.* Kyoto: Hōzōkan, 2012.

Krämer, Hans Martin. *Shimaji Mokurai and the Reconception of Religion and the Secular.* Honolulu, HI: University of Hawai'i Press, 2015.

L. C. "Un office bouddhique au Musée Guimet." *Revue de l'histoire des religions* 23 (1891): 212-217.

Lopez Jr., Donald S. *Buddhism and Science: A Guide for the Perplexed.* Chicago, IL: University of Chicago Press, 2008.

Maejima Shinji. *Indogaku no akebono.* Tokyo: Sekai seiten kankō kyōkai, 1985.

Marchand, Suzanne L. *German Orientalism in the Age of Empire: Religion, Race, and Scholarship.* Cambridge: Cambridge University Press, 2009.

Masako Satō. *Karl Florenz in Japan: Auf den Spuren einer vergessenen Quelle der modernen japanischen Geistesgeschichte und Poetik.* Hamburg: Gesellschaft für Natur- und Völkerkunde Ostasiens, 1995.

Müller, Friedrich Max. "Kenjin Kasawara." *The Times* (25 September 1883).

Müller, Friedrich Max. *Chips from a German Workshop*, vol. 2. London: Longmans, Green and Co., 1904.

Murakami Mamoru, *Shimaji Mokurai den: Ken o taishita itan no hijiri.* Kyoto: Minerva Shobō, 2011.

Nanjō Bun'yū. *Kaikyūroku.* Tokyo: Daiyūkaku, 1927.

Nève, Félix. *Le bouddhisme, son fondateur, et ses écritures.* Paris: Charles Douniol, 1853.

Ōta Yūzō. *B. H. Chenbaren: Nichiō-kan no ōfuku undō ni ikita sekaijin.* Tokyo: Riburupōto, 1990.

Paramore, Kiri. "Religion, Secularism and the Japanese Shaping of East Asian Studies." In *Religion and Orientalism in Asian Studies*, edited by Kiri Paramore, 129-143. London: Bloomsbury, 2016.

Paul, Herman. "What Is a Scholarly Persona? Ten Theses on Virtues, Skills, and Desires." *History and Theory* 53 (2014): 348-371.

Paul, Herman. "Introduction: Scholarly Personae in the History of Orientalism, 1870-1930," in this volume.

Reed, Edward James. *Japan: Its History, Traditions, and Religions. With the Narrative of a Visit in 1879*, vol. 1. London: John Murray, 1880.

Richard, Timothy. *The New Testament of Higher Buddhism*. Edinburgh: T. & T. Clark, 1910.

Rüttermann, Markus. "Japanologie – Genese und Struktur." In *Grundriß der Japanologie*, edited by Klaus Kracht and Markus Rüttermann, 1-35. Wiesbaden: Harrassowitz, 2001.

Schoebel, Charles. *Le Bouddha et le bouddhisme.* Paris: Benjamin Duprat, 1857.

Specht, Edouard. "Deux traductions chinoises du Miliñdapanho." In *Transactions of the Ninth International Congress of Orientalists*, vol. 1, edited by E. Delmar Morgan, 518-529. London: International Congress of Orientalists, 1893.

Sueki Fumihiko. "Siebold, Hoffmann und die japanischen Religionen." *Bochumer Jahrbuch zur Ostasienforschung* 26 (2002): 175-192.

Takagai Shunshi. *Takakusu Junjirō sensei den*. Tokyo: Ōzorasha, 1993.

Thelle, Notto. *Buddhism and Christianity in Japan: From Conflict to Dialogue, 1854-1899.* Honolulu, HI: University of Hawai'i Press, 1987.

Tuneld, Ebbe. *Recherches sur la valeur des traditions bouddiques Palie et non-Palie*. Lund: P. Lindstedt, 1915.

Wachutka, Michael., *Historical Reality or Metaphoric Expression? Culturally Formed Contrasts in Karl Florenz' and Iida Takesato's Interpretations of Japanese Mythology.* Münster: LIT, 2001.

CHAPTER 7

Orientalists at War

Personae and Partiality at the Outbreak of the First World War

Christiaan Engberts

1   Introduction

"I don't feel hate, only a deep sadness, because I have revered and loved Snouck. He was an ideal of scholarly personality to me. A wonderful illusion has been shattered."[1] Carl Heinrich Becker, professor for Oriental philology in Bonn, wrote these disappointed words to his colleague Theodor Nöldeke in February 1915. Two days later Nöldeke would pass them on to the scholar Becker used to revere and love, the Leiden professor for Arabic, Christiaan Snouck Hurgronje.[2] Before the outbreak of the First World War these highly-respected Semitists had always appreciated each other's company and scholarly output. By early 1915, however, the relation between Snouck and Becker seemed to have incurably deteriorated and Nöldeke seemed to be caught up between the two unforgiving antagonists. The war had worked as a catalyst in disclosing a wide range of misunderstandings and disagreements about scholarly honesty, professional cooperation and political attitudes. In this chapter I will explore how the concept of scholarly personae may allow us a better understanding of both Becker's and Snouck's mutual recriminations as well as their eventual careful reconciliation. In order to do this, I will first shortly introduce the adversaries. Subsequently I will look into the wide range of disagreements between them. This overview will allow me to close with a reflection on how the analytical tool of the scholarly persona may be helpful to our understanding of this and other conflicts.

Christiaan Snouck Hurgronje was born in 1857 in the Dutch village of Oosterhout.[3] He studied Semitic languages with Michael Jan de Goeje in Leiden. After

---

1   Carl Heinrich Becker to Theodor Nöldeke, 24 February 1915, Universitätsbibliothek Tübingen (hereafter UBT): Md 782 A 16.
2   Nöldeke to Christiaan Snouck Hurgronje, 26 February 1915, Universiteitsbibliotheek Leiden (hereafter UBL), Or. 8952 A: 757.
3   A more extensive biographical sketch of Snouck Hurgronje can be found in Arnoud Vrolijk and Richard van Leeuwen, *Arabic Studies in the Netherlands: A Short History in Portraits, 1580-1950*, trans. Alastair Hamilton (Leiden: Brill, 2014), 117-150.

receiving his doctor's degree *cum laude* in 1880 he further added to his linguistic knowledge by studying with Nöldeke in Strassburg. Nöldeke would later look back at him as "surely his most significant student."[4] Though Snouck's first job was as a lecturer at the municipal Leiden college for the training of East Indian civil servants, De Goeje and Nöldeke had good reason to fear that their best student would turn his back on a scholarly career. In 1884 and 1885 he visited Jeddah and Mecca and in 1889 he accepted a position as an adviser to the colonial government in the Dutch East Indies. "It is a shame that Snouck attaches himself so much to the tropics," Nöldeke complained, "but when [he] really wants something, nobody can talk him out of it."[5] His scholarly reputation, however, grew steadily, both through his scathing criticisms of contemporary scholarship and through his highly regarded books, the most famous of which were *Mekka* (Mecca, 1888-1889), *De Atjehers* (The Acehnese, 1893-1894), and *Het Gajōland en zijne bewoners* (The Gajoland and Its Inhabitants, 1903). In 1905 he returned to the Netherlands. One year later he would succeed his teacher De Goeje as professor of Arabic in Leiden, while maintaining his function as an advisor to the Dutch colonial authorities and assuming an important role in the establishment of a new school for the training of East Indian civil servants.[6] Snouck died in 1936, but his personal life and the entanglement of his scholarly and political legacy have continued to cause controversy amongst later generations of scholars.[7]

Carl Heinrich Becker was born in a German merchant family in Amsterdam in 1876. He studied Oriental languages in Heidelberg with Carl Bezold. Bezold had been friends with Snouck ever since the time they both studied with Nöldeke in the early eighteen-eighties.[8] After Becker received his doctor's degree *cum laude* in 1899, he traveled through Egypt, Turkey, and Syria where he

---

[4] Nöldeke to Eduard Meyer, 28 March 1928, in: *Der Briefwechsel zwischen Theodor Nöldeke und Eduard Meyer (1884-1929)*, ed. Gert Audring, <https://www.geschichte.hu-berlin.de/de/bereiche-und-lehrstuehle/alte-geschichte/forschung/briefe-meyer/noeldeke> (last accessed 28 January 2019).

[5] Nöldeke to Michael Jan de Goeje, 25 January 1890, UBL: BPL: 2389.

[6] Cees Fasseur, *De Indologen: Ambtenaren voor de Oost 1825-1950* (Amsterdam: Bert Bakker, 1993), 390-411.

[7] See for example P. Sj. van Koningsveld, *Snouck Hurgronje en de Islam: Acht artikelen over leven en werk van een oriëntalist uit het koloniale tijdperk* (Leiden: Documentatiebureau Islam-Christendom, 1987) and Jan Just Witkam, "Inleiding," in Christiaan Snouck Hurgronje, *Mekka in de tweede helft van de negentiende eeuw: Schetsen uit het dagelijks leven* (Amsterdam: Atlas, 2007), 7-189.

[8] Enno Littmann, "Carl Bezold," *Zeitschrift für Assyriologie* 34 (1922), 103-104, at 103; Snouck Hurgronje to Nöldeke, 24 November 1922, in *Orientalism and Islam: The Letters of C. Snouck Hurgronje to Th. Nöldeke from the Tübingen University Library* ed. P. Sj. van Koningsveld (Leiden: Documentatiebureau Islam-Christendom, 1985), 299.

improved his knowledge of spoken Arabic, studied contemporary Islam, and visited a number of libraries.[9] Upon his return to Germany he started teaching Oriental languages as a *Privatdozent* in Heidelberg. Meanwhile his broad knowledge of the contemporary Near East had been pointed out to the founders of the Colonial Institute in Hamburg. In his eyewitness account of the history of scholarship in Hamburg, the former state senator Werner von Melle recounts the enthusiastic endorsement of Becker by the historian Erich Marcks: "He knows contemporary Islam and is interested in present-day developments. He would be very valuable for your colonial establishment."[10] From the founding of the Colonial Institute in 1908 onwards, Becker would occupy the chair for the History and Culture of the Near East. One of his most important accomplishments during his Hamburg years would be the founding of a journal dedicated to contemporary Islamic culture, *Der Islam*. Snouck was one of the scholars who contributed to its success by encouraging some of his best students to publish their work in Becker's journal.[11] In 1913 Becker accepted a professorial chair in Bonn, which he would hold only until 1916, when he would move to Berlin. Here his main interests would soon shift from scholarship to educational politics.

Snouck and Becker both moved in the same academic circles. Theodor Nöldeke, who can be considered as the *eminence grise* of early-twentieth-century German Orientalism, was not only proud of his former student Snouck, he also held a high opinion of Becker. He considered him to be a "very capable young man" with an "independent mind."[12] Carl Bezold was another shared acquaintance as well as the Hungarian Orientalist Ignaz Goldziher, who shared Snouck's and Becker's interest in living Islamic culture. Most importantly, Snouck and Becker frequently met each other. In the years before the outbreak of the First World War, Becker often enjoyed Snouck's hospitality. Whenever Becker had a reason to visit Leiden, he would be a guest in Snouck's household. The mutual affection showed in a warm letter of thanks Becker wrote after attending a congress in Leiden in 1912:

9   Erich Wende, *C. H. Becker: Mensch und Politiker: Ein biographischer Beitrag zur Kulturgeschichte der Weimarer Republik* (Stuttgart: Deutsche Verlags-Anstalt, 1959), 19-20.
10 Werner von Melle, *Dreißig Jahre Hamburger Wissenschaft: 1891-1921* (Hamburg: Kommissionsverlag von Broschek & Co., 1923), 480. More information about the political and economic goals of the Colonial Institute can be found in Jens Ruppenthal, *Kolonialismus als "Wissenschaft und Technik": Das Hamburgische Kolonialinstitut, 1908 bis 1919* (Stuttgart: Franz Steiner, 2007).
11 Snouck Hurgronje to Becker, 11 April 1913, Geheimes Staatarchiv Preußischer Kulturbesitz (hereafter GStA PK), VI. HA, Nl Becker, C. H., Nr. 4227.
12 Nöldeke to De Goeje, 8 July 1905, UBL: BPL: 2389; Nöldeke to Ignaz Goldziher, 4 January 1907, Library of the Hungarian Academy of Sciences (hereafter MTAK): GIL/32/01/193.

> Happily back in Hamburg, it has to be my first task, to heartily thank you for your more than collegial hospitality, I could even call it fatherly … Your hospitable and pleasant home, the continuous kindness of your honored sister, … the exquisite circle of friendly and knowledgeable men, the feeling of spiritual togetherness, … the idyllic milieu of the old university town, the loving reception by all involved Dutch circles – all these impressions and memories lacked only one thing and that was the presence of your wife, who I missed so sorely all of the time.[13]

One more quality that Snouck and Becker shared, except for friends and each other's company, was a tendency to harshly judge those colleagues that did not live up to their high scholarly standards. Not long after his finishing his dissertation, Snouck, for instance, famously and venomously attacked a new edition of a textbook on Islamic law by the Dutch legal scholar L. W. C. van den Berg.[14] His attack was so ferocious that his teacher De Goeje even worried about his future career: "He has made v[an] d[en] B[erg] into an enemy who will never forgive him … [E]specially in a small country one accomplishes more through mutual benignity and a pardoning of each other mistakes than through his method."[15] Later De Goeje would disapprovingly notice similar harsh tendencies in Becker's style of reviewing: "I have finally read Becker's booklet against Karabacek. In the main B[ecker] is absolutely right. He could have formulated it a lot friendlier, though."[16] Nöldeke on the other hand, did not mind their harsh ways of reviewing all that much and even supported their harsh judgements in his private correspondences.[17] Nöldeke's acceptance of sharp mutual criticism, together with his reputation as an elderly scholar who could stand above all parties, made him the ideal mediator when Snouck and Becker would eventually aim their arrows at each other.

2 The Politics of War

The first point of contention between Snouck and Becker was purely political: they had widely differing opinions about the German invasion of Belgium. While Snouck was rather shocked by what he considered to be an unjust act of

---

13 Becker to Snouck Hurgronje, 15 September 1912, UBL, Or. 8952 A: 145.
14 Witkam, "Inleiding," 22-24.
15 De Goeje to Nöldeke, 8 March 1884, UBL: BPL 2389.
16 De Goeje to Nöldeke, 12 December 1908, UBL: BPL 2389.
17 Nöldeke to De Goeje, 7 March 1884, UBL: BPL 2389; Nöldeke to Goldziher, 14 April 1907, MTAK: GIL/32/01/206.

violence against a neutral nation, Becker adamantly defended the measure, arguing that "great nations should not sacrifice their vital interests to sentimental considerations, not even to an admiring recognition of the accomplishments of a small nation." Somewhat patronizingly he added that he could, of course, understand that the Dutch might not yet be able "to elevate themselves to this point of view."[18] This notion of the smaller nations having to elevate themselves to the superior point of view of the greater nations affronted Snouck. He wrote to Nöldeke that Becker had written to him "in a way which one could almost call offensive in normal times."[19] To Goldziher he also complained in an indignant tone: "Becker regrets that I cannot elevate myself to his point of view that the smaller nations are destined to be absorbed by the greater nations, etc. etc. I can only hope, that the now prevailing frenzy of violence of all great powers will end in general exhaustion and repentance."[20] Even if Becker explicitly told Snouck that he wished above all "to continue the intellectual exchange about other issues than just the purely scholarly and the purely personal," the seeds for a painful conflict about exactly those kind of things had been sown.[21]

Soon it appeared that in times of war it was not easy to differentiate between political and scholarly disagreement. Immediately after the outbreak of the World War a remarkably high number of German academics, amongst them famous men like Georg Simmel, Werner Sombart and Wilhelm Wundt, published their justifications of the German war effort.[22] When the Ottoman Empire decided to align itself with Germany and its allies, Orientalists found good reason to join the public discussion as well. Before the end of 1914 Becker had published two political pamphlets about the close relations between Germany and the Near East: *Deutschland und der Islam* (Germany and Islam) and *Deutsch–türkische Interessengemeinschaft* (German–Turkish Community of Interest).[23] The alliance of Germany and the Ottoman Empire was mutually

---

18   Becker to Snouck Hurgronje, 8 October 1914, UBL: Or. 8952 A: 150.
19   Snouck Hurgronje to Nöldeke, 16 October 1914, in Van Koningsveld, *Orientalism and Islam*, 190.
20   Snouck Hurgronje to Goldziher, 14 October 1914, in *Scholarship and Friendship in Early Islamwissenschaft: The Letters of C. Snouck Hurgronje to I. Goldziher*, ed. P. Sj. van Koningsveld (Leiden: Documentatiebureau Islam-Christendom, 1985), 414.
21   Becker to Snouck Hurgronje, 8 October 1914, UBL: Or. 8952 A: 150.
22   Wolfgang J. Mommsen, "Einleitung: Die deutschen kulturellen Eliten im Ersten Weltkrieg," in *Kultur und Krieg: Die Rolle der Intellektuellen, Künstler und Schrifsteller im Ersten Weltkrieg*, ed. Wolfgang J. Mommsen (Munich: Oldenbourg, 1996), 1-15, at 2-3.
23   Carl Heinrich Becker, *Deutschland und der Islam* (Stuttgart: Deutsche Verlags-Anstalt, 1914); Carl Heinrich Becker, *Deutsch-türkische Interessengemeinschaft* (Bonn: Friedrich Cohen, 1914).

beneficial, he argued, because Germany's enemies were the same nations whose international political aspirations threatened the Ottoman Empire.[24] Most of these countries were colonial powers ruling over large numbers of Muslim subjects.[25] Becker hoped that the Ottoman Sultan, in his capacity as Caliph, would be able to mobilize Muslims against the enemies of the Central Powers. The support of the "oppressed and discontent" Muslim subjects of French North-Africa, Egypt, British India and the Turkish peoples in Russia might prove to be an invaluable asset in the struggle against the Allied Powers.[26] Becker's call to action stopped just short of advocating the declaration of Holy War by the Sultan–Caliph. He advised caution instead, because he recognized the danger of such a call. It could, for instance, endanger the position of the Christian Greeks, Syrians, and Armenians who he deemed to be essential for maintaining the economic strength of the Ottoman Empire.[27]

As Becker himself acknowledged, not all German publicists were careful enough to refrain from explicitly calling for a declaration of Holy War. This persuaded Snouck to publish a long polemical article in *De Gids*, the most influential Dutch cultural and literary periodical of the day. He gave his article the provocative title "Heilige Oorlog made in Germany" (Holy War Made in Germany).[28] He argued that the Ottoman Sultan did not have the right to present himself as Caliph and elaborately pointed out that there did not exist any self-evident community of interest between Germany and the Ottomans. He referred to the less than helpful attitude of Germany when the Ottoman borders had been threatened earlier in the twentieth century at the Bulgarian declaration of independence and during the First Balkan War. He even argued that the most likely outcome of German–Ottoman cooperation would be that Turkey would become in all but name a German protectorate.[29] Snouck closed his argument by calling attention to the earlier writings of German authors which seemed to be at odds with the now commonly acclaimed call for German–Turkish cooperation. Becker was one of the scholars that he quoted on this issue. After reading "Heilige Oorlog Made in Germany," Becker was so upset and angry about what he called Snouck's unexpected "revolver journalism"

---

24   Becker, *Deutsch-türkische Interessengemeinschaft*, 10-12.
25   Becker did not consider Germany to be one of those powers as well. He stated that the "Negermoslime" in the German colonies in Africa "did not play a role in these questions. Becker, *Deutschland und der Islam*, 24.
26   Becker, *Deutsch-türkische Interessengemeinschaft*, 21-22; Becker, *Deutschland und der Islam*, 24-29.
27   Becker, *Deutschland und der Islam*, 30.
28   Christiaan Snouck Hurgronje, "Heilige Oorlog Made in Germany," *De Gids* 79 (1915), 115-147.
29   Ibid., 138.

that he closed off all further private correspondence with him.[30] The quarrel would, however, linger on in the periodicals.[31]

It is hard to disentangle scholarship and political advocacy in the ensuing discussion between the two antagonists. Questions about the legitimacy of the Ottoman Caliphate and an eventual proclamation of Holy War were presented as scholarly questions, but their political importance was clear to all. In fact, Snouck and Becker did not at all try to hide their political agendas. Becker, for example, commented on the encouraging of Pan-Islamic protest: "[I]t makes our enemies, who know their weaknesses even better than we do, nervous; it forces them to take security measures and to keep troops at hand."[32] Meanwhile, Snouck did not just look at the effects that an Islamic uprising could have on the war in Europe. He also kept an eye on the Muslim population of the Dutch Indies. Becker had emphasized the existence of a cohesive global Muslim community and had underlined the importance of the Sultan–Caliph who "is known even in the remotest districts of the Dutch Indies and of whom ... the liberation from the Europeans is expected."[33] Snouck, however, reassuringly stated in *De Gids* that "[f]ortunately we don't have to worry about our Muslims in the Dutch Indies ... In their eyes, the Sultan ... is still only a legendary creature."[34] This apparent confidence, however, mainly served to conceal the very real worries he actually harbored.[35]

A number of modern-day authors have made efforts to analyze the debate. The importance of political considerations is central to Peter Heine's analysis of the affair, in which he argues that the dispute shows the great differences in attitudes towards the Islamic world in applied Oriental studies.[36] Looking at this same quarrel, however, Wolfgang Schwanitz has argued that Snouck's and Becker's attitudes to Islam did not differ all that much: both were convinced

---

30 Becker to Nöldeke, 14 January 1915, UBT Md 782 A 16.
31 See for example Carl Heinrich Becker, "Islampolitiek," *De Gids* 79 (1915), 311-317; Carl Heinrich Becker, "Deutschland und der Heilige Krieg," *Internationale Monatsschrift für Wissenschaft Kunst und Technik* 9 (1915), 632-662; Christiaan Snouck Hurgronje, "Deutschland und der Heilige Krieg: Erwiderung," *Internationale Monatsschrift für Wissenschaft Kunst und Technik* 9 (1915), 1025-1033.
32 Becker, *Deutschland und der Islam*, 30.
33 Ibid., 15.
34 Snouck Hurgronje, "Heilige Oorlog," 145-146.
35 For a detailed account of Snouck's colonial considerations at the outbreak of the First World War, see Léon Buskens, "Christiaan Snouck Hurgronje, 'Holy War' and Colonial Concerns," in *Jihad and Islam in World War I: Studies on the Ottoman Jihad on the Centenary of Snouck Hurgronje's "Holy War Made in Germany,"* ed. Erik-Jan Zürcher (Leiden: Leiden University Press, 2016), 29-51.
36 Peter Heine, "C. Snouck Hurgronje versus C. H. Becker: Ein Beitrag zur Geschichte der angewandten Orientalistik," *Die Welt des Islams* 23/24 (1984), 378-387, at 383.

that its strength was to be found in its ability to adapt to new developments.[37] Within this shared interpretive frame Snouck and Becker had always had their differences but, as Ludmila Hanisch also suggests, this had never before led to any hostilities or mutual recriminations.[38] Just a few months before the outbreak of the World War, Snouck and Becker had even been able to gentlemanly agree to disagree on issues of colonial policy by accepting "a dissension, which may very well not be based on an intellectual but on an intuitive basis."[39] Their subsequent correspondence also shows that the vehemence of their eventual fall-out cannot be explained by exclusively pointing at a combination of political and scholarly differences. Instead, these surmountable differences got mixed up with personal and professional disagreements.

Relatively minor differences turned into major points of contention. One of these initially minor issues was Snouck's annoyance with the fact that Becker had attributed the Tabari-edition of his teacher De Goeje to a German academic tradition.[40] After the outbreak of the war Snouck extensively elaborated on how Becker's disregard of Dutch scholarship was just another example of the same haughty disposition that had led to the unjust German invasion of Belgium.[41] Other issues proved even more painful, such as the fact that part of Snouck's criticism of Becker in "Heilige Oorlog Made in Germany" was based on a misreading of the two words "*aus Unkenntnis*" (out of ignorance) in Becker's *Deutschland und der Islam*.[42] Snouck attacked what he assumed to be Becker's self-acclaimed past ignorance, while Becker had only pointed at the ignorance of the German government during the *Kaiser*'s visit to the Ottoman Empire in 1898.[43] Becker complained indignantly about this misreading in his letters to his and Snouck's friends and colleagues.[44] For a renowned linguist like Snouck who had even published his *magnum opus* about Mecca in German, this must have been very embarrassing.

---

37   Wolfgang G. Schwanitz, "Djihad »Made in Germany«: Der Streit um den Heiligen Krieg 1914-1915," *Sozial.Geschichte* 18 (2003), 7-34, at 10.
38   Ludmila Hanisch, "Gelehrtenselbstverständnis, wissenschaftlichen Rationalität und politische 'Emotionen,'" *Die Welt des Islams* 32 (1992), 107-123, at 115-117.
39   Becker to Snouck Hurgronje, 17 June 1914, UBL: Or. 8952 A: 149.
40   Becker to Snouck Hurgronje, 17 September 1914, UBL: Or. 8952 A: 149; Snouck Hurgronje to Nöldeke, 26 January 1915, in Van Koningsveld, *Orientalism and Islam*, 205.
41   Snouck Hurgronje to Becker, 19 September 1914, GStA PK, VI. HA, Nl Becker, C. H., Nr. 4227.
42   Becker, *Deutschland und der Islam*, 19.
43   Snouck Hurgronje, "Heilige Oorlog," 143.
44   Becker to Nöldeke, 14 January 1915, UBT Md 782 A 16; Becker to Goldziher, 12 January 1915, MTAK: GIL/03/15/052.

3 The *Encyclopaedia of Islam* and the Limits of International Cooperation

The most painful dispute, however, concerned an ambitious international co-operative effort: the *Encyclopaedia of Islam*. This idea had first been brought up by the British scholar William Robertson Smith, who had been editor-in-chief of the *Encyclopaedia Brittanica*. At the Orientalist Congress in London in 1892, he proposed to put together an Oriental Encyclopaedia as well. After Robertson Smith's death in 1894 Goldziher was appointed as the editor-in-chief.[45] Goldziher proved to be a rather hesitant organizer and he was supported behind the scenes by Snouck's teacher, de Goeje, who convinced the Leiden publishing house Brill to publish the *Encyclopaedia* and advised Goldziher about who he could invite as contributors.[46] Finally, in 1898, Goldziher's repeated requests to step down as editor-in-chief were answered. De Goeje had convinced his former student Theodor Houtsma, by then professor of Hebrew in Utrecht, to take Goldziher's place.[47] De Goeje continued to support the enterprise behind the scenes and was soon appointed as the director of the Supervisory Committee.[48] In 1908, his successor in Leiden, Snouck, would take over his place.[49] One of the most important tasks of the Supervisory Committee was to secure funding for the project. De Goeje and Snouck had been able to obtain support all over Europe. One of their most helpful peers had been Becker, who had been successful in negotiating funding from the Hamburg parliament as well as the *Kolonialgesellschaft*.[50] The broad international support came at a cost. The Supervisory Committee had to agree to publish the *Encyclopaedia* in three languages and therefore had to employ an English, a French, and a German co-editor.[51] The English and French editors would work from their home town. The German co-editor, however, who would be the only one to receive a fixed salary, would be Houtsma's right hand man and was supposed

---

45 Daniel van der Zande, "Martinus Th. Houtsma, 1851-1943: Een bijdrage aan de geschiedenis van de oriëntalistiek in Nederland en Europa" (PhD thesis, Utrecht University, 1999), 227-229.
46 De Goeje to Goldziher, 3 December 1895, MTAK: GIL/13/01/018.
47 De Goeje to Goldziher, 12 June 1898, MTAK: GIL/13/01/025.
48 Van der Zande, "Martinus Th. Houtsma," 246-247.
49 De Goeje to Nöldeke, 13 December 1908, UBL: BPL: 2389.
50 See for example Becker to Snouck Hurgronje, 1 February 1913, UBL: Or. 8952 A: 146 as well as the letter from Becker to Snouck in UBL: Or. 18.099.
51 Martinus Th. Houtsma and Johannes H. Kramers, "De wordingsgeschiedenis van de Encyclopaedie van den islam," *Jaarboek Oostersch Instituut* 5 (1941), 9-20, at 14-15.

to work from Leiden.[52] The international character of the project made it of course vulnerable to hostile sentiments in times of war.

Just before the beginning of the war the German co-editor Hans Bauer had been granted provisional permission to work from his home town Halle. At the outbreak of the war, however, Bauer signed up for voluntary work at a local emergency hospital. Though he still received his fixed salary, he now hardly contributed anything to the *Encyclopaedia* anymore. On Houtsma's recommendation, Snouck therefore informed Bauer that his contract would not be extended. This infuriated Becker, who wrote an angry letter to Houtsma, in which he complained that the "parity of the editions" was violated this way.[53] Houtsma forwarded this letter to Snouck, who indignantly wrote to Nöldeke: "I don't want to bother you with more saddening things than necessary, but because you would probably hear about this part of Becker's behavior against me anyway, I think I should inform you about just how far he goes in looking for an opportunity to personally grieve me."[54] Snouck had a long list of complaints: Becker should have written to him instead of Houtsma, Becker presented himself as if he was speaking on behalf of the whole of Germany and finally his accusations were unjust and mainly showed a lack of knowledge of the organizational structure of the project. Nöldeke was now forced into the role of mediator. He only reluctantly accepted this position, because Snouck's harsh criticism of Germany's war policies had hurt his patriotic feelings as well: "[I]f our enemies raise hell to ruin us completely, German politics cannot afford to be too selective," he argued.[55] He even repeatedly admitted to Becker that he was so angry and disappointed with Snouck's article that he seriously considered breaking all ties with him.[56] The fact that the article in question came from the successor of his good friend De Goeje made it even more painful for Nöldeke.[57] Notwithstanding his initial reluctance, he eventually accepted the mediating role that Snouck and Becker had bestowed on him: "Immediately after receiving your last letter I wrote to Becker about the *Encyclopaedia*. I have

---

52 Snouck Hurgronje to Nöldeke, 16 February 1915, in Van Koningsveld, *Orientalism and Islam*, 212.
53 Ibid., 214.
54 Ibid., 212.
55 Nöldeke to Snouck Hurgronje, 12 January 1915, UBL: Or. 8952 A: 757.
56 Nöldeke to Becker, 17 January 1915, 28 January 1915, 6 May 1915, GStA PK, VI. HA, Nl Becker, C. H., Nr. 3138.
57 Nöldeke to Goldziher, 9 November 1914, MTAK: GIL/32/01/287; Nöldeke to Goldziher, 12 December 1914, MTAK: GIL/32/01/291; Nöldeke to Goldziher, 10 November 1915, MTAK: GIL/32/01/299.

sent him your letter as well, even though I have torn off its last page because of the strong expressions against him."[58]

Becker soon answered Snouck's reproaches, though he of course did this by writing to Nöldeke rather than to Snouck himself.[59] He explained that even if he did not speak on behalf of the whole of Germany, he had indeed been encouraged by his colleagues Carl Brockelmann and Enno Littmann to write about Bauer's position at the *Encyclopaedia*. He also set out that he had written to Houtsma instead of Snouck because of "Heilige Oorlog Made in Germany," which had caused him to doubt Snouck's goodwill towards his German collaborators. He also admitted that he did indeed not know the organizational structure of the project very well. He had for instance always wrongly assumed that the English and French co-editors, Thomas W. Arnold and René Basset, had the same employee status as Bauer. He also bemoaned the deterioration of his relationship with Snouck, remarking that "he had always revered and loved" Snouck. This was also the letter in which he lamented the loss of his "ideal of scholarly personality." Finally, he explicitly asked Nöldeke for advice about Bauer and his work for the *Encyclopaedia*. Without a clear idea of what the future might bring, Becker counted on Nöldeke's influence on Snouck: "I have now completely entrusted myself to Nöldeke's guidance and I am eager to see what he will accomplish," he wrote to Goldziher.[60]

Now that Nöldeke had read Becker's reply to Snouck's accusations, it was time to try to assuage him.[61] After admitting that Snouck and Houtsma did indeed have the formal right to refuse Bauer's reappointment, he emphasized Bauer's delicate situation. He had accepted the job in Leiden while he was on a one year leave from Halle University, where he was employed as a *Privatdozent*. If he would not teach there for more than a year, however, his chances of an academic career in Germany would be in danger. Bauer's wish to work from Germany therefore deserved sympathetic consideration. Next, he excused Becker for turning to Houtsma instead of to Snouck, "because not only does he, *like all of us*, feel offended by your article, he is especially hurt by your very deprecating polemic against him." Nöldeke underlined Becker's good will by stating that he was already looking for a potential replacement for Bauer. This may have been a deliberate misrepresentation of Becker's letter of two days earlier.[62] In this letter Becker had indeed reflected on the possible future involvement of Carl Brockelmann and Rudolf Tschudi, but he envisioned them

---

58 Nöldeke to Snouck Hurgronje, 26 February 1915, UBL: Or. 8952 A: 757.
59 Becker to Nöldeke, 24 February 1915, UBT: Md 782 A 16.
60 Becker to Goldziher, 4 March 1915, MTAK: GIL/03/15/054.
61 Nöldeke to Snouck Hurgronje, 26 February 1915, UBL: Or. 8952 A: 757.
62 Becker to Nöldeke, 24 February 1915, UBT: Md 782 A 16.

as members of the Supervisory Committee rather than as co-editors.[63] Their status as full professors would have made them very unlikely candidates for the position of co-editor for the *Encyclopaedia* anyway, since this task had always been fulfilled by young promising *Privatdozenten* instead.

Nöldeke's insistence that Snouck should give in to Becker slowly started to pay off. In his first reply to Nöldeke, Snouck made clear that he "has not just loved Becker" but that he actually "still loved him."[64] Snouck also got in touch with Houtsma. The latter pointed out that the job description of the German co-editor was such that he could reasonably be expected to live in Leiden. This was not explicitly mentioned, but only tacitly assumed when the rules of procedure were drawn up.[65] Therefore these rules of procedure show that even if the tasks of the co-editor would most likely force him to work from Leiden, this was not an explicit requirement.[66] Houtsma could therefore argue that it would be within the bounds of the rules to keep working with Bauer if he would renounce his fixed salary and accept to only be paid for what he would actually deliver. Snouck seems to still have been under the assumption that the place of residence of the co-editor was included in the rules of procedure, as his next letter to Nöldeke shows.[67] However, he stated that if Becker would not be able to find a replacement for Bauer, he was prepared to continue to work with Bauer, if he would agree on the conditions stipulated by Houtsma. And this is exactly what happened. Becker had probably never actively looked for a new co-editor – his search for one was Nöldeke's rather than his own claim – so Bauer kept working for the *Encyclopaedia*. His name keeps popping up in the annual balance until the early nineteen-twenties, when he was offered a professorship in Halle and stopped working on the *Encyclopaedia*.[68]

Now that Nöldeke had successfully mediated in the quarrel about the position of Hans Bauer, there was one final important issue left to deal with: the mutual misgivings caused by "Heilige Oorlog Made in Germany." Becker sent

---

[63] At this moment Carl Brockelmann was full professor in Halle and Rudolf Tschudi, a former student of Becker, now occupied his former chair in Hamburg.
[64] Snouck Hurgronje to Nöldeke, 1 March 1915, in Van Koningsveld, *Orientalism and Islam*, 225.
[65] Snouck Hurgronje, transcript of Houtsma's letter of 2 March 1915, in Van Koningsveld, *Orientalism and Islam*, 229-230.
[66] Geschäftsordung für die Kommission zur Überwachung der Enzyklopädie des Islām, revised version, 9 April 1912, UBL: Or. 18.099.
[67] Snouck Hurgronje to Nöldeke, 3 March 1915, in Van Koningsveld, *Orientalism and Islam*, 228-229.
[68] Bericht über die Kassenführung des Kassierers der Enzyklopädie des Islam während des Jahres 1920, UBL: Or. 18.099; <http://www.catalogus-professorum-halensis.de/bauerhans.html> (last accessed 28 January 2019).

draft versions of his replies to Snouck to Nöldeke for proofreading and mellowed them down on his advice.[69] Meanwhile, Nöldeke pushed Snouck to get rid of his offensive mocking title and to officially apologize to his German friends and colleagues, whom he had badly offended with what was generally seen as an anti-German rant.[70] Even though Snouck was too proud and stubborn to radically change his argument or to make any straightforward apologies, he tried to be as accommodating as possible in his last published contributions to the debate.[71] He wrote to Nöldeke: "My wife, who has read the article before submittal, spontaneously shared her impression, that crudities were truly avoided, and in this respect women are more demanding than we are."[72]

More than by this self-acclaimed kindness, however, Becker was reassured by the fact that it had become increasingly clear that Snouck's criticism was to be understood in the light of Dutch colonial interests. As Becker had indignantly pointed out to Nöldeke, Snouck had stated in *De Gids* that "we don't have to worry about our Muslims in the Dutch Indies."[73] Over the next months, however, it clearly showed that he did actually worry about this quite a bit. In his letters to Nöldeke he hinted at the consequences that the German *Islampolitik* might have for the Dutch colonies. He argued in favor of "a calm development of Muslim society, which is a patriotic cause for me as well" and portrayed the pressure on the Sultan-Caliph to incite Muslims worldwide as "an incident that threatened Dutch vital interests as well as my life work."[74] In a letter to Goldziher he underlined that he thought that any call for Holy War was as a matter of course also directed against Dutch interests.[75] All this was pointed out to Becker by Richard Hartmann, Bauer's predecessor as co-editor of the *Encyclopaedia*. The "psychological key" to Snouck's demeanor, Hartmann explained, was the realization that "the belligerent mobilization of Islam is grist to the mill of Snouck's political enemies in the struggle about the treatment of Islam in the Dutch Indies."[76]

---

69   Becker to Nöldeke, 26 January 1915, UBT: Md 782 A 16; Becker to Nöldeke, 30 January 1915, UBT: Md 782 A 16.
70   Nöldeke to Snouck Hurgronje, 17 March 1915, UBL: Or. 8952 A: 757.
71   Snouck Hurgronje, "Deutschland und der Heilige Krieg: Erwiderung."
72   Snouck Hurgronje to Nöldeke, 14 March 1915, in Van Koningsveld, *Orientalism and Islam*, 223.
73   Becker to Nöldeke, 14 January 1915, UBT: Md 782 A 16.
74   Snouck Hurgronje to Nöldeke, 1 March 1915, in Van Koningsveld, *Orientalism and Islam*, 226; Snouck Hurgronje to Nöldeke, 14 March 1915, ibid., 232.
75   Snouck Hurgronje to Goldziher, 27 January 1915, in Van Koningsveld, *Scholarship and Friendship*, 429-430.
76   Becker to Goldziher, 4 March 1915, MTAK: GIL/03/15/054.

Some weeks later he explained to his friend Ernst Eisenlohr that Snouck's point of view should be understood in relation to Dutch colonial policy and that "[w]e are now on our way to mutual understanding without giving up our own points of view."[77] He considered Snouck's last published reply to be "conciliatory and keen."[78] Nöldeke and Littmann agreed with this judgement and praised Snouck's conciliatory closing paragraphs in particular.[79] In his last public comments Becker finally aimed to make sure that he would "fully acknowledge Snouck's colonial-political point of view as legitimate," without for that reason accepting his argument as an adequate reaction to his own pamphlets about the relation between Germany and the Ottoman Empire. Three weeks later Becker would resume his correspondence with Snouck. For the first time in more than 4 months he wrote him a letter, in which he explicitly declared that for him "this painful episode is now closed."[80] Snouck gratefully accepted Becker's attempt at reconciliation, which he welcomed as the "starting point of the resumption of our friendly relations."[81] From this moment onwards their correspondence would indeed continue for years without even one mention of the painful polemics in early 1915.

4   Personae and Partiality

This chapter started off with Becker bemoaning his loss of an ideal of scholarly personality. This ideal might not fully amount to what we nowadays call a scholarly persona. Still, his reflection on the loss of Snouck as the personification of an ideal of scholarship invites us to look at this episode through the prism of today's literature on scholarly personae. Lorraine Daston and Otto Sibum describe a persona as "a cultural identity that simultaneously shaped the individual ... and creates a collective with a shared and recognizable physiognomy."[82] The idea of a persona as a model or ideal-type is further emphasized by Herman Paul, who describes it as "a template to which scholars are invited to conform."[83] These templates can be understood as "constellations

---

[77]   Becker to Ernst Eisenlohr, 24 March 1915, <http://carl-heinrich-becker.de/korrespondenz-ernst-eisenlohr-1915> (last accessed 28 January 2019).
[78]   Becker to Goldziher, 19 April 1915, MTAK: GIL/03/15/056.
[79]   Nöldeke to Becker, 26 March 1915, GStA PK, VI. HA, Nl Becker, C. H., Nr. 3138.
[80]   Becker to Snouck Hurgronje, 12 May 1915, UBL: Or. 8952 A: 152.
[81]   Snouck Hurgronje to Becker, 14 May 1915, GStA PK, VI. HA, Nl Becker, C. H., Nr. 4227.
[82]   Lorraine Daston and H. Otto Sibum, "Introduction: Scientific Personae and Their Histories," *Science in Context* 16 (2003), 1-8, at 2.
[83]   Herman Paul, "What is a Scholarly Persona? Ten Theses on Virtues, Skills and Desires," *History and Theory* 53 (2014), 348-371, at 353.

of commitments, or models of what it takes to be committed to a certain cluster of concretely identified goods."[84] Such constellations may include very different goods. Certain goods, such as a lust for knowledge and an appreciation of a critical stance towards both your own and other researchers' findings are commonly associated with scholarly pursuits. However, scholars are also attached to commitments with a professional rather than a strictly epistemological character, such as the desire to be part of a tightly-knit professional community, a wish to further one's career, a hope to contribute to society at large or the aspiration to pursue one's own professional interests free of any outside interference. And finally, scholars are not free from those commitments that are widely shared outside of scholarly and professional communities either, such as their expectations of friendship and their political convictions. A closer look at the commitments that Snouck and Becker did and did not share, might not only allow us a better understanding of the temporary derailment presented by their quarrel, it may also show us something about the way in which personae are not only a heuristic tool for modern-day historians, but also important elements of the lived experience of the people studied by these same historians.

The initially close relation between Snouck and Becker was supported by a large number of shared commitments. One important scholarly commitment shared by both was a profound interest in living Islamic culture rather than a focus on philologically assessing the works of medieval or even earlier origin, even if they had both showed their prowess in that field as well. A shared political commitment was their willingness to put their knowledge of contemporary Islamic societies to the use of colonial administrations, even if they did not fully agree about the extent to which colonized people should be integrated into administrative structures: Becker argued that this disagreement with Snouck's ideas about the assimilation of the colonial subjects of the Dutch Indies was the result of temperamental rather than intellectual differences.[85] Becker and Snouck also shared personal commitments: not only were they good friends of each other, they were also both part of a group of Orientalists that had taken shape around the patriarchical figure of Theodor Nöldeke. This group included, amongst others, Carl Bezold and Ignaz Goldziher. Not only did the members of this group acknowledge the importance of the study of contemporary Islamic culture, most of them also kept their relationship alive by regular visits to Nöldeke at his favorite holiday residence in Herrenalb in the

---

84   Ibid., 364.
85   Becker to Snouck Hurgronje, 17 June 1914, UBL: Or. 8952 A: 149.

Black Forest.[86] Finally, as was mentioned in the introduction and underlined by their quarrel, they both shared a willingness to engage in sharp polemics to make their points.

Another thing both men could agree on was a commitment to both their own nation and to a cosmopolitan community of scholars. Becker's passionate defense of the German war means and aims provides the most obvious illustration of his nationalist vigor. In his arguments with Snouck he also underlined the extent to which the future of German Orientalism depended on the outcome of the war: "If Germany will win the war, Orientalism will thrive here; but it will be a national science. And if we lose, it will be altogether superfluous."[87] This envisioned decline of German Orientalism seems even more unfortunate if seen in the context of earlier conceptions of the distinctly German contribution to the field. In the nineteenth century it was not uncommon amongst German Orientalists to favorably compare their own rigorous scholarship to the supposedly shoddy work of especially their French peers. Nöldeke's earlier letters to De Goeje, for example, often clearly express this notion.[88] Finally, Becker's defense of Hans Bauer, the German contributor to the *Encyclopaedia* can be interpreted as another example of his patriotism. Even if the wartime discussions don't emphasize Snouck's patriotic feelings he was no stranger to national pride either. This clearly showed in his vigorous defense of the Dutch origins of De Goeje's Tabari edition and his passionate plea for the rights of the smaller nations. Most of all, of course, it is illustrated by the fact that his position in the debate with Becker was determined by Dutch colonial interests as much as a supposedly impartial cosmopolitanism.

It is exactly this cosmopolitanism that is most salient in Snouck's correspondence with Becker and Nöldeke in which he tried to present himself as a sincere opponent of nationalist sentiment and the accompanying violence: "We hope that the terrible suffering, which this revival of barbarity imposes on all countries, will soon make the belligerents understand that things cannot go on this way and they have to convert themselves to another way to solve the problems of world history."[89] In December 1914 he even referred to his newly born daughter as "a new cosmopolitan."[90] This ideal of cosmopolitan scholarship

---

[86] See for example Nöldeke to De Goeje, 10 August 1907, UBL: BPL 2389; Becker to Snouck Hurgronje, 4 September 1913, UBL: Or. 8952 A: 148.

[87] Becker to Snouck Hurgronje, 17 September 1914, UBL: Or. 8952 A: 149.

[88] See for example Nöldeke to De Goeje, 15 September 1859, UBL, BPL: 2389; Nöldeke to De Goeje, 16 March 1897, UBL, BPL: 2389; Nöldeke to De Goeje, 1 April 1900, UBL, BPL: 2389.

[89] Snouck Hurgronje to Becker, 19 September 1914, GStA PK, VI. HA, Nl Becker, C. H., Nr. 4227.

[90] Snouck Hurgronje to Nöldeke, 10 December 1914, in Van Koningsveld, *Orientalism and Islam*, 197.

was as least as old as the German notion of excellence. Philologically inclined Orientalists had always relied on international cooperation to work with manuscripts kept in different European countries. From the eighteen-seventies onwards international Orientalist congresses had been organized, initially on French initiative.[91] Finally, it was not uncommon for international teams of scholars to work on cooperative projects, of which De Goeje's Tabari edition and the *Encyclopaedia of Islam* are typical examples. Becker's support to secure funds for these projects emphasizes that he also valued this internationalist approach to scholarship. Even his worries about Bauer's position as co-editor of the *Encyclopaedia* can be interpreted as a commitment to an international endeavor rather than as an example of unswerving nationalism. He also did not cheer on the aforementioned prospect of German Orientalism becoming a national science, because "precisely the international nature of our science has benefited us so much."[92] After resuming his correspondence with Snouck in May 1915, he also kept an amicable interest in the fortunes of their French colleague Louis Massignon, who volunteered in the French army: "If you have any news about him, please let me know, and if you write him, please tell him that I often remember him warmly."[93] Though he recognized a "glowing feeling of patriotism" in his French peer, Becker felt a strong professional and personal connection to him, even if they could not stay in touch during the War.[94] Becker was therefore happy to find that Snouck could facilitate his communication with this beloved French peer.

Even if Snouck and Becker seemed to share a commitment to both their own nation and to an international community of scholars, their diverging appreciation of exactly these commitments appeared to be at the root of their dispute. This observation suggests three things about the study of scholarly personae. In the first place it suggests that the commitments that make up a scholarly persona are often clearly noticeable only in times of crisis. In times of peace it proved easy to Snouck and Becker to think of themselves as cosmopolitan scholars and to even affirm this self-image by supporting international cooperative efforts. Even their support for their countries colonial efforts did not necessarily have to be the product of any sort of perceived national rivalry between the Netherlands and Germany. Only when confronted with a major crisis, the outbreak of the First World War, was an appropriate occasion to

---

91 Pascale Rabault-Feuerhahn, "« Les grandes assises de l'orientalisme ». La question interculturelle dans les congrès internationaux des orientalists (1873-1912)," *Revue germanique international* 12 (2010), 47-67, at 47-48.
92 Becker to Snouck Hurgronje, 17 September 1914, UBL: Or. 8952 A: 149.
93 Becker to Snouck Hurgronje, 25 June 1915, UBL: Or. 8952 A: 152.
94 Becker to Snouck Hurgronje, 4 October 1915, UBL: Or. 8952 A: 152.

showcase their patriotism provided. This crisis encouraged Becker to share his ideas about smaller and greater nations, which he had never mentioned to the horrified Snouck before. This same crisis convinced Snouck to take his stand against Germany's *Islampolitik*, which could only appear to Becker as "cheap self-opinionatedness at an unfair time."[95] Of course Snouck and Becker would have recognized some national pride in each other before, but they had not been able to perceive the importance of this commitment before the outbreak of the war.

The second lesson this narrative teaches us about scholarly persona is also concerned with the relative weight of different commitments. A crisis does not just make latent commitments visible, it can also change the importance people attach to these commitments. Before the outbreak of the war Snouck may have thought of himself as a cosmopolitan, but in his correspondences with his German peers heartfelt expressions of this cosmopolitanism were rare. Only from August 1914 onwards would he begin to stress his neutral, cosmopolitan disposition over and over again, arguing that his "sympathy is not on the side of the Russians, Serbs etc., but not on the other side either" and that he "cannot consider one party more guilty than the other."[96] Becker even explicitly acknowledged that the outbreak of the war had recalibrated his commitments: "For us Germans even our scholarly ideals fade into the background as insignificant in this great time, now that our fatherland is struggling for its existence."[97] This shows something about the nature of scholarly persona as well. The fact that outside events can influence the relative weight of the commitments that make up these personae, means that these personae are not static constellations of commitments: they are subject to change.

Finally, the development of the relations between Snouck and Becker supports my earlier claim that the scholarly persona is not just an analytical tool for historians, but also teaches us something about the actual ideals and experiences of past scholars. Becker's moaning of the loss of "an ideal of scholarly personality" shows that before this loss Snouck had actually provided him with a model of good scholarship. Until the outbreak of the war it seemed as if Becker had successfully modeled himself on this example. During the war, however, latent differences between the scholarly personae of Snouck and Becker became visible. What is more, the war forced Becker to reevaluate the relative weight of his different commitments. His conclusion was that in times like

---

[95] Becker to Nöldeke, 11 January 1915, GStA PK, VI. HA, Nl Becker, C. H., Nr. 3138.
[96] Snouck Hurgronje to Nöldeke, 16 October 1914, in Van Koningsveld, *Orientalism and Islam*, 189-190.
[97] Becker to Snouck Hurgronje, 17 September 1914, UBL: Or. 8952 A: 149.

these Snouck no longer, alas, provided the most convincing and appropriate model of good scholarship. Becker's decision to break with Snouck was very painful for him, because it was a break with someone who he had always considered to be very similar to himself. A striking description of the painfulness of disputes between people so close to each other had been offered only a few years earlier by one of those other ardent academic supporters of the German war effort, Georg Simmel:[98]

> The more we as whole persons have in common with another, the more readily will our wholeness link up every single connection with that person; thus the completely disproportionate vehemence with which otherwise thoroughly controlled people sometimes allow themselves to be carried away when it comes to their closest intimates. All the joy and the depth in the connections to another person with whom we feel ourselves, as it were, identified: so that no single connection, no single word, no single common action or trouble actually remains single, but each is a garment for the whole soul that stretches over the other and is welcomed – just this makes an emerging dispute among such persons often so passionately expansive....[99]

5 Conclusion

Even if all their shared commitments made the break between Snouck and Becker very painful, these same shared commitments would eventually allow the restoration of their relation. Some of these commitments were primarily based on their shared scholarly interests. "As far as scholarship is concerned I am willing to acknowledge Snouck as some kind of pope" Becker wrote to Goldziher.[100] His comment about the loss of an ideal of scholarship was followed by the humble observation that he would "always acknowledge [Snouck's] scholarly superiority happily and gratefully."[101] At least as impor-

---

98 More information about Georg Simmel during the First World War can be found in Patrick Watier, "Georg Simmel et la guerre," in *Kultur und Krieg: Die Rolle der Intellektuellen, Künstler und Schrifsteller im Ersten Weltkrieg*, ed. Wolfgang J. Mommsen (Munich: Oldenbourg, 1996), 31-47.

99 Georg Simmel, *Soziologie: Untersuchungen über die Formen der Vergesellschaftung* (Leipzig: Duncker & Humblot, 1908), 273. This translation is taken from Georg Simmel, *Sociology: Inquiries into the Construction of Social Forms*, vol. 1, trans. and ed. Anthony J. Blasi, Anton K. Jacobs and Mathew Kanjirathinkal (Leiden: Brill, 2009), 250.

100 Becker to Goldziher, 4 March 1915, MTAK: GIL/03/15/054.

101 Becker to Nöldeke, 24 February 1915, UBT: Md 782 A 16.

tant as Becker's professional respect for Snouck, however, was their shared commitment to specific people. They both vented their frustrations to Ignaz Goldziher, but if one single factor deserves to be emphasized as a contributor to the eventual careful restoration of their relations, it is their mutual love and respect for their older friend and reluctant mediator, Theodor Nöldeke.

Bibliography

Audring, Gert, ed. *Der Briefwechsel zwischen Theodor Nöldeke und Eduard Meyer (1884-1929)*, <https://www.geschichte.hu-berlin.de/de/bereiche-und-lehrstuehle/alte-geschichte/forschung/briefe-meyer/noeldeke> (last accessed 28 January 2019).

Becker, Carl Heinrich. *Deutschland und der Islam*. Stuttgart: Deutsche Verlags-Anstalt, 1914.

Becker, Carl Heinrich. *Deutsch-türkische Interessengemeinschaft*. Bonn: Friedrich Cohen, 1914.

Becker, Carl Heinrich. "Deutschland und der Heilige Krieg." *Internationale Monatsschrift für Wissenschaft Kunst und Technik* 9 (1915): 632-662.

Becker, Carl Heinrich. "Islampolitiek." *De Gids* 79 (1915): 311-317.

Buskens, Léon. "Christiaan Snouck Hurgronje, 'Holy War' and Colonial Concerns." In *Jihad and Islam in World War I: Studies on the Ottoman Jihad on the Centenary of Snouck Hurgronje's "Holy War Made in Germany,"* ed. Erik-Jan Zürcher, 29-51. Leiden: Leiden University Press, 2016.

Daston, Lorraine and H. Otto Sibum. "Introduction: Scientific Personae and Their Histories," *Science in Context* 16 (2003): 1-8.

Fasseur, Cees. *De Indologen: Ambtenaren voor de Oost 1825-1950*. Amsterdam: Bert Bakker, 1993.

Hanisch, Ludmila. "Gelehrtenselbstverständnis, wissenschaftlichen Rationalität und politische 'Emotionen.'" *Die Welt des Islams* 32 (1992): 107-123.

Heine, Peter. "C. Snouck Hurgronje versus C. H. Becker: Ein Beitrag zur Geschichte der angewandten Orientalistik." *Die Welt des Islams* 23/24 (1984): 378-387.

Houtsma, Martinus Th. and Johannes H. Kramers. "De wordingsgeschiedenis van de Encyclopaedie van den islam." *Jaarboek Oostersch Instituut* 5 (1941): 9-20.

Littmann, Enno. "Carl Bezold," *Zeitschrift für Assyriologie* 34 (1922): 103-104.

Mommsen, Wolfgang J. "Einleitung: Die deutschen kulturellen Eliten im Ersten Weltkrieg." In *Kultur und Krieg: Die Rolle der Intellektuellen, Künstler und Schrifsteller im Ersten Weltkrieg*, edited by Wolfgang J. Mommsen. Munich: Oldenbourg, 1996, 1-15.

Paul, Herman. "What is a Scholarly Persona? Ten Theses on Virtues, Skills and Desires," *History and Theory* 53 (2014): 348-371.

Rabault-Feuerhahn, Pascale. "« Les grandes assises de l'orientalisme ». La question interculturelle dans les congrès internationaux des orientalists (1873-1912)." *Revue germanique international* 12 (2010): 47-67.

Ruppenthal, Jens. *Kolonialismus als "Wissenschaft und Technik": Das Hamburgische Kolonialinstitut: 1908 bis 1919*. Stuttgart: Franz Steiner, 2007.

Schwanitz, Wolfgang G. "Djihad »Made in Germany«: Der Streit um den Heiligen Krieg 1914-1915," *Sozial.Geschichte* 18 (2003): 7-34.

Simmel, Georg. *Soziologie: Untersuchungen über die Formen der Vergesellschaftung*. Leipzig: Duncker & Humblot, 1908.

Simmel, Georg. *Sociology: Inquiries into the Construction of Social Forms*, vol. 1. Translated by and ed. Anthony J. Blasi, Anton K. Jacobs and Mathew Kanjirathinkal. Leiden: Brill, 2009.

Snouck Hurgronje, Christiaan. "Deutschland und der Heilige Krieg: Erwiderung." *Internationale Monatsschrift für Wissenschaft Kunst und Technik* 9 (1915): 1025-1033.

Snouck Hurgronje, Christiaan. "Heilige Oorlog Made in Germany." *De Gids* 79 (1915): 115-147.

van Koningsveld, P. Sj., ed. *Orientalism and Islam: The Letters of C. Snouck Hurgronje to Th. Nöldeke from the Tübingen University Library*. Leiden: Documentatiebureau Islam-Christendom, 1985.

van Koningsveld, P. Sj., ed. *Scholarship and Friendship in Early Islamwissenschaft: The Letters of C. Snouck Hurgronje to I. Goldziher*. Leiden: Documentatiebureau Islam-Christendom, 1985.

van Koningsveld, P. Sj. *Snouck Hurgronje en de Islam: Acht artikelen over leven en werk van een oriëntalist uit het koloniale tijdperk*. Leiden: Documentatiebureau Islam-Christendom, 1987.

van der Zande, Daniel. "Martinus Th. Houtsma, 1851-1943: Een bijdrage aan de geschiedenis van de oriëntalistiek in Nederland en Europa." PhD thesis, Utrecht University, 1999.

von Melle, Werner. *Dreißig Jahre Hamburger Wissenschaft: 1891-1921*. Hamburg: Kommissionsverlag von Broschek & Co., 1923.

Vrolijk, Arnoud and Richard van Leeuwen. *Arabic Studies in the Netherlands: A Short History in Portraits, 1580-1950*. Translated by Alastair Hamilton. Leiden: Brill, 2014.

Watier, Patrick. "Georg Simmel et la guerre." In *Kultur und Krieg: Die Rolle der Intellektuellen, Künstler und Schrifsteller im Ersten Weltkrieg*, edited by Wolfgang J. Mommsen, 31-47. Munich: Oldenbourg, 1996.

Wende, Erich. *C. H. Becker: Mensch und Politiker: Ein biographischer Beitrag zur Kulturgeschichte der Weimarer Republik*. Stuttgart: Deutsche Verlags-Anstalt, 1959.

Witkam, Jan Just. "Inleiding." In Christiaan Snouck Hurgronje, *Mekka in de tweede helft van de negentiende eeuw: Schetsen uit het dagelijks leven*, 7-189. Amsterdam: Atlas, 2007

Index

Akamatsu Renjō 13, 158-159, 166
Alekseev, V.M. 137
Algazi, Gadi 6
Althoff, Friedrich 59, 110
al-Yāziğī, Ibrāhīm 1, 7-8, 10-11, 14, 143
Anesaki Masaharu 166
Anscombe, G.E.M. 65
App, Urs 146
Aristotle 65
Arnold, Matthew 49, 54
Arnold, Thomas W. 182
Aston, William George 149, 151-153, 165
Aufrecht, Theodor 108
Aylmer, Charles 118, 122
Ayscough, Florence 131

Backhouse, Edmund Trelawny 137
Bacon, Francis 119
Barbour, Kim 4-5
Barrett, Timothy 12, 118-142
Barth, Jacob 11, 18-19, 23, 25, 37-40
Barth (née Hildesheimer), Rosa 37
Barton, Sidney 137
Basset, René 182
Bauer (née Kerschbaumer), Eugenie 35
Bauer, Hans 11, 18-19, 23, 33-40, 181-184, 187-188
Baumstark, Anton 26
Becker, Carl Heinrich 2, 7, 13, 18, 37, 172-191
Benfey, Theodor 26, 105-106, 108
Berg, L.W.C. van den 175
Bezold, Carl 173-174, 186
Bhandarkar, Ramkrishna Gopal 111-112, 115, 143
Bickell, Gustav 11, 17-19, 23-30, 32-33, 35-37, 39-40
Bickell, Johann Wilhelm 24
Binyon, Laurence 132-133, 137
Bleek, Wilhelm 110
Blunt, Anne 84-85
Blunt, Wilfrid 84-85
Boehtlingk, Otto 113
Bopp, Franz 103, 108
Bosch, Mineke 4-5
Braudel, Fernand 5

Brockelmann, Carl 21, 36, 38, 182
Brown, Robbins 13, 154
Bruce, J. Percy 130
Bühler, Georg 110-111, 113, 115
Bunsen, Christian 107-110
Burckhardt, Jean Louis 77
Burnouf, Eugène 156-158

Carlyle, Thomas 54
Carus, Paul 158
Chalmers, John 124
Chamberlain, Basil Hall 149, 151-153, 160, 165
Chaudhuri, Nirad C. 48-49, 53
Clark, William 66
Conway, Moncure 48
Couling, C.E.C. 131
Couling, Samuel 130-131, 133

Darwin, Charles 28
Daston, Lorraine 5-6, 45-46, 64, 185
Dawkins, Richard 49
Delitzsch, Friedrich 33-34
Deussen, Paul 161
Dillmann, August 21
Doughty, Charles 68
Douglas, R.K. 124
Dozy, Reinhart Pieter Anne 1-3, 7-11
Duyvendak, Jan Julius Lodewijk 3

Edkins, Joseph 127-128
Eisenlohr, Ernst 185
Elisséeff, Serge 151
Elphinstone, Mountstuart 108
Emerson, Ralph Waldo 54
Engberts, Christiaan 13, 172-192
Euting, Julius 12, 30-31, 67-95
Ewald, Heinrich 7, 103-105, 108-111, 113-114

Fleischer, Heinrich Leberecht 2-3, 7, 18, 37
Florenz, Karl 148-149, 151-153, 165, 168
Foot, Philippa 65
Freedman, Maurice 130
Freiligrath, Ferdinand 93
Freud, Sigmund 85
Fruin, Robert 5

Fujieda Takutsū 160
Fujishima Ryōon 160-162

Galison, Peter 64
Gandhi, Indira 49
Garbe, Richard 110
Geiger, Theodor 34-35
Geldner, Karl 115
Giles, Herbert 12-13, 118-138
Giles, Lionel 122-123
Girardot, Norman J. 127, 129
Goeje, Michael Jan de 1, 38, 172-173, 175, 179-181, 187-188
Goffman, Erving 4
Goldstücker, Theodor 108
Goldziher, Ignác 1, 3, 174, 176, , 180, 182, 184, 186, 190-191
Gordon, Marquis Lafayette 149
Graham, A.C. 138
Granet, Marcel 130
Guimet, Émile 164
Gzella, Holger 11-12, 14, 17-44

Haas, Hans 13, 149, 153-154, 156
Hanisch, Ludmila 179
Hardy, Robert Spence 157
Hartmann, Martin 1, 3
Hartmann, Richard 184
Haug, Martin 12, 99-116
Hawkes, David 138
Heine, Heinrich 90-91, 93-94
Heine, Peter 178
Hepburn, James C. 13, 154
Hillebrandt, Alfred 115
Hiller, W.C. 125
Hodgson, Brian Houghton 157-158
Hoffmann, Johann Joseph 147, 151
Holloway, John 54
Holt, Henry F. 129
Houtsma, Theodor 180-183
Howard, E.I. 109
Huber, Charles 67-68, 72, 78, 80-83, 85-86, 88, 91, 94

Iida Takesato 165, 168
Imamura Gen'emon 147
Irwin, Robert 10

Jacobi, Hermann 115
Jamaspji, Destur Hoshengji 112, 115
John, Griffith 124

Kaempfer, Engelbert 147, 150
Kampffmeyer, Georg 2
Karabacek, Joseph von 175
Karwan, Richard 4
Kasawara Kenju 13, 159, 163-164, 166
Kepler, Johannes 6
Kielhorn, Franz 110-111
Kingsmill, Thomas W. 129
Kivistö, Sari 66
Krämer, Hans Martin 13-14, 143-171
Krencker, Daniel 73-75

Lange, Rudolf 156
Lassen, Christian 106, 108
Legge, James 120, 126, 129, 143
Lévi, Sylvain 160-161
Lidzbarski, Mark 11, 17-19, 23, 29-33, 35-37, 39-40
Lindgren-Utsi, Ethel John 137
Littmann, Enno 12, 69-71, 73, 81-83, 86-89, 95, 182, 185
Lloyd, Arthur 149
Lowell, Percival 149

Mangold, Sabine 2
Marchand, Suzanne 2, 10, 143-145, 148
Marcks, Erich 174
Marshall, P. David 4-5
Massignon, Louis 188
Mauss, Marcel 5
McMullen, D.L. 123
Melle, Werner von 174
Migne, Jacques Paul 57
Minford, John 118, 137
Molendijk, Arie L. 8, 12, 47-63
Mommsen, Theodor 56, 59
Müller, Friedrich Max 8, 12, 45-61, 107-108, 110-113, 154-156, 159, 161-164, 166
Müller (*née* Grenfell), Georgina 53
Mülsow, Martin 66
Munzinger, Karl 149

Nanjō Bun'yū 13, 159-166
Nève, Félix 157

INDEX

Nietzsche, Friedrich   72
Nöldeke, Theodor   21-22, 26-28, 30-31, 36-38, 68-70, 79, 172-176, 181-187, 191
Nolde, Eduard von   81-83

Olcott, Henry Steel   155-156
Oldenberg, Hermann   59, 115, 161
Olshausen, Justus   22, 25
Ostwald, Joh. Martin   149

Paramore, Kiri,   165
Parkes, Harry Smith   151-152
Pattison, Mark   108-109, 111
Paul, Herman   1-16, 46-47, 145, 185
Pelliot, Paul   118, 135-136
Pfizmaier, August   13, 149-151, 154-155, 166
Pischel, Richard   115
Planck, Max   46-47
Porter, James   72
Pound, Ezra   137

Rabault-Feuerhahn, Pascale   12, 99-117
Reed, James   158
Reiske, Johann Jacob   20, 33
Renan, Ernest   68
Richard, Timothy   123, 125
Richards, I.A.   127
Ritter, Carl   78
Robertson Smith, William   57, 180
Rosen, Friedrich   103
Rosny, Léon de   13, 144, 149-151, 154, 156, 160, 166
Ross, E. Denison   124
Roth, Rudolf   104-106, 108, 110, 112-114
Ruskin, John   54
Rüttermann, Markus   149-150

Sachau, Eduard   29
Sagan, Carl   60
Sansom, George   134
Satow, Ernest   149, 151-153, 165
Saussaye, Pierre Daniel Chantepie de la   156, 160
Saussure, Ferdinand de   48
Sâyana   112
Schaub, Martin   124
Schiller, Emil   149
Schlegel, Gustaaf   2
Schrader, Eberhard   29

Schwanitz, Wolfgang   178
Sibum, H. Otto   5-6, 45-46, 185
Siebold, Philipp Franz von   147, 150
Simmel, Georg   176, 190
Smith, Adam   119
Snouck Hurgronje, Christiaan   1-3, 7, 13, 38, 79-80, 172-191
Sombart, Werner   176
Spinner, Wilfrid   149
Staël-Holstein, Alexander von   127
Stanley, Arthur Penrhyn   59
Strachey, Lytton   133
Sueki Fumihiko   147

Takakusu Junjirō   161-162
Temple, Richard Carnac   123
Ten Kate, Herman   149
Thibaut, Georg   110-111
Thoreau, Henry David   54
Tong Man   118, 137
Trubetzkoy, Nikolai   36
Trüper, Henning   12, 64-98
Trumpp, Ernst   110
Tschudi, Rudolf   182

Utsi, Mikel   137

Veit, Friedrich   101-102

Wachutka, Michael   168
Wade, Thomas   118, 121, 125
Waley, Arthur   131-134, 138
Wang Tao   143
Weber, Albrecht   108, 113-114
Wellhausen, Julius   23, 28, 31, 35-36
Whitney, William Dwight   48-50, 113
Wilamowitz-Möellendorf, Ulrich   72
Wilde, Oscar   128
Williams, Bernard   65
Williams, Monier   155
Windisch, Ernst   161
Winter, Pieter van   5
Witte, Johannes   149
Woesler, Winfried   93
Wood, Charles   108
Wundt, Wilhelm   176

Zimmern, Heinrich   34, 38

Printed in the United States
By Bookmasters